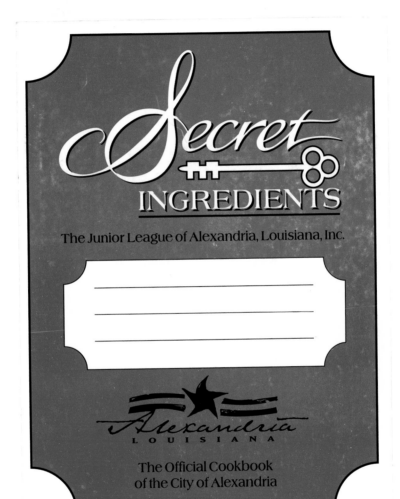

Secret INGREDIENTS

The Junior League of Alexandria, Louisiana, Inc.

Alexandria
LOUISIANA

The Official Cookbook
of the City of Alexandria

Secret INGREDIENTS

The Junior League of Alexandria, Louisiana, Inc.

HIBERNIA

Front cover and title page sponsor

Copyright © 2000
The Junior League of Alexandria, Louisiana, Inc.
1082 Alexandria Mall
3437 Masonic Drive
Alexandria, Louisiana 71301
318-443-6975

Library of Congress Number: 99-097170
ISBN: 0-9675255-0-0

Photographer: Greg Mayo
Illustrator: Darrin Dickerson
Food Stylist: Denise Wood
Art Direction: Merrilyn Norem, Catherine Pears
Text: Missy Laborde, Merrilyn Norem, Catherine Pears, Denise Wood

Designed, Edited, and Manufactured by
Favorite Recipes® Press
an imprint of

FRP

P.O. Box 305142
Nashville, Tennessee 37230
1-800-358-0560

Art Director and Book Design: Steve Newman
Jacket Illustrator: Barbara Ball
Project Manager: Susan Larson

Manufactured in the United States of America
First Printing: 2000   15,000 copies

Introduction

Secret Ingredients is a celebration of central Louisiana. Through traditions, humanity, and pure determination, we insist on preserving our uniquely southern lifestyle. We have a comfortable pace to our life, with family and friends at the center, where courtesy and respect reflect our sentiment. Here we celebrate our diversity through food and festivals, determined to remember those cultures whose flavor have added spice to our lives.

For these reasons, **Secret Ingredients** was the perfect title for a cookbook that was meant to be more than just a cookbook. It is an open door to a place where the world stops when you sit down at the dinner table, where life is a spin around the dance floor with a gracious partner, where all of the ingredients are essential in our gumbo of life.

The Junior League of Alexandria, Inc., is happy to share these recipes from family and friends with you. Proceeds from the sale of **Secret Ingredients** will be reinvested into the community we treasure so much. We hope you get a glimpse of all we love here in the heart of Louisiana. Enjoy!

The Junior League of Alexandria, Inc.

The Junior League of Alexandria, Inc., is an organization of women committed to promoting voluntarism and to improving the community through the effective action and leadership of trained volunteers. Its purpose is exclusively educational and charitable.

The Junior League of Alexandria, Inc., is committed to promoting voluntarism and to significantly improving the community in the areas of Child Abuse and Domestic Violence Against Women.

Contents

Brunch & Breads

Family and friends are the key ingredients that make life in Alexandria a joy.
Many families trace their roots back to the city's earliest settlement on the Red River
and still have strong ties here. Many families boast four generations still living and
growing in our area. These families are very active in civic and philanthropic endeavors
and have been the secret behind much of the community's success. Some have donated
landholdings for public projects or set up foundations to fund the needs of
our community or to ensure cultural opportunities for our citizens.

In addition to the families who have lived in Alexandria for generations,
there are many new, young families. Young people have been drawn to central Louisiana
because it has much to offer—both professionally and personally—and because it is
an outstanding place to raise a family. Friends here support one another like family.
There are still neighborhoods where kids can ride their bikes around the block.
Friends take turns cooking on Friday nights while all the kids
run around the yard into the night. This is the life we cherish.

Alexandrians are strongly committed to this community.
Community service and voluntarism is prevalent and is an avenue
for building close, lasting friendships. Our citizens have provided shelters
for the abused, day care for the young and old, assistance for the unfortunate,
advocacy for children, job training, assistance to inexperienced mothers,
food for the hungry, and much more for the welfare of our community.
The Junior League of Alexandria is proud to have played a part in building
up the community while we have built relationships with one another.

Breaking bread with family and friends is at the center of our lifestyle.
We offer these selections for starting out your day with style.

*Friends here support
one another like family.
There are still neighborhoods
where kids can ride their bikes
around the block.*

Natchitoches Meat Pies

1 pound lean ground beef
1 pound lean ground pork
1 medium onion, chopped
1 medium green bell pepper, chopped
1 bunch green onions, chopped
4 to 5 cloves garlic, minced
1 tablespoon flour
1 teaspoon salt
1/2 teaspoon black pepper
1/2 teaspoon ground red pepper
Pastry
Vegetable oil for deep-frying

⚷ Brown the ground beef and pork in a skillet over medium heat, stirring until crumbly. Remove the ground beef and pork from the skillet, reserving the drippings.

Cook the onion, bell pepper, green onions and garlic in the reserved drippings in the skillet over medium-high heat until tender, stirring constantly. Stir in the ground beef and pork. Add the flour, salt, black pepper and red pepper and mix well. Remove from heat.

Divide the pastry into 4 portions. Roll each portion 1/8 inch thick on a floured surface. Cut 5 circles from each portion using a 6-inch saucer as a guide. Spoon 1/4 cup of the meat mixture over half of each circle. Moisten the edges with water. Fold the pastry over the meat mixture, pressing the edges to seal. Crimp the edges with a fork dipped in flour.

Pour the oil into a Dutch oven to a depth of 3 inches. Heat to 375 degrees. Cook the pies 4 at a time in the hot oil until brown, turning once. Drain on paper towels. Serve immediately.

Yield: 20 pies.

Pastry

8 cups flour
2 teaspoons baking powder
4 teaspoons salt
1 cup shortening
2 eggs, beaten
2 1/4 cups milk

⚷ Combine the flour, baking powder and salt in a large bowl and mix well. Cut in the shortening until crumbly. Combine the eggs and milk in a bowl and mix well. Add to the flour mixture gradually, mixing with a fork until the mixture forms a ball.

To make sour cream, stir 1 tablespoon fresh lemon juice into 1 cup heavy cream in a glass bowl. Let the mixture stand at room temperature for ten to thirty minutes or until it has thickened. Cover the bowl and refrigerate until ready to use.

Breakfast Wellington

1 pound ground hot sausage
1/2 (10-ounce) package frozen chopped onions
Pepper to taste
1 (10-ounce) package frozen chopped broccoli
1 (8-ounce) package garlic cheese, chopped
1/2 cup sour cream
2 (8-count) cans crescent rolls
1 egg (optional)
1 1/2 teaspoons water (optional)

Brown the sausage with the onions in a skillet, stirring until the sausage is crumbly; drain. Season with pepper. Stir in the broccoli and cook until tender-crisp. Add the cheese and cook until it begins to melt, stirring constantly.

Stir in the sour cream. Cook until the cheese melts, stirring constantly. Remove from heat. Let stand for 10 to 15 minutes or until mixture begins to thicken.

Unroll the crescent roll dough onto a baking sheet, forming a rectangle and pressing the perforations together. Spoon the sausage mixture down the center. Cut slits 2 to 3 inches from the outer edge to the filling, every 1 to 2 inches. Fold the strips alternately across the filling.

Beat the egg and water in a small bowl. Brush over the top. Bake at 375 degrees for 10 to 15 minutes or until golden brown.

Yield: 6 to 8 servings.

Breakfast Burritos

8 ounces bulk pork sausage
1 cup hashed brown potatoes with onions
2 cups hot water
6 eggs, beaten
1/2 teaspoon salt
Freshly ground pepper to taste
6 (8-inch) flour tortillas
2 tablespoons butter
3/4 cup shredded Cheddar cheese
Picante sauce (optional)

Brown the sausage in a skillet, stirring until crumbly; drain. Combine the hashed brown potatoes and water in a bowl and mix well. Let stand, covered, for 15 minutes; drain. Add the sausage, eggs, salt and pepper and mix well.

Wrap the tortillas tightly in foil. Warm in a 350-degree oven for 10 minutes or until completely heated.

Melt the butter in a large skillet. Add the egg mixture. Cook over low heat until the eggs are set, stirring gently. Spread 1/2 cup of the egg mixture down the center of each tortilla. Sprinkle with 2 tablespoons of the cheese. Roll up to enclose the filling. Place seam side down on a serving platter. Spoon picante sauce over the tortillas.

Yield: 6 servings.

· Store cheese tightly wrapped in a vinegar-dampened cloth in the refrigerator.
· Cheddar cheese grates more easily if it is placed in the freezer for ten to twenty minutes.
· One pound hard cheese yields four to five cups of grated cheese.

Crab Meat Cheesecake with Pecan Crust

3/4 cup pecan halves
1 cup flour
1/2 teaspoon salt
5 tablespoons butter, chilled
3 tablespoons ice water
1/2 small onion, finely chopped
Butter
4 ounces crab meat
8 ounces cream cheese, softened
1/3 cup Creole cream cheese, or equal parts
*   yogurt and sour cream*
2 eggs
Salt to taste
White pepper to taste
Hot sauce to taste
2 tablespoons chopped shallots
4 ounces sliced mixed wild mushrooms
1 tablespoon lemon juice
6 tablespoons Worcestershire sauce
2 tablespoons hot sauce
6 tablespoons heavy cream
3 tablespoons unsalted butter, softened
24 crab claw fingers
Black pepper to taste

Process the pecans, flour and
1/2 teaspoon salt in a food processor until fine.
Cut 5 tablespoons butter into the pecan mixture
until crumbly. Add the water and mix well;
mixture will be crumbly. Press the dough over
the bottom and up the side of a 9-inch tart pan.
Bake at 350 degrees for 20 minutes.

Cook the onion in a small amount of butter
in a skillet over medium heat until translucent.
Stir in the crab meat. Cook until heated through;
set aside. Beat the cream cheese in a mixer bowl
until smooth. Beat in the Creole cream cheese
until smooth.

Add the eggs 1 at a time, mixing well after
each addition. Fold in the crab meat mixture.
Season with salt to taste, white pepper and hot
sauce to taste. Spoon into the prepared crust. Bake
at 300 degrees for 30 minutes or until set.

Sauté the shallots in a small amount of
butter in a skillet until translucent. Add the
mushrooms. Cook until the moisture from the
mushrooms is evaporated. Add the lemon juice,
Worcestershire sauce and 2 tablespoons hot sauce.
Cook until reduced by 3/4. Add the cream. Cook
until reduced by 1/2. Whisk in 3 tablespoons
unsalted butter.

Place the crab claws in a skillet. Season
with salt and black pepper. Pour the sauce over
the crab claws.

Serve each slice of cheesecake with 3 crab
claws and 2 tablespoons of the sauce.

Yield: 8 servings.

Crab Cakes with Tomato Salsa

1 pound fresh crab meat
1/2 cup chopped red bell pepper
1/2 cup chopped green onions
3 tablespoons chopped fresh basil
2 tablespoons fresh lemon juice
2 tablespoons mayonnaise
1 tablespoon Dijon mustard
1/2 teaspoon hot pepper sauce
Dash of Worcestershire sauce
Salt and pepper to taste
*3 1/4 cups bread crumbs from French bread
    with the crusts trimmed*
1 egg, lightly beaten
2 tablespoons butter
2 tablespoons vegetable oil
Tomato salsa

Combine the crab meat, bell pepper, green onions, basil, lemon juice, mayonnaise, Dijon mustard, hot pepper sauce and Worcestershire sauce in a bowl and mix well. Season with salt and pepper. Add 1/4 cup of the bread crumbs and egg and mix well. Shape into eight 2 1/2-inch-diameter patties, using a scant 1/2 cup of the crab mixture for each pattie.

Place the remaining 3 cups bread crumbs in a shallow dish. Dredge the crab cakes in the bread crumbs, pressing to coat.

Heat 1 tablespoon of the butter with 1 tablespoon of the oil in a skillet over medium heat until the butter melts. Add 4 crab cakes and cook for 4 minutes per side or until golden brown, turning once. Repeat with the remaining 1 tablespoon butter, 1 tablespoon oil and 4 crab cakes. Serve with tomato salsa.

Yield: 4 servings.

Hotel Bentley

Along the banks of the Red River in Alexandria, Louisiana, stands the "Biltmore of the Bayou" or the "Waldorf of the Red River" as the Hotel Bentley is often referred. The Bentley was built in 1908 and is listed on the National Register of Historic Hotels.

The legend of its construction begins oddly enough with eating–Louisiana's not-so-secret pasttime. Joe Bentley was an independent, rugged lumberman who was partly responsible for the development of the lumber industry in central Louisiana. After a day of hard work, he was refused admittance to the Hotel Rapides dining room because he came to dinner without a coat. Angered by this and his refusal to conform to late-Victorian manners, Mr. Bentley vowed to build his own hotel, bigger and grander, where a man would not have to put up with rules and regulations. The Hotel Bentley, truly an architectural gem, adds such elegance to our downtown.

Crawfish Cardinale

3 green onion bulbs, chopped
6 tablespoons butter
2 tablespoons flour
1 cup light cream
1/4 cup catsup
3/4 teaspoon salt
1/4 teaspoon white pepper
1/2 teaspoon Tabasco sauce
2 teaspoons lemon juice
2 tablespoons brandy
1 pound boiled peeled crawfish tails or shrimp
8 thin lemon slices
Paprika to taste

Sauté the green onions in 4 tablespoons of the butter in a skillet for 5 minutes.

Heat the remaining 2 tablespoons butter in a saucepan until melted. Stir in the flour. Whisk in the cream and catsup. Cook until sauce thickens, stirring constantly. Stir in the salt, pepper, Tabasco sauce and lemon juice.

Place the brandy in a heatproof bowl. Ignite the brandy, letting the flames subside. Stir into the sauce gradually. Stir the green onions into the sauce. Add the crawfish tails and mix well.

Divide evenly among 8 ramekins. Bake at 350 degrees for 12 to 15 minutes or until heated through. Top each with a lemon slice and sprinkle with paprika.

Yield: 8 servings.

Country Morning Eggs

18 eggs
1 teaspoon salt
1/4 cup milk
1/4 cup (1/2 stick) butter
1/2 green bell pepper, chopped
1 (10-ounce) can cream of mushroom soup, warm
1 tablespoon sherry
4 ounces grated sharp cheese
8 ounces mushroom caps
Paprika to taste

Beat the eggs, salt and milk in a mixer bowl. Heat the butter in a skillet until melted. Add the egg mixture, stirring gently. Cook until almost set. Spoon the eggs over the bottom of a 9x13-inch baking dish.

Sprinkle the bell pepper over the eggs. Combine the soup, sherry and cheese in a bowl and mix well. Pour over the layers. Arrange the mushroom caps over the top. Chill, covered, for 8 hours or longer.

Sprinkle with paprika. Let stand until at room temperature. Bake at 325 degrees for 50 minutes.

Yield: 10 servings.

Country Club Omelette

8 ounces thinly sliced roasted turkey breast
4 slices bacon, crisp-cooked, crumbled
1 tomato, chopped
2 tablespoons chopped green onion tops
6 eggs
1 tablespoon butter
Salt to taste
Hollandaise Sauce

 Cut the turkey into bite-size pieces. Combine the turkey, bacon and tomato in a skillet. Cook over low heat until heated through. Remove from heat. Stir in the green onions. Beat the eggs in a bowl until smooth and creamy.

Heat ¹/₂ tablespoon of the butter in a skillet until melted, swirling to coat the bottom. Pour half of the eggs into the skillet, swirling to coat the bottom and part of the edge. Sprinkle with salt. Spoon one-third of the turkey mixture in a line over the eggs just to the left or right of the center, starting and stopping ¹/₂ inch from the edge. Roll the omelette over three times, enclosing the filling. Cook for 2 minutes or until cooked through. Slide the omelette out of the skillet seam side down and onto an ovenproof serving platter. Repeat the process with the remaining eggs. Keep the cooked omelette warm in a 250-degree oven.

Spoon the Hollandaise Sauce over the omelettes. Spread the remaining turkey mixture over the top.

Yield: 2 servings.

Hollandaise Sauce

¹/₂ cup (1 stick) butter, softened
3 egg yolks
1 tablespoon lemon juice
¹/₂ teaspoon sugar
¹/₈ teaspoon onion powder
¹/₈ teaspoon salt
Dash of paprika
Dash of white pepper
¹/₂ cup boiling water

 Cream the butter in a mixer bowl. Add the egg yolks 1 at a time, mixing well after each addition. Add the lemon juice, sugar, onion powder, salt, paprika and white pepper. Add the boiling water gradually, stirring until creamy. Pour into the top of a double boiler. Cook over boiling water until thick, stirring constantly.

If you have a recipe that calls for only egg whites or only yolks, it's easy and safe to save the leftovers. Whites will keep for up to four days if you store them in a covered container in the refrigerator.

Store leftover egg yolks in water in a covered container in the refrigerator and be sure to use them within a day or two.

Stuffed French Toast

6 (1-inch-thick) French bread slices
3/4 cup peach preserves
6 tablespoons cream cheese, softened
6 eggs
1/2 cup milk
1 tablespoon flour
1/2 cup fresh white bread crumbs
1/2 cup packed brown sugar
1 tablespoon cinnamon
2 tablespoons (about) vegetable oil

Slit the top of each slice of bread to within 1 inch of the edge making a pocket. Spoon 2 tablespoons of the preserves and 1 tablespoon of the cream cheese into each pocket.

Combine the eggs, milk and flour in a bowl; whisk until smooth. Mix the bread crumbs, brown sugar and cinnamon in a separate bowl.

Heat a large nonstick skillet over medium heat and brush with some of the oil. Dip the bread slices in the egg mixture and then into the bread crumb mixture, coating completely. Cook in the skillet for 2 minutes per side or until golden brown, brushing the skillet with additional oil as needed. Serve with maple syrup.

Yield: 6 servings.

To determine if an egg is fresh, place it in a pan of cold water. If it lies on its side, it's fresh. If it tilts, it's about 3 to 4 days old. If the egg stands upright, it's probably about 10 days old. If the egg floats to the top, it's old and should not be used.

Pesto Cheesecake

1 tablespoon butter, softened
1/2 cup fine dry bread crumbs
1/4 cup grated Parmesan cheese
2 1/2 cups fresh basil leaves
1/2 cup parsley leaves
1/2 teaspoon salt
1 clove garlic
1/4 cup olive oil
16 ounces ricotta cheese, at room temperature
32 ounces cream cheese, softened
2 cups grated Parmesan cheese
5 eggs
1/2 cup pine nuts, lightly toasted

Butter the bottom and side of a 10-inch springform pan. Combine the bread crumbs and 1/4 cup Parmesan cheese in a bowl and mix well. Sprinkle over the bottom and side of the pan.

Process the basil, parsley, salt and garlic in a food processor for 30 seconds. Add the olive oil gradually, processing for 1 minute or until smooth and scraping the side occasionally. Combine the ricotta cheese, cream cheese and 2 cups Parmesan cheese in a mixer bowl and beat for 2 minutes or until smooth. Beat in the eggs. Set aside 1/3 of the cheese mixture. Fold the basil mixture into the remaining 2/3 cheese mixture. Spoon into the prepared pan. Spread the reserved cheese mixture over the basil mixture. Sprinkle with the pine nuts.

Set the pan on a baking sheet. Bake at 325 degrees for 1 1/2 hours. Turn off the oven, leaving the cheesecake in the oven with the door ajar for 1 hour. Cool on a wire rack. Serve at room temperature or slightly warmed.

Yield: 12 to 14 servings.

Crêpe Cups with Goat Cheese and Walnuts

10 crêpes
3 leeks, chopped
3 tablespoons butter
3 tablespoons cream
Salt and pepper to taste
4 ounces California goat cheese
6 tablespoons chopped walnuts

⚷— Cut twenty 2-inch round or fluted circles from the crêpes using a cookie cutter. Fit each circle into a small buttered muffin cup. Place a small ball of aluminum foil in each crêpe cup to hold it open during baking. Bake at 350 degrees for 6 minutes or until crisp.

Sauté the leeks in the butter in a skillet until tender. Stir in the cream. Cook until thickened and bubbly, stirring constantly. Season with salt and pepper. Spoon into the prepared muffin cups.

Cut the goat cheese into 20 small pieces. Place 1 piece over the leek mixture. Sprinkle with the walnuts. May be served immediately or warmed in a 350-degree oven for 3 to 4 minutes.

Yield: 20 servings.

Deep-Fried Corn and Cheese Crêpes

6 ounces Cheddar cheese, shredded
3 ears fresh corn, kernels removed and cooked
3 spring onions, chopped
1/2 jalapeño chile, chopped
Salt and pepper to taste
Basic Crêpes
Flour
4 eggs, beaten
Bread crumbs
Vegetable oil for deep-frying

⚷— Mix the cheese, corn, onions, chile, salt and pepper in a bowl. Spread the filling down the middle of each crêpe. Fold over opposite ends and roll to enclose the filling.

Dip each filled crêpe in the flour, then the eggs and then the bread crumbs. Deep-fry in 350-degree oil until golden brown. Drain on paper towels. Cool for 10 minutes.

Yield: 20 servings.

Basic Crêpes

3 eggs
1/8 teaspoon salt
1 to 1 1/4 cups milk or beer
1 cup flour
4 to 5 tablespoons butter, melted

⚷— Combine the eggs, salt, milk, flour and butter in a blender container and process until smooth. Let stand for 1 hour. Place 2 tablespoons of the batter in a greased 6- to 7-inch skillet. Tilt the skillet to coat the bottom. Cook over medium heat until light brown. Turn and cook the other side. Repeat with the remaining batter.

Yield: 20 crêpes.

Hot Artichoke Loaf

1 (16-ounce) loaf French bread
1/4 cup (1/2 stick) margarine
3 cloves garlic, minced
1 (14-ounce) can artichoke hearts, drained,
    finely chopped
2 teaspoons basil
2 teaspoons garlic powder
1 cup shredded Monterey Jack cheese
1 cup grated Parmesan cheese
1/2 cup sour cream
Dash of red pepper
1/4 cup shredded Cheddar cheese
Paprika to taste

Cut the bread in half lengthwise. Scoop out the center in each half leaving a 1-inch shell. Crumble the removed bread and set aside.

Heat the margarine in a skillet over medium heat until melted. Add the garlic. Cook until light brown, stirring constantly. Remove from heat. Add the artichoke hearts, basil, garlic powder, Monterey Jack cheese, Parmesan cheese, sour cream, red pepper and reserved bread and mix well. Spoon into the bread shells. Sprinkle with the Cheddar cheese and paprika.

Place bread halves on a baking sheet. Cover with aluminum foil coated with nonstick cooking spray. Bake at 350 degrees for 25 minutes. Remove the foil. Bake for an additional 5 minutes or until the cheese has melted. Cut into slices.

Yield: 12 servings.

Crawfish Corn Bread

2 (7-ounce) packages yellow corn bread mix
1/3 cup vegetable oil
2 eggs
1 (17-ounce) can cream-style corn
1/3 cup chopped seeded jalapeño chiles
10 ounces shredded Cheddar cheese
1 onion, chopped
1 pound crawfish tails, chopped

Combine the corn bread mixes, oil, eggs, corn, chiles, cheese, onion and crawfish tails in a bowl and mix well. Spoon into a 9x13-inch baking dish coated with nonstick cooking spray.

Bake at 400 degrees for 35 to 40 minutes or until corn bread tests done.

Yield: 15 servings.

Don't throw away those orange, lemon, and grapefruit rinds. Grate and store in an airtight container in the refrigerator and use to flavor breads and cakes.

Orange Muffins with Smoked Turkey

Zest of 1 orange
1 cup raisins or currants
2 cups sifted flour
1/2 teaspoon salt
1 cup sugar
1/2 cup (1 stick) unsalted butter, softened
2 eggs
1 teaspoon baking soda
1 cup buttermilk
Juice of 1 orange
1/2 cup sugar
8 ounces thinly sliced smoked turkey breast
3/4 cup quince or mayhaw jelly

    Process the orange zest and raisins in a food processor until fine. Sift the flour and salt together. Cream 1 cup sugar and butter in a mixer bowl until light and fluffy. Add the eggs 1 at a time, mixing well after each addition. Combine the baking soda and buttermilk in a bowl and mix well. Add the flour and buttermilk alternately to the sugar mixture, mixing well after each addition. Stir the raisin mixture into the batter. Pour into miniature muffin cups sprayed with nonstick cooking spray.

    Bake at 400 degrees for 12 minutes or until golden brown. Brush the tops of the warm muffins with the orange juice. Sprinkle with 1/2 cup sugar. Cool in the pan for 5 minutes. Remove to a wire rack. Let stand until completely cooled.

    Cut the turkey into small pieces. Cut each muffin in half. Place a small amount of turkey on each muffin bottom. Place 1 teaspoon of jelly on the turkey. Place the muffin top over the jelly.

    Yield: 30 muffins.

Mushroom Croustades

24 slices firm white bread
1/4 cup (1/2 stick) margarine or butter
3 tablespoons chopped shallots or onion
8 ounces mushrooms, finely chopped
2 tablespoons flour
1 cup heavy cream
2 tablespoons snipped chives
1 tablespoon snipped parsley
1/2 teaspoon lemon juice
1/4 teaspoon salt
1/8 teaspoon ground red pepper
Dash of black pepper
2 tablespoons grated Parmesan cheese

    Cut a 2 1/2-inch circle from each slice of bread. Press each circle into a lightly greased muffin cup. Bake at 400 degrees for 10 minutes or until golden brown.

    Heat the margarine in a skillet over medium heat until melted. Add the shallots and cook for 4 minutes. Stir in the mushrooms. Cook for 15 minutes longer or until most of the liquid is evaporated. Stir in the flour. Add the cream. Cook until thickened and bubbly, stirring constantly. Cook for 1 minute longer, stirring constantly. Remove from heat. Stir in the chives, parsley, lemon juice, salt, red pepper and black pepper.

    Place the bread cups in a shallow baking pan. Spoon the mushroom mixture into the cups. Sprinkle with the cheese. Bake at 350 degrees for 15 minutes. Garnish with sour cream and additional snipped chives. May freeze cooled wrapped bread cups until needed.

    Yield: 12 servings.

Spiced Apples

1 gallon water
3 cups sugar
4 (4-ounce) packages red hot cinnamon
  candies
24 Red Delicious apples
3 tablespoons (about) red food coloring
1 (4-ounce) package cinnamon sticks

Bring the water to a boil in a large stockpot. Add the sugar. Cook until the sugar dissolves, stirring occasionally. Add the candy 1 package at a time, stirring frequently; do not let candy stick to the bottom. Cook until all the candy dissolves.

Peel and cut the apples into quarters. Add to the boiling candy mixture, stirring to cover with the mixture. Reduce the heat. Cook until apples are tender.

Remove apples to a large bowl or several small containers. Pour the liquid over the apples. Add the cinnamon sticks. Let stand until cooled. Chill, covered, for several weeks or until ready to serve.

Yield: 12 to 15 servings.

Potato Pancakes

1¹/2 tablespoons flour
1¹/4 teaspoons salt
2 tablespoons chopped chives (optional)
2 cups grated potatoes
3 eggs
1 to 3 teaspoons grated onion
Vegetable oil for deep-frying

Sift the flour and salt into a bowl. Stir in the chives. Drain the potatoes, squeezing out the excess moisture.

Beat the eggs in a large bowl. Add the potatoes to the eggs and mix well. Add the flour mixture and mix well. Stir in the onion. Shape into 3-inch-diameter patties ¹/4 inch thick.

Cook the patties in hot oil in a skillet until brown on both sides, turning once. Serve with applesauce and sour cream.

Yield: 6 to 8 servings.

A little salt sprinkled into a frying pan will prevent spattering.

Strawberry Cheese Ring

1 pound sharp Cheddar cheese, shredded
1 cup mayonnaise
1 cup chopped pecans
1 small onion, grated
Dash of black pepper
Dash of red pepper
Dash of garlic powder
Dash of salt
1 (12-ounce) jar strawberry preserves

Combine the cheese, mayonnaise, pecans, onion, black pepper, red pepper, garlic powder and salt in a bowl and mix well. Spoon into a large greased ring mold. Chill, covered, for 8 hours or longer.

Dip the mold in hot water for 5 seconds and run a knife around the edge. Invert onto a serving plate. Fill the center with the preserves. Serve with crackers.

May substitute 5 to 6 chopped green onions for the onion and seedless raspberry preserves for the strawberry preserves.

Yield: 6 to 8 servings.

Garlic Cheese Grits

1 cup quick-cooking grits
1 (6-ounce) roll garlic cheese
1/2 cup (1 stick) butter or margarine
2 eggs, beaten
3/4 cup milk
1/2 cup chopped green onions (optional)

Prepare the grits using the package directions. Cut the cheese and butter into pieces. Add to the hot grits, stirring until melted. Let stand until cooled. Spoon into a buttered 2-quart baking dish. Combine the eggs and milk in a bowl and mix well. Pour over the grits. Sprinkle the green onions over the top. Bake at 375 degrees for 1 hour.

Yield: 4 to 6 servings.

One of the scariest words in the English language is "brunch"—that meal that's neither breakfast nor lunch. Unlike breakfast (which can be bacon and eggs) or lunch (which can be tuna sandwiches), brunch implies something special. Brunch needs to be simple but creative, comforting yet sophisticated. It's usually something you reserve for company or, perhaps, special holidays.

Grits and Greens

Salt
1 bunch mustard greens or 1 (10-ounce)
  package frozen mustard greens
2 cups water
2 cups milk
1/2 teaspoon salt
1 cup quick-cooking grits
1/4 cup (1/2 stick) butter
1 (6-ounce) roll garlic or jalapeño cheese
2 eggs, beaten
1 tablespoon Worcestershire sauce
1 cup diced cooked ham

Bring enough water to cover the greens to a boil in a saucepan. Add a small amount of salt. Add the greens and cook until tender; drain. Cut into small pieces.

Combine 2 cups water, milk and 1/2 teaspoon salt in a saucepan. Bring to a boil. Stir in the grits gradually. Reduce the heat. Cook, covered, for 5 minutes or until done. Cut the butter and cheese into pieces. Add to the hot grits, stirring until melted. Cool slightly. Beat in the eggs and Worcestershire sauce. Stir in the ham and cooked greens. Spoon into a 1 1/2-quart baking dish. Bake for 40 to 45 minutes or until firm in the center.

Yield: 6 servings.

Baked Hominy and Cheese

1 egg
2 (15-ounce) cans white or yellow hominy,
  rinsed, drained
12 ounces American process cheese,
  cut into cubes
3/4 cup milk
1/2 small onion, finely chopped
3 slices bacon, crisp-cooked, crumbled
1 tablespoon butter or margarine, melted
1/4 teaspoon pepper

Beat the egg in a large bowl. Add the hominy, cheese, milk, onion, bacon, butter and pepper and mix well. Spoon into a greased 7x11-inch baking dish.

Bake at 350 degrees for 45 minutes or until bubbly and brown. Let stand for 5 to 10 minutes before serving. Garnish with parsley.

Yield: 8 servings.

Mushroom Spoon Bread

1 (10-ounce) can cream of mushroom soup
3/4 cup milk
1/2 cup white cornmeal
1 tablespoon butter
1/4 teaspoon salt
2 egg yolks, beaten
2 egg whites, stiffly beaten

⚷— Combine the soup and milk in a saucepan and mix well. Stir in the cornmeal. Bring to a boil slowly, stirring constantly. Boil for 5 minutes. Remove from heat. Add the butter and salt, stirring until the butter melts. Stir a small amount of the hot mixture into the eggs yolks. Stir the yolks into the hot mixture. Fold in the egg whites. Pour into a 1 1/2-quart baking dish. Bake at 350 degrees for 1 hour. Serve immediately.

Yield: 4 servings.

Broccoli Corn Bread

4 eggs
1/2 cup (1 stick) butter, melted
1 teaspoon salt
6 ounces cottage cheese
1 (6-ounce) package corn bread mix
1 (10-ounce) package frozen broccoli, thawed
3/4 cup chopped onion
1 cup shredded Cheddar cheese

⚷— Mix the eggs, butter, salt and cottage cheese in a bowl. Add the corn bread mix, broccoli, onion and Cheddar cheese and mix well. Spoon into a 9x13-inch baking dish. Bake at 400 degrees for 30 to 40 minutes.

Yield: 10 servings.

The Burning of Alexandria

The city of Alexandria was burned on Friday 13, 1864 or 1865 by Union troops who had been bitterly defeated by Confederate troops at Mansfield, north of Alexandria on the Red River. Father Bellier of the Catholic Church had secreted the Episcopal altar vessels, along with the vessels from the Catholic Church, in a hole under the church floor because of the looting that occurred. Some say that when the troops came to burn the church he stood at the door brandishing a sword, commanding them to depart. He had been an officer in the French army before he came to America and that experience proved most useful in defending the church. Other stories of the event relate the Father standing at the tabernacle with a sidearm to protect the church from being burned. What we do know for certain is that through Father Bellier's heroic actions, the Catholic Church in Alexandria was one of three buildings spared in the burning of Alexandria.

Applesauce Pecan Cake

2 cups sifted flour
1 teaspoon salt
1 teaspoon baking soda
1 teaspoon cinnamon
$1/2$ teaspoon nutmeg
$1/4$ teaspoon cloves
$1^1/2$ cups finely chopped pecans
$1/2$ cup raisins
1 cup sugar
$1/2$ cup shortening
$1^1/2$ cups applesauce

 Sift the flour, salt, baking soda, cinnamon, nutmeg and cloves together. Combine the pecans and raisins in a bowl. Add a small amount of the sifted dry ingredients and toss to coat. Cream the sugar and shortening in a mixer bowl until light and fluffy. Add the sifted dry ingredients alternately with the applesauce, mixing well after each addition. Stir in the pecan mixture. Pour into a greased and floured loaf pan.

Bake at 325 degrees for $1^1/4$ hours or until a wooden pick inserted in the center comes out clean.

Yield: 12 servings.

Classic Sour Cream Coffee Cake

2 cups flour
1 tablespoon baking powder
$1/4$ teaspoon salt
1 cup (2 sticks) butter, softened
2 cups sugar
2 eggs
2 cups sour cream
1 tablespoon vanilla extract
$3/4$ cup sugar
2 cups pecan halves, chopped
1 tablespoon cinnamon

Sift the flour, baking powder and salt together. Cream the butter and 2 cups sugar in a mixer bowl until light and fluffy. Add the eggs 1 at a time, mixing well after each addition. Add the sour cream and vanilla and mix well. Beat in the sifted dry ingredients just until blended.

Combine $3/4$ cup sugar, pecans and cinnamon in a bowl and mix well. Pour half of the batter into a greased and floured 10-inch bundt pan. Sprinkle with half of the pecan mixture. Pour the remaining batter over the pecan mixture. Sprinkle with the remaining pecan mixture.

Bake at 350 degrees for 1 hour or until a wooden pick inserted in the center comes out clean. Serve warm.

Yield: 10 servings.

Deluxe Pound Cake

3 cups flour
1/2 teaspoon baking powder
1/2 teaspoon salt
1 cup (2 sticks) butter, softened
1/2 cup shortening
3 cups sugar
5 eggs
1 cup milk
2 teaspoons coconut flavoring
1 teaspoon rum flavoring

Sift the flour, baking powder and salt together. Cream the butter, shortening and sugar in a mixer bowl until light and fluffy. Add the eggs 1 at a time, mixing well after each addition. Add the sifted dry ingredients and milk alternately, mixing well after each addition. Stir in the coconut and rum flavorings. Pour into a greased and floured 10-inch tube pan.

Bake at 350 degrees for 50 to 60 minutes or until a wooden pick inserted in the center comes out clean.

Yield: 16 servings.

Treasure Cake

2 (10-count) cans biscuits
8 ounces cream cheese
1 cup sugar
1 tablespoon orange zest
1 cup (2 sticks) butter, melted

Cut the biscuits in half. Cut the cream cheese into 40 pieces. Place one piece of cream cheese on each biscuit half. Fold each biscuit half around the cream cheese, sealing the edge.

Combine the sugar and orange zest in a shallow dish and mix well. Dip each biscuit half into the melted butter and then the sugar mixture. Place biscuit halves into a greased bundt pan.

Bake at 350 degrees for 40 minutes. Serve warm.

Yield: 12 to 15 servings.

Another way to beat the heat was to crank down the window, crank up the radio, and take in the scenery. After church services and enjoying crispy fried chicken, biscuits, and cream gravy, folks would pile in the family car for the Sunday drive–truly a southern Sunday.

Parmigiano-Reggiano

Typically this ever-popular Italian cow's milk cheese is grated and used in cooking, but a well-aged piece is sensational just eaten on its own. Offer it on a marble board with a sharply pointed Parmesan knife to chip away at a wedge of this hard cheese, rather than slice it. The chips have the splintery texture that is part of the cheese's appeal. Some fresh figs and a glass of Italian red wine, such as Chianti or Barolo, are great with Parmesan's salty, nutty, assertive flavor.

Parmesan Bread

1/4 cup grated Parmesan cheese
1 teaspoon basil
1 (25-ounce) package frozen dinner rolls
3 tablespoons butter or margarine, melted

Spray a 12-cup bundt pan with nonstick cooking spray. Butter the sprayed pan.

Combine the cheese and basil in a small bowl and mix well. Sprinkle one-third over the bottom of the prepared pan. Layer the frozen dinner rolls, butter and remaining cheese mixture half at a time in the prepared pan. Let rise in a warm place for 2 hours or until doubled in bulk; must be doubled.

Bake at 350 degrees for 20 minutes. Cover with aluminum foil. Bake for an additional 10 minutes. Invert onto a serving platter. Serve immediately.

Yield: 8 servings.

Banana Nut Bread

3 cups flour
2 cups sugar
1 teaspoon baking soda
1 teaspoon salt
1 teaspoon cinnamon
1 1/2 cups vegetable oil
1 1/2 teaspoons vanilla extract
3 eggs
5 bananas, mashed
1 cup chopped pecans
1 (8-ounce) can crushed pineapple, drained

Combine the flour, sugar, baking soda, salt and cinnamon in a large bowl and mix well. Add the oil, vanilla, eggs and bananas and mix well. Stir in the pecans and pineapple.

Spoon into 2 greased and floured loaf pans. Bake at 350 degrees for 50 minutes or until a wooden pick inserted in the center comes out clean.

Yield: 24 servings.

Poppy Seed Bread

1 (2-layer) package white cake mix
4 eggs
1/4 cup poppy seeds
1/2 cup vegetable oil
1 (6-ounce) package vanilla instant
    pudding mix
1 cup hot water

Combine the cake mix, eggs, poppy seeds, oil, pudding mix and water in a mixer bowl and mix well. Beat at medium speed for 4 minutes. Pour the batter into 2 greased 5x9-inch loaf pans.

Bake at 350 degrees for 45 minutes or until a wooden pick inserted in the center comes out clean.

Yield: 24 servings.

Vidalia Onion Bread

3 cups self-rising flour
1/2 teaspoon basil
1/2 teaspoon thyme
1/2 teaspoon oregano
1/4 teaspoon garlic powder
1/4 teaspoon paprika
3 tablespoons sugar
2 eggs or 1/2 cup egg substitute
1/2 cup puréed Vidalia onions
1/2 cup grated Parmesan cheese
10 ounces beer

Spray a 5x9-inch loaf pan with nonstick cooking spray. Dust with cornmeal.

Combine the flour, basil, thyme, oregano, garlic powder, paprika and sugar in a bowl and mix well. Add the eggs and onions and mix well. Add the cheese and beer and mix well. Pour into the prepared pan.

Bake at 350 degrees for 35 minutes or until a wooden pick inserted in the center comes out clean. Cool in the pan for 10 minutes. Remove to a wire rack to cool completely.

Yield: 12 servings.

When choosing onions, select firm bulbs with even-colored skins and no signs of sprouting. Avoid any that look damp or smell musty. Leeks and scallions should have dark green leaves and fresh looking roots.

Making a Perfect Cup of Tea

Much is made of preparing tea properly, but my theory is, if you can boil water, you can make tea. Fill a kettle with fresh, cold water. Bring it to a full boil, then turn off immediately. To prewarm the teapot, pour in a small amount of the hot water, swirling it about. Discard. Add the tea leaves to the pot, one spoon per cup, plus one for the pot, and then fill with the hot water. Stir to circulate. Put lid back and, depending on the size of the leaves, let stand for three to seven minutes for the tea to release its flavor. Then pour through a tea strainer into cups. You can use this method to make floral and herbal teas, substituting flowers like anice hyssop, nasturtiums, rose petals, or violets for the tea leaves.

Almond Tea

2 cups boiling water
3 tea bags
1 cup sugar
6 tablespoons lemon juice concentrate
1¹/₂ teaspoons almond extract
1 teaspoon vanilla extract
6 cups cold water

Pour boiling water over the tea bags in a large drink container. Steep to the desired strength. Remove the tea bags. Add the sugar, lemon juice concentrate, almond extract and vanilla. Stir until sugar dissolves. Add cold water. Refrigerate until chilled. Serve over ice.

Yield: 2 quarts.

Breakfast Scones

2³/₄ to 3¹/₄ cups flour
6 tablespoons sugar
1¹/₂ tablespoons baking powder
¹/₂ teaspoon salt
¹/₂ cup (1 stick) unsalted butter, chilled
³/₄ cup raisins
1 cup heavy cream, chilled
2 eggs
Sugar

Sift the flour, 6 tablespoons sugar, baking powder and salt into a bowl. Cut in the butter until crumbly. Stir in the raisins. Beat the cream and eggs in a separate bowl until well blended. Pour over the crumb mixture and mix well. Pat into a 1-inch-thick circle on a lightly floured surface. Cut into eight 3-inch-diameter pieces. Sprinkle with sugar. Place the scones on a greased and floured baking sheet.

Bake at 400 degrees for 10 minutes. Reduce the oven temperature to 350 degrees. Bake for 13 minutes or until golden brown. Serve with jelly or jam.

Yield: 8 scones.

Iced tea is served up virtually everywhere you go in the South. It can be as simple as "sweet tea" or exotic blends using extracts such as almond, vanilla, or peppermint. Whatever the variety it is always a surefire thirst quencher.

Raspberry Corn Muffins

1/2 cup (1 stick) unsalted butter, softened
1/2 cup packed brown sugar
2 eggs
1 1/2 teaspoons vanilla extract
1/2 teaspoon cinnamon
1 cup white cornmeal
1 cup unbleached or all-purpose flour
1 1/2 teaspoons baking powder
1/2 cup sour cream
1 cup fresh raspberries
Orange Honey

⚬—⚟ Cream the butter and brown sugar in a mixer bowl until light and fluffy. Add the eggs and beat for 2 minutes. Stir in the vanilla and cinnamon. Add the cornmeal, flour and baking powder and beat for 1 minute. Add the sour cream and beat for 1 minute. Fold in the raspberries. Spoon into muffin cups sprayed with nonstick cooking spray.

Bake at 350 degrees for 20 to 25 minutes or until brown. Serve with the Orange Honey, refrigerating any remaining honey in an airtight container.

Yield: 12 muffins.

Orange Honey

1 cup honey
1/3 cup unsalted butter, softened
Juice of 1 orange (about 1/3 cup)
Zest of 1 orange (about 1 1/2 tablespoons)

⚬—⚟ Combine the honey, butter, orange juice and orange zest in a bowl and mix well.

Cheddar and Chive Biscuits

1 3/4 cups flour
2 teaspoons baking powder
1/2 teaspoon baking soda
1/2 teaspoon garlic powder
1/4 teaspoon salt
1/4 teaspoon pepper
5 tablespoons cold unsalted butter
1/2 cup shredded sharp Cheddar cheese
2 tablespoons minced chives
3/4 cup buttermilk

⚬—⚟ Sift the flour, baking powder, baking soda, garlic powder, salt and pepper into a large bowl. Cut in the butter until crumbly. Add the cheese and chives and mix well. Make a well in the center. Pour the buttermilk into the well. Stir vigorously for 1 minute or until the dough comes away from the side of the bowl.

Drop 2 tablespoons at a time 2 to 3 inches apart on a lightly greased baking sheet. Bake at 400 degrees for 12 to 15 minutes or until golden brown. May substitute crisp-cooked crumbled bacon for the chives.

Yield: 20 biscuits.

Biscuits

6 cups self-rising flour
3 tablespoons baking powder
1 1/2 teaspoons salt
1 cup (2 sticks) margarine
2 1/4 cups milk

Combine the flour, baking powder and salt in a bowl and mix well. Cut in the margarine until crumbly. Add the milk and stir quickly with a fork just until the dough begins to form a ball.

Knead the dough 10 to 12 times on a lightly floured surface. Roll to 3/4-inch thickness. Cut with a 2 1/2-inch biscuit cutter. Place on a baking sheet with the sides touching. Let rise, covered, in a warm place for 30 minutes.

Bake at 450 degrees for 10 to 12 minutes or until golden brown. May be frozen and reheated in the microwave.

Yield: 30 biscuits.

Sausage Gravy

1 pound bulk pork sausage
2 tablespoons finely chopped onion
6 tablespoons flour
4 cups milk
1/2 teaspoon poultry seasoning
1/4 teaspoon salt
Dash of Worcestershire sauce
Dash of Tabasco sauce

Brown the sausage with the onion in a skillet, stirring until the sausage is crumbly. Drain, reserving 2 tablespoons of the drippings. Stir in the flour.

Cook over medium-low heat for 6 minutes or until golden brown, stirring constantly. Stir in the milk, poultry seasoning, salt, Worcestershire sauce and Tabasco sauce. Cook until thickened, stirring constantly. Serve over biscuits.

Yield: 4 to 6 servings.

Lumpy gravy? Try this–add a pinch of salt to the flour before mixing with water.

Breakfast Cinnamon Rolls

1 (16-ounce) loaf thinly sliced bread
8 ounces 1/3-less-fat cream cheese, softened
1 egg white
1/2 cup confectioners' sugar
1 cup sugar
1 tablespoon cinnamon
1/2 cup (1 stick) margarine, melted

⚷— Trim the crusts from the bread. Beat the cream cheese, egg white and confectioners' sugar in a mixer bowl at medium speed until smooth. Spread evenly on 1 side of each bread slice. Roll each slice up to enclose the filling.

Combine the sugar and cinnamon in a shallow dish. Dip each bread roll in the margarine and then in the sugar mixture. Place on a greased baking sheet.

Bake at 350 degrees for 15 to 20 minutes or until brown. Cool on a wire rack.

Yield: 24 rolls.

Cinnamon Sticky Buns

1/2 (1-pound) frozen loaf sweet roll dough, thawed
3/4 cup (1 1/2 sticks) butter, softened
2 cups packed brown sugar
3 tablespoons dark corn syrup
3 tablespoons butter, melted
1 tablespoon cinnamon
1/3 cup chopped pecans

⚷— Place the sweet roll dough in a greased bowl, turning to coat the surface. Let rise, covered, in a warm place until doubled in bulk.

Beat 3/4 cup butter, 1 1/2 cups of the brown sugar and corn syrup in a mixer bowl until smooth. Spread evenly over the bottom of a buttered 8x12-inch baking pan.

Roll the dough into a 12x16-inch rectangle 1/3 inch thick on a lightly floured surface. Brush with the melted butter. Combine the remaining 1/2 cup brown sugar, cinnamon and pecans in a bowl and mix well. Sprinkle evenly over the buttered dough, pressing in gently. Roll up to enclose the filling, beginning at the long end. Cut into 12 slices.

Arrange the slices cut side down with the sides touching in the prepared pan. Let rise, covered, until doubled in bulk.

Bake at 375 degrees for 25 minutes or until golden brown. Cool in the pan for 5 minutes. Invert onto a serving platter. Serve warm.

Yield: 12 buns.

French Breakfast Puffs

1 1/2 cups flour
1 1/2 teaspoons baking powder
1/2 teaspoon salt
1/4 teaspoon ground nutmeg
1/3 cup butter or margarine, softened
1/2 cup sugar
1 egg, lightly beaten
1/2 cup milk
1/4 cup sugar
1/2 teaspoon cinnamon
2 tablespoons butter or margarine, melted

⚷— Combine the flour, baking powder, salt and nutmeg in a bowl and mix well. Cream 1/3 cup butter and 1/2 cup sugar in a mixer bowl until light and fluffy. Add the egg and mix well. Add the flour mixture alternately with the milk, beginning and ending with the flour mixture and mixing well after each addition; batter will be thick. Spoon into greased miniature muffin cups, filling 2/3 full.

Bake at 350 degrees for 18 to 20 minutes or until golden brown. Remove from pan immediately. Combine 1/4 cup sugar and cinnamon in a shallow dish. Dip the tops of the puffs in the melted butter and then in the sugar mixture.

Yield: 28 puffs.

Hot 'n Tots

1 cup (2 sticks) margarine, softened
8 ounces sharp Cheddar cheese, shredded
1 1/2 teaspoons Tabasco sauce
1/4 teaspoon salt
1/2 teaspoon cayenne pepper
2 cups flour
3 tablespoons cold water

⚷— Beat the margarine and cheese in a mixer bowl until blended. Stir in the Tabasco sauce, salt and cayenne. Add the flour and mix well. Add the water and mix well. Roll 1/8 inch thick on a floured surface.

Cut into circles with a round cookie cutter. Fold circles over and shape into crescents on an ungreased baking sheet.

Bake at 350 degrees for 25 minutes. Serve hot or at room temperature. May add 1/2 cup crumbled crisp-cooked bacon to dough.

Yield: 6 dozen.

Biscotti

4 cups (about) flour
2 teaspoons baking soda
1 teaspoon baking powder
$1/2$ teaspoon salt
$1/2$ cup (1 stick) butter, softened
2 cups sugar
3 eggs
2 teaspoons almond extract
$1^1/2$ cups slivered almonds
1 teaspoon lemon zest
$1/2$ cup dried cranberries (optional)
$1/2$ cup golden raisins (optional)
1 tablespoon candied ginger (optional)
1 tablespoon candied orange peel (optional)

Combine the flour, baking soda, baking powder and salt in a bowl and mix well. Cream the butter and sugar in a mixer bowl until light and fluffy. Add the eggs 1 at a time, mixing well after each addition. Add the almond extract, almonds and lemon zest and mix well. Add the flour mixture and beat until a soft dough is formed. Stir in the cranberries, raisins, candied ginger and/or candied orange peel.

Roll into three $2^1/2$x12-inch rectangles 1 inch thick on a lightly floured surface. Place the loaves on light-colored greased baking sheets; do not use dark-colored baking sheets. Bake at 350 degrees for 25 to 30 minutes or until firm. Cool on a wire rack.

Slice diagonally into $3/4$-inch slices. Place cut side down on a baking sheet. Bake for 15 minutes. Turn over and bake an additional 10 minutes or until light brown. Cool on a wire rack. Store in airtight containers.

Yield: 40 biscotti.

Open Houses

An Open House in the 1940s and 1950s was not reserved for the real estate market, but rather an invitation to a cocktail party. Although the term seems casual, these parties were by engraved invitation only, and quite the social event in the Alexandria Garden District.

When preparing for an open house make sure you have seating for about 25 percent of your guest list. You should also serve six to eight different hors d'oeuvre, allowing five to seven per guest.

Appetizers & Beverages

Central Louisiana is often called the Crossroads of the State because so many ethnic cultures influence our region. Although Creole and Cajun foods are probably Louisiana's best-known cuisine, numerous cultural influences create a flavor that is uniquely Louisiana. As different groups migrated up and down Louisiana's rivers and bayous, their recipes, herbs, and spices came with them. Because we are in the heart of the state, central Louisiana enjoys the influences of many cultures.

Creole cooking originated from the southern part of the state, bringing European, French, and Spanish influence. Cajun flavor was brought to the area by the French settlers from Nova Scotia. German, Czech, Lebanese, Italian, and Syrian settlers all contributed their secrets as well. These cultures blend with the home cooking styles from the African American and Native American populations to form a delicious style of cooking that offers something for every appetite.

Not only did these many cultures contribute to our cooking styles; they also contributed to our unique lifestyle. Cultural practices from different peoples have been incorporated into our way of life. Festivals throughout Louisiana celebrate our love for this diversity. The most popular celebration, Mardi Gras, also known as Fat Tuesday, began as the feast before the fast of Lent. Now nearly every town in Louisiana has secret krewes whose masquerading members ride atop elaborate floats throwing trinkets and beads while revelers shout "throw me something, mister" as the parade rolls by.

This information about the different cultures in central Louisiana is just a prelude to all that contributes to our food and lifestyle. Spice up your gatherings with these terrific recipes.

As different groups migrated up and down Louisiana's rivers and bayous, their recipes, herbs, and spices came with them. Because we are in the heart of the state, central Louisiana enjoys the influences of many cultures.

Appetizers & Beverages Key Sponsor

Security
First
National Bank

Crab Boat Dip

6 green onions, chopped
2 teaspoons minced garlic
1/2 cup (1 stick) butter
2 (4-ounce) cans lump crab meat, rinsed,
 drained
2 cups mayonnaise
1 envelope ranch dip mix
1 1/2 cups shredded Cheddar cheese
Dash of hot sauce
1 loaf of French bread or other crusty bread

Sauté the green onions and garlic in the butter in a skillet until tender. Stir in the crab meat and mix well.

Combine the mayonnaise, dip mix, cheese and hot sauce in a bowl and mix well. Fold in the crab meat mixture.

Cut the top off the bread. Scoop out the center, leaving a shell. Reserve the center portion for another purpose. Spoon the crab mixture into the shell. Place on a baking sheet. Bake at 350 degrees for 15 to 20 minutes or until the dip is bubbly and light brown. Serve with chips or crackers.

Yield: 6 to 8 servings.

Crab Meat Evangeline

1/4 cup (1/2 stick) butter
1/4 cup flour
1 cup cream
1/4 cup sherry
Salt and black pepper to taste
1 pound white crab meat
3/4 cup grated sharp cheese
1/8 to 1/4 teaspoon cayenne pepper

Heat the butter in a saucepan until melted. Stir in the flour. Whisk in the cream. Cook until thickened, stirring constantly. Stir in the sherry. Season with salt and black pepper. Remove from heat. Stir in the crab meat. Spoon into a buttered baking dish. Sprinkle the cheese over the crab meat mixture. Sprinkle with the cayenne pepper.

Bake at 325 degrees until the cheese melts. Serve with crackers. May substitute 8 ounces crab meat and 8 ounces chopped cooked shrimp for the 1 pound crab meat.

Yield: 6 to 8 servings.

Crab Meat Louisiane

1/4 cup chopped green onions
1/4 cup chopped parsley
1/2 cup (1 stick) butter
8 ounces cream cheese, chopped
1 pound white lump crab meat
Dash of lemon juice
Salt to taste
Red pepper to taste

Sauté the green onions and parsley in the butter in a skillet until tender. Add the cream cheese and cook until melted, stirring constantly. Stir in the crab meat. Season with lemon juice, salt and red pepper. Spoon into a microwave-safe bowl. Chill, covered, until ready to serve. May be reheated in a microwave. Serve with plain crackers.

Yield: 12 servings.

Curry Dip

1 cup mayonnaise
1/2 clove garlic, crushed
1 teaspoon curry powder
1 teaspoon grated onion
1 teaspoon prepared horseradish
1 teaspoon tarragon vinegar

Combine the mayonnaise, garlic, curry powder, onion, horseradish and vinegar in a bowl and mix well. Chill, covered, for 8 to 10 hours. Serve with fresh vegetables.

Yield: 4 servings.

Keeping Your Cool— Make a Fresh Start Each Day

Take twenty minutes for yourself each morning in order to get your day straight, and to exercise, etc.

Each week, have a family dinner night. Also take one morning to organize your week, clean out your car, and do similar chores.

Hummus

1 (16-ounce) can garbanzos, drained
3 tablespoons tahini
1/4 to 1/2 cup lemon juice
1 clove garlic
1/8 teaspoon cumin
1/2 teaspoon salt
Olive oil (optional)

Place the beans, tahini, lemon juice, garlic, cumin and salt in a blender container. Add enough water to come just below the top of the beans. Purée, adding additional water if a thinner consistency is desired. Pour onto a serving dish. Garnish with finely chopped parsley and/or pomegranate seeds.

Place 1 tablespoon of the hummus at a time on a plate. Pour a small amount of olive oil over the top. Serve with Arabic bread.

Yield: 4 to 6 servings.

Onion Soufflé

24 ounces cream cheese, softened
1/2 cup mayonnaise
1 (12-ounce) package frozen onions, thawed, drained
2 cups grated Parmesan cheese
1/2 cup chopped artichoke hearts, drained (optional)
Dash of Creole seasoning or cayenne pepper (optional)

⚷— Combine the cream cheese and mayonnaise in a bowl and mix until smooth. Add the onions, Parmesan cheese, artichokes and seasoning and mix well. Spoon into a greased 8-inch baking dish. Bake at 400 degrees for 10 to 15 minutes or until bubbly. Serve with corn chips.

Yield: 12 to 15 servings.

Smoked Oyster Dip

3 ounces cream cheese, softened
2 tablespoons mayonnaise
2 tablespoons milk
1 tablespoon finely chopped onion
2 teaspoons chopped pimento
1 (4-ounce) can smoked oysters, drained, chopped

⚷— Combine the cream cheese, mayonnaise and milk in a bowl and mix until smooth. Stir in the onion, pimento and oysters. Chill, covered, until ready to serve. Serve with crackers or chips.

Yield: 4 servings.

Spicy Shrimp Salsa

1 pound large shrimp, peeled, deveined, cooked
2 Roma tomatoes, seeded, diced
1/4 cup chopped red onion
1/4 cup chopped cilantro
1/2 jalapeño chile, minced
1 tablespoon chopped parsley
Juice of 1 lime
1/4 cup olive oil
Salt and freshly ground pepper to taste

⚷— Cut each shrimp into 4 or 5 pieces. Combine the shrimp, tomatoes, onion, cilantro, chile and parsley in a bowl and mix well. Add the lime juice and olive oil and toss to coat. Season with salt and pepper. Chill, covered, until ready to serve. Serve with tortilla chips. May add additional jalapeño chiles for a hotter version.

Yield: 4 servings.

Revive stale chips or crackers in the microwave oven by microwaving on full power for 45 to 60 seconds.

Tex-Mex Tabouli with Spicy Pita Triangles

3/4 cup fresh chopped tomatoes
1 cup bulgur
1/2 cup chopped green onions
1/2 cup finely chopped red bell pepper
3/4 cup chopped cilantro
1 (4-ounce) can chopped green chiles, drained
3 tablespoons lemon juice
1 1/2 teaspoons oregano
1/4 teaspoon ground cumin
3/4 teaspoon salt
1/2 teaspoon pepper
Spicy Pita Triangles

⚸— Combine the tomatoes, wheat, green onions, bell pepper, cilantro and chiles in a large bowl and mix well. Whisk the lemon juice, oregano, cumin, salt and pepper in a small bowl. Pour over the tomato mixture and mix gently. Chill, covered, until ready to serve.

Place the tabouli bowl on a large platter and surround the bowl with the Spicy Pita Triangles.

May substitute drained, dried, oil-pack tomatoes for the fresh tomatoes and substitute the tomato oil for the olive oil in the Spicy Pita Triangles.

Yield: 8 servings.

Cool Summer Camps

In the years before air-conditioning, families would close up their houses for the summer and move out to the camp. You could find these camps along various creeks and swimming holes, which provided cool relief from the heat of summer. The camps were recognizable by their names, like ThisLDu or Foote Rest. Many families still find sanctuary on the water, but you can bet the camp has air-conditioning.

Spicy Pita Triangles

1/2 teaspoon ground cumin
1 teaspoon chili powder
1 teaspoon garlic salt
4 pita breads
1/2 cup olive oil

⚸— Combine the cumin, chili powder and garlic salt in a bowl and mix well. Cut each pita into halves. Cut each pita half into two pieces. Arrange the pita pieces on a baking dish. Brush with the oil. Sprinkle with the chili powder mixture. Bake at 350 degrees for 10 minutes or until crisp.

Basil Parmesan Terrine

1/4 cup slivered sun-dried tomatoes
8 ounces cream cheese, softened
4 ounces goat cheese, softened
1 cup loosely packed fresh spinach leaves
3/4 cup loosely packed fresh Italian parsley
1/4 cup loosely packed fresh basil leaves
1 teaspoon minced garlic
1/4 cup olive oil
1 cup freshly grated Parmesan cheese
1/4 cup finely chopped walnuts

Coat the bottom and sides of a 2x5-inch loaf pan with oil. Line with plastic wrap, allowing the extra wrap to hang over the sides.

Combine the tomatoes with enough hot water to cover in a bowl. Let stand until plumped. Drain and pat dry.

Combine the cream cheese and goat cheese in a bowl and mix until smooth. Combine the spinach, parsley, basil and garlic in a food processor container.

Add the olive oil in a fine stream, processing constantly until smooth. Stir in the Parmesan cheese, forming a crumbly mixture; do not process into a paste.

Spread 1/3 of the cheese mixture evenly over the bottom of the prepared pan. Layer the spinach mixture, walnuts, sun-dried tomatoes and remaining cheese mixture one-half at a time over the cheese mixture. Chill, covered, for 24 hours.

Let stand at room temperature for 30 minutes. Invert onto a serving platter. Serve with crackers and French bread.

Yield: 4 servings.

Catfish Mousse with Shrimp Sauce

8 ounces skinned fresh catfish fillets, cut into
1-inch pieces
1 egg
1 egg yolk
1/4 cup milk
1/2 cup heavy cream
1/2 teaspoon salt
1/8 teaspoon cayenne pepper
1/2 teaspoon seasoned salt or Cajun seasoning
Juice of 1/2 lemon
Shrimp Sauce (page 43)

Process the fish in a food processor fitted with the steel blade until smooth. Pulse 8 times. Process continuously for 1 minute, scraping the work bowl as necessary. Press through a fine sieve.

Whisk the egg, egg yolk, milk and cream in a bowl. Whisk in the processed catfish. Add the salt, cayenne pepper, seasoned salt and lemon juice and mix well. Divide evenly among 4 buttered 3/4-cup molds.

Place the molds in a large baking pan. Add enough boiling water to come halfway up the sides of the molds. Bake at 325 degrees for 30 minutes or until set. Unmold onto individual plates. Serve with Shrimp Sauce.

Yield: 4 servings.

Shrimp Sauce

3 tablespoons olive oil
3 tablespoons safflower oil
1 pound medium shrimp
$1/2$ cup loosely packed parsley leaves
1 medium carrot, cut into 1-inch pieces
1 medium leek, white part only, cut into
    1-inch pieces
1 medium rib celery, cut into 1-inch pieces
1 medium clove garlic, crushed
1 teaspoon fresh thyme leaves, or
    $1/8$ teaspoon dried thyme
$1/3$ cup bourbon
1 cup dry white wine
$1^1/2$ tablespoons tomato paste
$1^1/2$ cups heavy cream
Salt to taste
Freshly ground white pepper to taste

Heat the olive oil and safflower oil in a large skillet. Add the shrimp. Cook, covered, for 2 minutes, shaking the skillet often. Turn the shrimp. Cook, covered, for 2 to 3 minutes longer, shaking the skillet often. Remove from the heat. Remove the shrimp. Shell the shrimp, leaving the tails intact and reserving the shells. Set the shrimp aside. Reserve the oil in the skillet.

Chop the reserved shells in a food processor fitted with the steel blade by pulsing 8 to 10 times. Remove to a bowl. Process the parsley in the food processor for 15 seconds or until finely chopped. Add to the shrimp shells in a bowl. Chop the carrot, leek and celery in the food processor by pulsing 6 to 8 times. Add to the shrimp shells.

Add the shrimp shell mixture, garlic and thyme to the reserved oil in the skillet used to cook the shrimp. Cook over medium heat for 5 minutes, stirring frequently.

Stir in the bourbon. Cook for 2 minutes or until reduced by $1/2$. Stir in the wine and tomato paste. Bring to a boil. Cook for 4 to 5 minutes or until reduced by $1/3$.

Stir in the cream. Reduce the heat. Simmer for 7 to 10 minutes. Season with salt and white pepper.

Strain the sauce into a bowl, pressing down with a wooden spoon to extract as much liquid as possible. Stir in the shrimp.

Chèvre originated in France, but there are now many artisanal cheesemakers in the United States producing the goat's-milk cheese. Sonoma's Laura Chenel has mastered the aging process that creates the rich, tangy taste of excellent chèvre, a taste that is set off well by salty olives and a bit of bread. Cut the soft cheese with a spreader.

Cream Cheese Cake with Shrimp Rémoulade Sauce

16 ounces cream cheese, softened
12 ounces cocktail sauce
1 teaspoon prepared horseradish
1 teaspoon lemon juice
1 1/2 cups finely chopped cooked shrimp
10 ounces mozzarella cheese, shredded
1 red bell pepper, finely chopped
3 tomatoes, seeded, finely chopped
6 green onion tops, chopped

Line a 9-inch round baking pan or pie plate with plastic wrap. Spread the cream cheese evenly in the prepared pan. Chill, covered, for 30 minutes or longer. Invert onto a serving plate. Remove the plastic wrap.

Combine the cocktail sauce, horseradish and lemon juice in a bowl and mix well. Spoon over the cream cheese, spreading to the edge. Sprinkle with the shrimp and mozzarella cheese. Combine the bell pepper, tomatoes and green onions in a bowl and mix well. Sprinkle over the layers. Serve with crackers. May substitute 3/4 cup cooked shrimp and 3/4 cup cooked crab meat for the 1 1/2 cups shrimp.

Yield: 12 servings.

Party Loaf

1 cup sour cream
8 ounces cream cheese, softened
1 tablespoon Worcestershire sauce
16 ounces shredded Cheddar cheese
1/2 cup chopped green onions
1 cup chopped ham
2 (4-ounce) cans chopped green chiles
1 loaf French bread
Paprika

Combine the sour cream, cream cheese and Worcestershire sauce in a bowl and mix until smooth. Stir in the cheese, green onions, ham and chiles.

Cut the top off the bread. Scoop out the center of the bread, leaving a shell. Reserve the center portion for another purpose. Spoon the cream cheese mixture into the shell. Place on a baking sheet coated with nonstick cooking spray.

Bake at 350 degrees for 1 hour. Place on a serving platter. Sprinkle with paprika. Serve with assorted crackers or corn chips.

Yield: 8 to 10 servings.

Smoked Oyster Loaf

1 clove garlic, crushed
1 tablespoon finely chopped onion
16 ounces cream cheese, softened
1 tablespoon mayonnaise
1 tablespoon milk
2 teaspoons Worcestershire sauce
1/4 teaspoon salt
1/8 teaspoon ground white pepper
Dash of Tabasco sauce
2 (4-ounce) cans smoked oysters, drained
1/2 cup finely chopped pistachios, pecans or
    walnuts

Process the garlic, onion, cream cheese, mayonnaise, milk, Worcestershire sauce, salt, pepper and Tabasco sauce in a food processor until well blended.

Cover a baking sheet with foil. Spread the cream cheese mixture over the foil in a 1/8- to 1/4-inch-thick rectangle. Purée the oysters. Spread over the cream cheese mixture. Chill, loosely covered with plastic wrap, for 8 to 10 hours.

Roll to enclose the oyster layer, smoothing any cracks and sealing the edge. Roll in the pistachios to coat. Chill, covered, until ready to serve. Garnish with dill or parsley. Serve with crackers or small toasts.

Yield: 12 servings.

Smoky Salmon Spread

1 (15-ounce) can salmon, drained
8 ounces cream cheese
2 tablespoons lemon juice
1 1/2 teaspoons prepared horseradish
2 teaspoons grated onion
1/4 teaspoon salt
1/4 teaspoon pepper
1/2 teaspoon liquid smoke
2 tablespoons finely chopped parsley

Remove the bones from the salmon and flake. Combine the cream cheese, lemon juice, horseradish, onion, salt, pepper and liquid smoke in a bowl and mix well. Add the flaked salmon and mix well. Chill, covered, for 1 hour. Shape into a roll. Sprinkle with the parsley, pressing lightly into the roll. Wrap in plastic wrap. Chill for 6 to 10 hours. Serve with assorted crackers.

Yield: 12 servings.

Menu planning: Plan twelve hors d'oeuvre per person if the event is being held after 5:30 p.m.

Artichoke Canapés

4 slices white bread, toasted, crusts trimmed
1 (8-ounce) jar marinated artichoke hearts,
    drained
6 tablespoons mayonnaise
2 teaspoons minced shallots
1 tablespoon grated Parmesan cheese

⚷— Cut four 1¹/₂-inch circles from each piece of toast. Cut the artichoke hearts into 16 pieces. Combine the mayonnaise, shallots and cheese in a bowl and mix well.

Place 1 artichoke piece on each toast round. Top with a spoonful of the mayonnaise mixture, covering the artichoke and toast completely. Place on a baking sheet.

Broil under a preheated broiler until golden brown and bubbly. Serve hot.

Yield: 16 appetizers.

Years ago, mothers of teenage girls in Alexandria sponsored (and chaperoned) Tea Dances. They were from four to six at The Sky Roof Garden downtown and featured live music and dancing. On these occasions, each girl invited the boy of her choice, making this a great way to check out that secret crush.

Tea sandwich fillings may include: Chicken salad and orange marmalade; applesauce and nutmeg; cheese spread and sliced tomatoes; chopped egg, minced onion, minced anchovies and mayonnaise; Parmesan cheese and mayonnaise; mashed avocado, tarragon vinegar, salt, pepper and chili sauce; grated raw vegetables and salad dressing.

Bacon Tomato Quesadillas

2 tablespoons margarine, softened
6 (8-inch) flour tortillas
4 cups shredded Monterey Jack cheese
1 pound bacon, crisp-cooked, crumbled
1 tomato, peeled, chopped
1/4 cup finely chopped pickled jalapeño chiles
1/4 cup salsa

⚷— Spread the margarine over 1 side of each tortilla. Place margarine side up on a baking sheet. Bake at 400 degrees for 3 minutes.

Combine the cheese, bacon, tomato, chiles and salsa in a bowl and mix well. Spread evenly over the baked tortillas. Bake at 400 degrees for 5 minutes or until the cheese is bubbly. Cut each tortilla into fourths.

Yield: 24 appetizers.

Crabbies

1 cup white crab meat
1 (5-ounce) jar Old English sharp cheese
1 tablespoon mayonnaise
1/4 teaspoon salt
1 teaspoon garlic powder
1/2 cup (1 stick) margarine, softened
6 English muffins, split

⚷— Combine the crab meat, cheese, mayonnaise, salt, garlic powder and margarine in a bowl and mix well. Spread over the muffin halves. Cut into quarters. Arrange on a broiler pan. Broil until bubbly. Serve immediately.

Yield: 48 appetizers.

Crawfish in Phyllo Triangles

16 ounces cream cheese, softened
1 pound cooked crawfish, shelled,
    coarsely chopped
3 scallions, chopped
1 tablespoon chopped fresh cilantro
1 tablespoon chopped fresh tarragon
1/2 teaspoon chopped garlic
1/2 teaspoon red chili paste or red
    pepper flakes
1/8 teaspoon salt
Juice of 1/2 lime
1 (16-ounce) package frozen phyllo dough
3/4 cup (1 1/2 sticks) melted butter
1 cup bread crumbs

Combine the cream cheese, crawfish, scallions, cilantro, tarragon, garlic, chili paste, salt and lime juice in a bowl and mix well.

Place 1 sheet of phyllo dough on a lightly floured surface. Brush lightly with melted butter. Sprinkle with bread crumbs. Place another sheet of dough over the bread crumbs. Brush lightly with melted butter. Sprinkle with bread crumbs. Place a third sheet of dough over the layers. Cut horizontally to form 3 rectangles. Place a rounded tablespoonful of the filling mixture on a corner of each rectangle. Fold each rectangle like a flag, forming triangles. Brush the tops of the triangles with melted butter. Repeat the process until all ingredients are used.

Place triangles on a baking sheet. Bake at 400 degrees for 12 minutes.

Yield: 24 appetizers.

Edible Flowers

Edible flowers can transform the presentation of your food with colors that are vivid and varied. This is especially true if you are doing a buffet, tea party, or cocktail party where all the dishes are set out on the table at once, offering a visual feast as well as an edible one. Use flowers to embellish the tops of pâtés, wheels of cheese, or any food with a flat top. You can make designs using leaves and whole sprigs of herbs. Fruits cut into shapes and whole flower heads also look appetizing.

Editor's Note: Thaw phyllo dough, unopened, in the refrigerator overnight. It dries out very quickly, so do not open the package until the filling has been prepared. Unroll the phyllo and cover it with waxed paper topped with a damp towel. Keep the unused portion covered until needed.

Creole Tartar Sauce

1 cup mayonnaise
1 teaspoon minced garlic
1 tablespoon chopped parsley
2 tablespoons chopped green onion tops
1/4 teaspoon cayenne pepper
*1 tablespoon Creole mustard or whole-
    grain mustard*
1 teaspoon salt

Combine the mayonnaise, garlic, parsley, green onions, cayenne pepper, mustard and salt in a bowl and mix well. Chill, covered, for 1 hour or longer; use within 24 hours.

Crawfish Beignets

2 1/2 teaspoons chopped garlic
2 cups mayonnaise
Cayenne pepper to taste
Salt to taste
Black pepper to taste
2 tablespoons catsup
1 pound crawfish, cut into halves
2 eggs
1 tablespoon dry mustard
1 teaspoon cayenne pepper
1 1/2 teaspoons salt
1/2 cup flour
1/2 cup chopped green onions
12 ounces angel hair pasta, hot, cooked
Vegetable oil for deep-frying

Combine the garlic, mayonnaise, cayenne pepper to taste, salt to taste, black pepper and catsup in a bowl and mix well. Set aside.

Combine the crawfish, eggs, mustard, 1 teaspoon cayenne pepper, 1 1/2 teaspoons salt, flour and green onions in a bowl and mix well. Stir in the pasta. Shape into 1-inch balls, pressing to form.

Deep-fry in hot oil for 2 minutes or until brown. Serve with the mayonnaise mixture or Creole Tartar Sauce.

Yield: 50 to 60 appetizers.

Cucumber Sandwiches

3 small cucumbers, peeled, seeded, minced
16 ounces cream cheese, softened
3 tablespoons minced fresh Italian parsley
2 teaspoons minced fresh mint
1/2 teaspoon minced fresh oregano
1 1/2 teaspoons lime zest
2 teaspoons green peppercorns, crushed
1/2 teaspoon salt
1 medium shallot, chopped
1 clove garlic, minced
36 wheat or white bread slices
1/2 cup chopped fresh parsley
9 fresh parsley sprigs

Drain the cucumbers, pressing between layers of paper towels to remove the excess moisture.

Combine the cream cheese, Italian parsley, mint, oregano, lime zest, green peppercorns and salt in a bowl and mix well. Stir in the cucumber, shallot and garlic. Chill, covered, for 4 hours.

Cut the bread slices into rounds using a 3-inch cutter. Spread the cream cheese mixture evenly over half the bread rounds. Top with the remaining rounds. Roll the sides of 9 sandwiches in the chopped parsley, coating the edge. Top the remaining sandwiches with a parsley sprig.

Yield: 18 appetizers.

The perfect cut for tea/cucumber sandwiches can be achieved by using the open end of a liquid medicine cup. Pressing down much like a cookie cutter and rotating gently in the bread will yield 3 to 4 perfect circles per slice of bread.

Cucumber Memories

Munching on cucumber and cream cheese sandwiches brings back memories of parties at the Fishville Camp, a favorite summer rustic retreat for the young mothers and their children. The cool spring creek helped restore the psyches after broken summer romances. The evenings and afternoons were filled with wading in the creek, which was followed by playing Liverpool rummy, the latest card craze of the day. Isn't it wonderful the images evoked from such an unsuspecting sandwich.

Eggplant Cookies with Goat Cheese and Tomato Basil Sauce

2 teaspoons olive oil
1 large clove garlic, minced
1 small shallot, minced
1 tablespoon tequila, preferably golden
1 1/2 tablespoons dry red wine
2 large tomatoes, peeled, seeded, chopped
1/8 teaspoon each salt and freshly
    ground pepper
2 tablespoons julienned fresh basil
2 oriental eggplant, peeled, cut into
    1/2-inch rounds
1/2 cup flour, sifted
1 egg, lightly beaten
1/2 cup fresh bread crumbs
6 tablespoons olive oil
4 ounces cylindrical goat cheese, cut into
    12 rounds

Heat the 2 teaspoons olive oil in a saucepan over medium heat. Add the garlic and shallot. Cook for 1 minute or until tender but not brown, stirring constantly. Add the tequila and wine.

Cook for 1 minute or until the liquid is almost completely absorbed. Stir in the tomatoes, salt and pepper.

Cook for 5 minutes or until slightly thickened. Stir in the basil. Remove from heat. Cover to keep warm.

Dredge the eggplant rounds in the flour to coat. Dip in the egg. Dredge in the bread crumbs to coat. Heat 2 of the 6 tablespoons olive oil in a large heavy skillet over medium-high heat.

Add 1/3 of the eggplant slices. Cook for 4 minutes on each side or until crisp and golden brown. Drain on paper towels. Repeat the process with the remaining olive oil and eggplant.

Place 1 round of goat cheese between 2 hot cooked eggplant slices. Repeat with the remaining cheese and eggplant slices. Spread the tomato sauce over the bottom of a heated serving platter. Arrange the eggplant "cookies" over the sauce. Serve warm.

Yield: 12 appetizers.

Jalapeño Tongue Twisters

¹/₂ cup minced onion
¹/₂ cup minced celery
¹/₂ cup minced green bell pepper
¹/₂ cup (1 stick) margarine
8 ounces shrimp, shelled, deveined, cut into
*   small pieces*
1 tablespoon minced garlic
1 tablespoon flour
¹/₂ cup milk or water
1¹/₂ to 2 cups seasoned bread crumbs
8 ounces crab meat
¹/₂ cup minced green onion tops
1 tablespoon chopped parsley
¹/₄ teaspoon hot pepper sauce
2 teaspoons Creole seasoning
¹/₂ teaspoon Worcestershire sauce
¹/₂ teaspoon salt
¹/₂ teaspoon freshly ground pepper
2 (28-ounce) cans whole jalapeño chiles,
*   drained*
¹/₂ cup milk
2 eggs, beaten
2 cups flour
³/₄ teaspoon baking powder
Vegetable oil for deep-frying

Sauté the onion, celery and bell pepper in the margarine in a large skillet over medium heat. Stir in the shrimp and garlic.

Cook over low heat for 15 minutes. Stir in the flour. Stir in the milk. Cook until thickened, stirring constantly. Stir in enough bread crumbs to absorb the liquid.

Add the crab meat, green onions, parsley, hot pepper sauce, Creole seasoning, Worcestershire sauce, salt and pepper and mix well. Add water if needed for the desired consistency. Add additional seasonings to taste. Let stand until cooled.

Cut the chiles from top to bottom on 1 side, removing the seeds; drain. Stuff with the bread crumb mixture.

Combine the milk and eggs in a shallow dish and mix well. Combine the flour and baking powder in a shallow dish and mix well. Dredge each stuffed chile in the flour mixture to coat. Dip in the milk mixture. Dredge in the flour mixture again.

Deep-fry the coated chiles in hot oil until brown; drain. Serve with cold ranch salad dressing.

Yield: 50 appetizers.

To prepare fresh chiles, cut them lengthwise into halves. Scrape out the seeds with a small knife, removing the membrane with them.

Flatten the chile with the palm of your hand and slice lengthwise into strips with a chef's knife.

To dice, hold the strips firmly together and slice into equal-size cubes.

Handling Peppers

· When handling all but the mildest of peppers, use rubber gloves. Some of the hotter varieties can cause burning pain just by coming in contact with unbroken skin. Never touch your eyes or other sensitive areas after handling peppers.

· What to do if you get burned? If it's your skin that is burning, try a little vegetable oil. If it's your mouth that's aflame, try milk, sour cream, yogurt, ice cream, tomato juice, lemon or lime juice, bread or rice. Water, surprisingly, can actually fan the flame by distributing the capsaicin (the heat-causing compound) to more areas of the mouth.

Armadillo Eggs

1 (15-ounce) can whole seeded jalapeño chiles
16 ounces finely shredded cheese
1 pound hot ground pork
1 1/2 cups baking mix
2 eggs, beaten
1 (6-ounce) package pork flavor Shake'n Bake

Rinse and pat dry each chile. Remove the stems. Stuff each chile with the cheese, reserving any remaining cheese.

Mix the pork, baking mix and remaining cheese in a bowl. Shape into patties. Wrap each patty around a stuffed chile, sealing the edges.

Dip into the eggs. Dredge in the Shake'n Bake to coat. Place on a greased baking sheet. Bake at 350 degrees for 30 minutes.

Yield: 15 to 20 appetizers.

Meatballs in Cranberry Sauce

2 cups bread crumbs
1/2 cup milk
1 tablespoon soy sauce
1/2 teaspoon garlic salt
1/4 teaspoon onion salt
1 pound ground beef
1 (6-ounce) can water chestnuts, drained, finely chopped
1 (16-ounce) can cranberry sauce
1 (12-ounce) jar chili sauce
2 tablespoons brown sugar
1 tablespoon lemon juice

Combine the bread crumbs, milk, soy sauce, garlic salt and onion salt in a bowl and mix well. Add the ground beef and water chestnuts and mix well. Shape into 1-inch balls. Place on a 10x15-inch baking pan.

Bake at 350 degrees for 18 to 20 minutes or until cooked through. Drain on paper towels.

Combine the cranberry sauce, chili sauce, brown sugar and lemon juice in a large saucepan. Cook until the mixture is smooth and the cranberry sauce is melted, stirring frequently. Add the meatballs, stirring to coat. Spoon into a chafing dish or electric casserole dish. Serve with wooden picks.

Yield: 5 dozen appetizers.

Sausage in Puff Pastry

12 ounces lean ground pork or veal
1/2 medium onion, chopped
3/4 cup chopped cooked potato
2 tablespoons chopped parsley
1 1/2 tablespoons crushed dried sage leaves
1/2 teaspoon salt
1/2 teaspoon black pepper
1/4 teaspoon crushed red pepper flakes
*1 (17-ounce) package frozen puff pastry,
    thawed*
1 egg, well beaten
1/2 cup Worcestershire sauce

⚷ Combine the pork, onion, potato, parsley, sage, salt, black pepper and red pepper flakes in a bowl and mix well. Spoon into a large pastry bag fitted with a large plain tip.

Unfold the pastry sheets. Cut each sheet into 3 rectangles, using the fold marks as a guide. Roll out slightly. Pipe the pork mixture along one of the long edges of each rectangle. Brush the opposite edges with some of the egg. Roll up each rectangle, starting at the edge with the sausage mixture and pressing the edge to seal. Cut each roll into 1 1/2-inch-thick slices.

Place the slices on a broiler pan or a wire rack set on top of a baking sheet. Brush the slices with the remaining egg. Bake at 350 degrees for 20 minutes or until golden brown. Serve warm with the Worcestershire sauce.

Yield: 50 appetizers.

Creamed Mushrooms

1/4 cup (1/2 stick) butter
2 pounds mushrooms, sliced
1/4 cup sherry
6 tablespoons milk
2 cups sour cream
1 cup grated Parmesan cheese
1/2 teaspoon salt
1/2 teaspoon pepper
3/4 teaspoon paprika
Buttered toast points

⚷ Heat the butter in a skillet until melted. Add the mushrooms and sauté for 5 minutes or until lightly cooked but not browned. Stir in the sherry. Cook over high heat for 1 minute. Add the milk, sour cream, Parmesan cheese, salt, pepper and paprika and stir to combine. Cook over low heat until smooth and slightly thickened, stirring constantly.

Divide the toast points among 6 plates. Pour the mushroom mixture over the toast points.

Yield: 6 servings.

Fried Oyster Mushrooms

1 1/2 cups flour
1/4 cup cornstarch
1/2 teaspoon paprika
3/4 teaspoon salt
1/2 teaspoon pepper
2 tablespoons minced parsley
2 eggs
1 1/3 cups milk
18 well-shaped whole oyster mushrooms
Vegetable oil for deep-frying
Avocado Mayonnaise or Whipped
    Horseradish Sauce

    Combine the flour, cornstarch, paprika, salt, pepper and parsley in a shallow dish and mix well. Combine the eggs and milk in a shallow dish and mix well. Dredge the mushrooms in the flour mixture to coat. Dip in the milk mixture. Dredge in the flour mixture again.

    Deep-fry in 365-degree oil for 5 minutes or until golden brown. Drain on paper towels. Serve with Avocado Mayonnaise or Whipped Horseradish Sauce.

    Yield: 18 appetizers.

Avocado Mayonnaise

1 cup mayonnaise
1 avocado, puréed
1 pimento, minced
1 tablespoon lemon juice
Salt to taste
Tabasco sauce to taste
1 bunch green onions, tops only, chopped
2 tablespoons chopped parsley

    Combine the mayonnaise, avocado, pimento, lemon juice, salt, Tabasco sauce, green onions and parsley in a bowl and mix well.

Whipped Horseradish Sauce

1/2 cup heavy cream
2 tablespoons prepared horseradish
1 to 2 tablespoons lemon juice
1 tablespoon lemon zest
1/8 teaspoon cayenne pepper
Salt and black pepper to taste

    Beat the cream in a mixer bowl until soft peaks form. Fold in the horseradish, lemon juice, lemon zest and cayenne pepper. Season with salt and black pepper. Chill for 30 minutes.

For avocados to be served as halves, with a dressing or filling in the central cavity, the skin is left intact. Cut the avocado lengthwise in half all around the stone. Twist the halves in opposite directions until separated. Carefully strike the pit with a knife. Twist to dislodge.

Oysters Alex

4 shallots, chopped
1/2 clove garlic, minced
2 tablespoons butter
3 cups sliced mushrooms
Dash of pepper
1/8 teaspoon dried thyme
1/4 cup dry white wine
1 1/2 cups heavy cream
2 tablespoons butter
1 cup chopped, deveined peeled shrimp or
    crawfish tails
20 shucked oysters, drained
1 1/2 cups heavy cream
1/8 teaspoon dried tarragon, crushed
3 egg yolks
1/4 cup sherry
Salt and pepper to taste
20 (1/2-inch-thick) slices baguette, toasted

Cook half the shallots and the garlic in 2 tablespoons butter in a large skillet over medium heat. Stir in the mushrooms, dash of pepper and thyme. Cook until the liquid is evaporated.

Add the wine and 1 1/2 cups cream. Bring to a boil. Reduce the heat. Simmer for 5 minutes. Remove from heat and keep warm.

Cook the remaining shallots in 2 tablespoons butter in a saucepan until tender. Stir in the shrimp. Cook for 2 to 3 minutes or until opaque. Remove with a slotted spoon. Set aside and keep warm.

Add the oysters to the saucepan. Cook over medium heat for 5 minutes or until the edges begin to curl. Remove with a slotted spoon. Set aside and keep warm. Pour 1 1/2 cups cream into the saucepan. Add the tarragon. Bring to a boil. Reduce the heat.

Combine the egg yolks and sherry in a bowl and mix well. Stir a small amount of the hot cream mixture into the egg yolk mixture. Stir the egg yolk mixture into the hot cream mixture.

Cook over low heat for 3 minutes or until thickened, stirring constantly. Stir in the shrimp. Remove from heat. Season with salt and pepper to taste.

Spoon a small amount of the mushroom mixture onto each piece of toast. Place one oyster over the mushroom mixture. Spoon a small amount of the cream mixture over the oysters. Serve immediately.

Yield: 20 appetizers.

Rockefeller Turnovers

1 pint freshly shucked oysters,
    coarsely chopped
1 pound fresh spinach
1/2 cup (1 stick) unsalted butter
1 rib celery, finely chopped
2 large shallots, finely chopped
1 clove garlic, finely chopped
1 teaspoon salt
1/4 cup fresh lemon juice
1/4 cup Herbsaint or Pernod, or 1/2 teaspoon
    ground fennel seeds
1/2 teaspoon Tabasco sauce
1/2 cup fine dry bread crumbs
2 tablespoons finely chopped anchovy fillets
1 (17-ounce) package frozen puff pastry,
    thawed but very cold
1 egg
2 tablespoons water

Place the oysters in a strainer set over a bowl. Drain in the refrigerator for 1 hour. Chop the spinach. Cook in a steamer; drain.

Heat the butter in a large nonreactive skillet until melted. Add the celery and shallots. Cook over medium heat for 5 minutes or until tender, stirring occasionally. Stir in the garlic, spinach and salt. Increase the heat to medium-high. Add the lemon juice, Herbsaint and Tabasco sauce. Cook for 5 minutes or until the liquid is almost evaporated and the spinach is reduced to a coarse purée. Remove from the heat. Fold in the oysters, bread crumbs and anchovies. Spoon into a large strainer and drain.

Roll the puff pastry into two 14-inch squares or one 14x28-inch rectangle 1/8 inch thick on a lightly floured surface. Cut into 3 1/2-inch squares. Place a rounded tablespoon of the oyster mixture in the center of each square. Moisten two adjacent edges of each square lightly with water. Fold the opposite corner over to form triangular turnovers. Crimp the sealed edges with the tines of a fork. Arrange the turnovers 1 inch apart on a baking sheet.

Combine the egg and the water in a bowl and mix well. Brush lightly over the top of each turnover; do not let the egg mixture drip down the sides. Reserve the remaining egg mixture. Refrigerate the turnovers, covered with plastic wrap, until completely chilled or for up to 1 day.

Brush the tops of the turnovers lightly with the reserved egg mixture. Bake at 400 degrees for 20 minutes or until golden brown. Serve hot.

May substitute one drained thawed 10-ounce package frozen chopped spinach for the fresh spinach. May substitute 18 ounces very cold all-butter puff pastry for the frozen puff pastry.

Yield: 32 appetizers.

When choosing leafy greens such as endive, Swiss chard, and spinach, choose those with crisp, fresh-looking greens. Leaves should feel springy to the touch; avoid any that appear limp or wilted. There should be no sign of insect damage. Spinach leaves are best when small and moist, with fine stalks.

Savory Pesto Rugalach

2¹/₄ cups flour
1 cup (2 sticks) butter, cut into pieces
8 ounces cream cheese, cut into pieces
¹/₂ teaspoon salt
Basil Pesto

⊶ Combine the flour, butter, cream cheese and salt in a food processor container. Pulse until the dough leaves the side of the container. Divide into 8 equal portions. Wrap each portion in plastic wrap. Chill for 1 hour or longer.

Roll 1 portion into an 8-inch circle on a lightly floured surface. Spread with 3 tablespoons of the Basil Pesto, leaving a 2-inch circle uncovered in the center. Cut into 8 wedges. Roll each wedge up, starting at the wide end. Place point side down on a lightly greased baking sheet. Repeat the process with the remaining dough portions and pesto. May be frozen for up to 1 week.

Bake at 350 degrees for 15 to 20 minutes or until golden brown.

Yield: 64 appetizers.

Basil Pesto

1 cup fresh basil leaves
5 ounces pine nuts
1 cup freshly grated Parmesan cheese
2 cloves garlic, sliced
¹/₈ teaspoon salt
¹/₂ cup olive oil

⊶ Combine the basil, pine nuts, cheese, garlic, salt and olive oil in a food processor container. Process for 1 minute or until of uniform texture.

Mardi Gras

It is no secret that Mardi Gras has strong roots in Louisiana. By the early 1700s the French were already celebrating Mardi Gras in the New World. The observance began as masked balls and lascivious street processions. By 1806 the celebration became so lewd and rowdy that Mardi Gras festivities were forbidden, but the law was ignored. Masks were declared illegal in 1817 as another attempt to end the revelry. In true Louisiana style, the persistence of the celebrants paid off. Mardi Gras was declared legal again in 1823, and masquerading was legalized in 1826. The Mystick Krewe of Comus was the first to parade the streets of New Orleans in the 1830s. The parade consisted of a secret society of krewe members and two floats.

Bloody Marys

Bloody Marys or Virgin Marys (fondly called Bloodys or Marys depending on if they are virgins or not) is a traditional start for a spicy Louisiana brunch. Here are the basics:
Tomato juice or V-8 juice
Vodka (leave this out for the
Virgin Mary)
Prepared horseradish
Tabasco sauce
Worcestershire sauce
Celery salt
Black pepper
For the perfect finishing touch, add a celery stick or pickled green bean and 1 wedge each of lemon and lime.

Crawfish Bloody Mary

2 ounces vodka
Bloody Mary Mix to taste
1 tablespoon picante sauce
1 teaspoon prepared horseradish sauce
Dash of Worcestershire sauce
Drop of Salsa de Chile Habanero or Louisiana
Hot Sauce
Creole Crab Boil

Combine the vodka, Bloody Mary Mix, picante sauce, horseradish sauce, Worchestershire sauce and Salsa de Chile Habanero in a drink container and mix well. Pour over ice in 2 glasses. Serve with a celery stick. Sprinkle lightly with Creole Crab Boil.

Yield: 2 servings.

Amaretto Freeze

1 quart vanilla ice cream, softened
1/3 cup amaretto
2 tablespoons Triple Sec
1/4 cup crème de cacao

Combine the ice cream, amaretto, Triple Sec and crème de cacao in a food processor container fitted with a steel blade. Process until smooth. Chill until cold. Pour into drink glasses.

Yield: 2 servings.

Old-Fashioned

1 1/2 ounces Southern Comfort bourbon
1 teaspoon Simple Syrup
1 teaspoon orange marmalade
1 teaspoon maraschino cherry juice
Dash of bitters
Dash of club soda (optional)
1 maraschino cherry with stem

Combine the bourbon, Simple Syrup, marmalade, cherry juice and bitters in a double old-fashioned glass and mix well. Add enough ice to fill the glass 2/3 full and stir. Add the club soda. Place the cherry in the glass.

Yield: 1 serving.

Simple Syrup

2 parts sugar
1 part water

Combine the sugar and water in a saucepan. Bring to a boil. Boil for 5 minutes. Store in the refrigerator.

Brandy Alexander

2 ounces each crème de cacao, brandy and heavy cream
Cracked ice

Combine the crème de cacao, brandy, cream and cracked ice in a cocktail shaker and shake well. Strain into a brandy snifter. May substitute light cream for the heavy cream or use a fruit-flavored brandy.

Yield: 4 servings.

Piña Colada Punch

1 (46-ounce) can unsweetened pineapple juice, chilled
1 (34-ounce) bottle club soda, chilled
1 (16-ounce) can cream of coconut, chilled

Mix the pineapple juice, club soda and cream of coconut in a punch bowl.

Yield: 24 servings.

Decorative ice cubes can be made by placing fresh berries, mint leaves, pineapple chunks, maraschino cherries, cucumber wedges, stuffed ripe olives, mandarin oranges, or citrus fruit twists in ice cube trays with water.

Mardi Gras

Mardi Gras officially begins on the twelfth day after Christmas and ends the day before Lent, or Fat Tuesday as it is known by those who celebrate Mardi Gras. Each day from January 6 through Fat Tuesday is a day of celebration. Another name for January 6 is Kings Day. Some Christians call January 6 the Epiphany, or Little Christmas. Since the third century, the Epiphany or Little Christmas, has been observed as the day the Wise Men found the Baby Jesus.

The colors of Mardi Gras are purple for justice, green for faith, and gold for power. Instituted as the official colors of Mardi Gras in 1872, they were adopted from the house of Romanoff in honor of Russian Grand Duke Alexis Romanoff's visit to New Orleans during the Mardi Gras season.

Mardi Gras Punch

2 cups vanilla ice cream, softened
1½ ounces praline liqueur
1 ounce vodka

Combine the ice cream, liqueur and vodka in a blender container. Process until smooth.

Yield: 4 servings.

New Orleans Milk Punch

1½ cups milk
1½ cups half-and-half
½ cup white crème de cacao
½ cup bourbon
2 tablespoons confectioners' sugar
2 egg whites
Cinnamon to taste

Combine the milk, half-and-half, crème de cacao, bourbon, confectioners' sugar and egg whites in a blender container. Process until frothy. Pour over cracked ice in 4 drink glasses. Sprinkle with cinnamon.

Yield: 4 servings.

Spring Punch

2 cups sugar
2 1/2 cups water
1 cup lemon juice
1 cup orange juice with pulp
1 (6-ounce) can frozen pineapple juice
*   concentrate*
1 quart ginger ale

Bring the sugar and water to a boil in a saucepan. Boil for 10 minutes. Remove from heat. Add the lemon juice, orange juice and pineapple juice concentrate, stirring until the concentrate has dissolved. Refrigerate until completely chilled. Stir in the ginger ale. Pour into a punch bowl. Garnish with cherries frozen in orange juice cubes.

Yield: 16 to 20 servings.

Sangria

1 (750-milliliter) bottle burgundy
1 bottle Champagne
1 (6-ounce) can frozen lemonade concentrate,
*   thawed*
1 (6-ounce) can frozen orange juice
*   concentrate, thawed*
2 liters club soda

Combine the wine, Champagne, lemonade concentrate, orange juice concentrate and club soda in a punch bowl and mix well. Garnish with apple and orange slices. Serve over ice.

Yield: 20 to 25 servings.

Try freezing small blossoms or herbs in ice cube trays or decorative ice molds; floating them in beverages makes for a lovely little surprise. Tiny rose heads or violets in ice cubes can be added to such drinks as plain water or iced tea. Mint or lemon balm leaves in cubes are the perfect complement to lemonade. Large ice molds dappled with flowers look elegant in silver or glass punch bowls filled to the brim with cold Champagne or fruit punch.

Soups & Salads

Alexandria offers a variety of activities for people of every age and interest. Museums, music, theatre, sports, and family fun are always on the menu here in central Louisiana.

Area festivals feature a wide variety of music, crafts, and demonstrations. Downtown rocks with citizens enjoying outdoor concerts featuring blues, rock, and pop sounds. The riverfront sings with the sound of the Rapides Symphony when they perform their annual Pops in the Park concert while the audience dines in the moonlight. We have community theatre opportunities for children as well as adults, with year-round performances. The downtown arts district features the Alexandria Museum of Art, the River Oaks Square Arts Center that includes art studios of many of our area artists, and the Arna Bontemps African-American Museum and Cultural Arts Center. The Tunica Biloxi tribe has annual powwows open to the public for education and enjoyment.

Sporting events have always been popular in central Louisiana. Besides nights at the ball field and mornings at the soccer field cheering on their kids, area residents can be found in historic Bringhurst field supporting the Alexandria Aces. Fans also gather in the Rapides Coliseum to hear the swish of the ice with the Warthogs hockey team. Professional sports have found a home here with spirited fans.

The Alexandria Zoo is a favorite meeting place for children and adults alike. It is home to more than 500 animals, including 20 endangered species, and the train at the Alexandria Zoo—Bayou LeZoo Choo Choo— provides a favorite family excursion around the entire zoo. The newest expansion of the zoo, the Louisiana Habitat, is one of the finest regional exhibits found anywhere in the South.

Wherever we go in central Louisiana, you can bet we've packed along some refreshments. These recipes should get things started nicely whether you want to soup it up or cool things down and keep it green.

Museums, music, theatre, sports, and family fun are always on the menu here in central Louisiana. The train at the Alexandria Zoo— Bayou LeZoo Choo Choo— provides a favorite family excursion around the entire zoo.

Cowboy Soup

1 1/2 pounds ground beef
1 cup chopped onion
2 tablespoons vegetable oil
1 envelope taco seasoning mix
1 envelope ranch salad dressing mix
1 (14-ounce) can diced tomatoes
1 (10-ounce) can tomatoes with green chiles
1 (8-ounce) can tomato sauce
1 (14-ounce) can pinto beans
1 (14-ounce) can red kidney beans
1 (14-ounce) can whole kernel corn

Brown the ground beef with the onion in the oil in a skillet, stirring until the ground beef is crumbly; drain. Stir in the seasoning and salad dressing mixes. Add the diced tomatoes, tomatoes with green chiles, tomato sauce, pinto beans, kidney beans and corn and mix well. Cook over low heat for 1 hour.

Serve over rice, corn chips or tortilla chips if desired. Garnish with sour cream and shredded cheese.

Yield: 8 servings.

The one outfit everyone in the South– possibly America–had as a child is the cowboy or cowgirl suit. You may think felt hats, fringed vests, bright red boots, and a shining sheriff's star were a product of the fifties, but the truth is that every kid secretly wishes for that ensemble at some point. So, go wild–make your kid's day.

Chicken Corn Chowder

4 slices bacon
1/2 cup chopped onion
3 tablespoons flour
3 cups half-and-half
2 cups chopped cooked chicken
1 tablespoon Creole seasoning
1/2 teaspoon thyme
1 (17-ounce) can whole kernel corn, drained
1 large potato, peeled, chopped, parboiled
1 carrot, peeled, chopped, parboiled
6 chicken bouillon cubes
1/4 teaspoon pepper
1 tablespoon flour (optional)
2 tablespoons water (optional)

Cook the bacon in a large saucepan until crisp. Remove the bacon and crumble. Sauté the onion in the bacon drippings until tender. Stir in 3 tablespoons flour. Add the half-and-half, whisking constantly. Add the chicken, Creole seasoning, thyme, corn, potato, carrot, bouillon cubes and pepper and mix well. Bring to a boil. Reduce the heat. Simmer for 30 minutes, stirring occasionally; do not boil again.

Combine 1 tablespoon flour and water in a bowl and mix well. Add to the chowder to thicken as needed. Ladle into soup bowls. Sprinkle with the bacon.

May substitute 1 1/2 cups half-and-half and 1 1/2 cups 2% milk for 3 cups half-and-half.

Yield: 8 to 10 servings.

Chicken and Sausage Gumbo

2 tablespoons vegetable oil
1 ham steak, cut into cubes
1 pound smoked sausage or andouille, sliced
$1/2$ cup chopped tasso (optional)
2 large onions, chopped
4 ribs celery, chopped
2 cloves garlic, minced
$1/2$ cup chopped parsley
$1/4$ cup vegetable oil
$1/4$ cup flour
3 quarts hot water
1 (3- to 4-pound) chicken or roasting hen
2 chicken bouillon cubes
Red pepper to taste
Black pepper to taste
White pepper to taste
Salt to taste
1 teaspoon thyme
1 bay leaf
2 tablespoons filé powder
$1/2$ cup chopped green onions
Hot cooked white rice

Heat 2 tablespoons oil in a Dutch oven. Add the ham, sausage, tasso, onions, celery, garlic and parsley. Sauté for 10 minutes. Remove with a slotted spoon and keep warm.

Add $1/4$ cup oil and flour to the pan drippings. Cook until dark brown, stirring constantly. Whisk in the hot water gradually. Add the chicken, bouillon cubes, red pepper, black pepper, white pepper, salt, thyme and bay leaf. Bring to a simmer. Simmer for 2 to 3 hours or until chicken is tender and cooked through.

Remove the chicken. Cut the meat into bite-size pieces, discarding the skin and bones.

Remove the gumbo from the heat. Stir in the chicken, sausage mixture, filé powder and green onions. Remove the bay leaf. Serve over rice.

Yield: 8 to 10 servings.

First You Make a Roux

A roux is the thickening agent for many Gulf Coast dishes, including gumbos, stews, and étouffées. The quickest and easiest way to make a roux is in the microwave. Whisk equal amounts of vegetable oil and flour in an 8-cup glass measure. Microwave for 30 seconds or until the color of a copper penny; stir the mixture. Microwave for 30 seconds longer if necessary, watching carefully to avoid burning. If it burns, discard the whole thing and begin again. You'll be wasting a week's wages on seafood if you put it into a burned roux! The completed roux, with vegetables, can be frozen for later use.

Chicken and Leek Soup

1 (2½-pound) chicken
2½ quarts water
1½ teaspoons salt
½ teaspoon freshly ground pepper
¼ teaspoon thyme
1 bay leaf
2 cloves garlic, minced
¼ cup (½ stick) unsalted butter
¼ cup flour
2 carrots, julienned
1 leek, julienned
2 ribs celery, julienned
½ cup julienned peeled potato
¼ cup julienned onion

Combine the chicken, water, salt, pepper, thyme, bay leaf and garlic in a stockpot. Cook until chicken is cooked through. Remove chicken from stock, reserving the stock. Let chicken cool. Strain the stock and set aside. Cut the chicken into bite-size pieces, discarding the skin and bones. Set aside.

Combine the butter and flour in a saucepan. Cook over medium heat until a light brown roux is made, stirring constantly. Whisk in the reserved stock gradually. Bring to a simmer. Simmer for 30 minutes.

Add the carrots, leek, celery, potato and onion. Simmer until tender. Add the chicken. Simmer until chicken is heated through. Ladle into soup bowls. Garnish with chopped fresh parsley.

Yield: 12 servings.

Smoked Salmon Bisque

3/4 cup chopped onion
½ cup chopped celery
¼ cup chopped parsley
¼ cup (½ stick) butter
3 cups finely chopped potatoes
2 tablespoons flour
1 cup clam juice
1 cup chicken broth
8 ounces chunk smoked salmon, flaked
Salt and white pepper to taste
2 cups heavy cream

Cook the onion, celery and parsley in the butter in a saucepan until tender, stirring frequently. Add the potatoes. Cook for 10 minutes, stirring frequently. Add the flour and stir to coat the vegetables.

Stir in the clam juice, broth, salmon, salt and white pepper. Simmer for 20 minutes. Pour in the cream. Cook for 15 minutes; do not boil.

Yield: 4 servings.

If you've over-salted soups or vegetables, add cut raw potatoes. They will absorb the salt. Discard the potatoes once the soup is fully cooked.

Crawfish Bisque

1/4 cup (1/2 stick) butter
1 medium onion, chopped
1/2 green bell pepper, chopped
1 clove garlic, minced
1 (15-ounce) can cream of mushroom soup
1 (8-ounce) can tomato sauce
4 ounces dark roux
4 cups hot water
8 ounces seasoned crawfish tails,
    finely chopped
1/4 cup minced parsley
1/4 cup chopped green onions
1/4 teaspoon thyme
1 bay leaf
1 pound seasoned crawfish tails
Salt to taste
Red pepper to taste
Black pepper to taste
Creole seasoning to taste
Crawfish Cakes

Heat the butter in a large heavy pot until melted. Add the onion, bell pepper and garlic. Sauté until tender.

Add the soup, tomato sauce and roux. Cook over medium-low heat until blended, stirring constantly. Whisk in the water gradually. Reduce the heat. Simmer for 15 minutes. Stir in the chopped crawfish tails, parsley, green onions, thyme and bay leaf. Simmer for 1 1/2 hours, stirring frequently.

Stir in 1 pound crawfish tails. Simmer for 15 to 20 minutes. Season with salt, red pepper, black pepper and Creole seasoning. Remove the bay leaf. Place 1 Crawfish Cake in the center of each of 6 shallow soup bowls. Ladle soup around the Crawfish Cake. Garnish with additional parsley or green onions. May serve with white rice.

Yield: 6 servings.

Crawfish Cakes

3 tablespoons olive oil
2 tablespoons minced onion
1 tablespoon minced red bell pepper
1 tablespoon minced green bell pepper
2 teaspoons minced garlic
1 tablespoon chopped parsley
1 tablespoon chopped green onions
8 ounces crawfish, coarsely chopped
1/2 teaspoon salt
1/4 teaspoon cayenne pepper
1/4 teaspoon black pepper
2 teaspoons Creole mustard
2 cups bread crumbs
1 egg, beaten
1 cup flour
1 teaspoon Creole seasoning
1/2 cup milk
1 egg, beaten

Heat 1 tablespoon of the olive oil in a large skillet. Add the onion and bell peppers. Sauté until tender. Add the garlic, parsley, green onions, crawfish, salt, cayenne pepper and black pepper. Sauté until crawfish turn red and are just cooked through. Remove from the heat. Stir in the mustard and 1 cup of the bread crumbs. Let stand until cool. Add 1 egg and mix well. Chill in the refrigerator.

Combine the flour and Creole seasoning in a shallow dish and mix well. Combine the milk and 1 egg in a shallow dish and mix well. Place the remaining 1 cup bread crumbs in a shallow dish.

Shape the crawfish mixture into 6 small 1/2-inch-thick cakes. Dredge each cake in the flour. Dip in the milk. Dredge in the bread crumbs.

Heat the remaining 2 tablespoons olive oil in a skillet. Add the cakes. Cook for 1 to 2 minutes per side or until brown.

Cream of Crab and Corn Soup

2 tablespoons butter
1/2 cup chopped green onions
2 cloves garlic, minced
1/2 to 1 teaspoon cayenne pepper
4 (10-ounce) cans cream of potato soup
16 ounces cream cheese, softened
3 3/4 cups milk
1 (14-ounce) can whole kernel corn
1 (14-ounce) can cream-style corn
1 pound lump crab meat

Heat the butter in a large saucepan until melted. Add the green onions and garlic. Sprinkle with the cayenne pepper. Sauté until the green onions are tender.

Add the soup, cream cheese and milk. Cook over medium heat, stirring until well blended. Stir in the corn and crab meat. Bring to a boil. Reduce the heat. Simmer for 10 minutes.

May substitute crawfish for the crab meat and add paprika for color. May be frozen.

Yield: 12 to 14 servings.

Lobster and Chive Bisque

1 tablespoon finely chopped onion
3 tablespoons butter
1 cup lobster meat
3 tablespoons flour
1/2 cup sherry
3 cups milk
1 teaspoon salt
Pinch of paprika
1 cup cream
2 tablespoons chopped chives

Sauté the onion in the butter in a large skillet until tender. Stir in the lobster meat. Add the flour. Cook until blended, stirring constantly. Stir in the sherry, milk, salt, paprika and cream.

Cook over low heat until thickened. Stir in the chives. Let stand over hot water until ready to serve. Ladle into soup bowls.

Yield: 6 servings.

To clarify butter, melt in a saucepan over low heat; do not brown. Remove from heat. Let stand for 2 to 3 minutes or until the solids settle. Skim off the clear liquid, discarding the sediment.

Oysters Rockefeller Soup

1/4 cup (1/2 stick) unsalted butter
2 cups minced white onion
1 to 1 1/2 cups minced celery
1/4 cup sherry
8 cups oyster water and/or bottled clam juice
2 teaspoons salt
1 teaspoon white pepper
3/4 cup clarified butter
3/4 cup flour
2 pounds fresh spinach, stemmed,
　　finely chopped
2 cups heavy cream
3 pints shucked oysters, drained,
　　coarsely chopped
2 tablespoons Tabasco or Louisiana hot sauce
2 tablespoons minced green onions tops

⊶ Heat the butter in a stockpot over medium-high heat until melted. Add the onion and celery. Sauté for 5 minutes. Add the sherry, stirring to deglaze the stockpot. Add the oyster water and/or clam juice. Bring to a simmer. Simmer for 15 minutes, skimming the top and stirring occasionally. Add the salt and pepper.

Combine the clarified butter and flour in a heavy skillet. Cook over low heat to make a blonde roux. Add to the stockpot, stirring until dissolved. Stir in the spinach. Simmer for 30 seconds. Stir in the cream, oysters and Tabasco sauce. Simmer for 3 to 4 minutes. Remove from heat. Season with additional salt and white pepper as needed.

Ladle into soup bowls. Sprinkle the minced green onions over the soup.

Yield: 12 servings.

Cream of Brown Scallop Soup

2 tablespoons chopped onion
1 quart diced fresh scallops
1/2 cup (1 stick) butter
1/4 cup flour
4 cups milk
Salt and coarsely ground pepper
1 cup cream
Blanched slivered almonds (optional)

⊶ Cook the onion and scallops in the butter in a large skillet, stirring until scallops are evenly browned. Add the flour. Stir until blended. Pour in the milk. Cook over low heat until thickened, stirring constantly. Season with salt and pepper.

Add the cream just before serving. Heat until very hot. Stir in almonds.

Yield: 8 servings.

The right wine to flavor any soup: sherry to crab, lobster and shrimp bisques; chablis to chowders; burgundy to minestrones and bean soups.

Shrimp Bisque Cardinale

1/4 cup (1/2 stick) butter
2 tablespoons (heaping) grated onion
3 tablespoons flour
1/2 teaspoon dry mustard
4 cups half-and-half, heated
2 cups milk, heated
2 tablespoons catsup
1 1/2 teaspoons tomato paste
2 teaspoons chopped parsley
1 pound cooked shrimp or crab meat
2 tablespoons dry sherry
2 teaspoons Worcestershire sauce
1/4 teaspoon Tabasco sauce
2 teaspoons salt
Dash of white pepper

⚷— Heat the butter in a heavy saucepan over medium heat until melted. Add the onion. Sauté for 5 minutes. Stir in the flour. Cook for 2 minutes. Stir in the dry mustard. Reduce the heat. Whisk in the half-and-half and milk gradually. Whisk in the catsup.

Combine 1/4 cup of the milk mixture with the tomato paste in a bowl and stir until smooth. Stir into the milk mixture in the saucepan. Stir in the parsley, shrimp, sherry, Worcestershire sauce, Tabasco sauce, salt and white pepper. Adjust the seasonings as needed.

Refrigerate, covered, for several hours or for up to 3 days to allow flavors to blend.

Serve cold or warm.

Yield: 8 servings.

Corn and Shrimp Soup

2/3 cup vegetable oil
6 tablespoons flour
2 onions, chopped
2 pounds shrimp, peeled
2 bell peppers, chopped
1/4 cup chopped parsley
Salt and pepper to taste
2 (16-ounce) cans tomatoes
2 (16-ounce) cans corn
2 cups water

⚷— Combine the vegetable oil and flour in a medium skillet and mix well. Cook over medium heat until golden brown, stirring constantly; do not burn. Stir in the onions. Cook for 10 minutes, stirring frequently.

Add the shrimp, bell peppers and parsley and mix well. Season with salt and pepper. Cook for 10 minutes, stirring occasionally. Stir in the tomatoes, corn and water. Cook for 1 hour, adding additional water as needed.

Yield: 6 to 8 servings.

Shrimp and Corn Chowder

1/4 cup (1/2 stick) butter
8 ounces fresh mushrooms, sliced
1 cup chopped green onions
8 ounces cream cheese
2 (10-ounce) cans niblet corn
2 (15-ounce) cans cream of potato soup
1 (15-ounce) can cream of mushroom soup
1 pound shrimp, peeled
2 cups half-and-half
Seasoned salt or Creole seasoning to taste
Hot sauce to taste

Heat the butter in a large saucepan until melted. Add the mushrooms and green onions. Sauté until tender. Reduce the heat to low. Add the cream cheese, stirring until blended. Add the corn, potato and mushroom soups, stirring until blended. Add the shrimp, half-and-half, seasoned salt and hot sauce and mix well. Cook for 25 to 30 minutes, stirring occasionally.

May substitute chicken, crawfish or crab for the shrimp.

Yield: 10 to 12 servings.

Cream of Artichoke Soup with Bleu Cheese

1 medium onion, chopped
3 tablespoons butter
1/4 cup flour
1 1/2 cups chicken stock
1/2 cup dry vermouth
1 (14-ounce) can artichoke hearts, drained, rinsed
2 tablespoons finely chopped parsley
1 1/4 cups half-and-half
1 (14-ounce) can artichoke hearts, drained, rinsed, chopped
Salt and pepper to taste
4 ounces crumbled bleu cheese

Sauté the onion in the butter in a large saucepan until tender. Add the flour. Cook for 2 minutes, stirring constantly. Remove from heat. Whisk in the stock and vermouth. Stir in 1 can artichoke hearts and parsley. Cook over medium heat for 5 minutes, stirring constantly.

Pour into a blender container. Process until puréed. Return to the saucepan. Add the half-and-half, chopped artichoke hearts, salt and pepper. Ladle into soup bowls. Sprinkle the bleu cheese over the soup.

Yield: 4 to 6 servings.

When choosing mushrooms, choose firm, fresh-looking ones that have a soft "bloom" and fresh smell. The stalk ends should be moist; if dry they may be slightly old.

White Bean Chili

16 ounces large white beans, rinsed
6 cups chicken broth
2 medium onions, chopped
2 (4-ounce) cans chopped green chiles
6 to 8 cloves garlic, minced
1 tablespoon olive oil
2 teaspoons ground cumin
1 1/2 teaspoons oregano
1 teaspoon cayenne pepper
4 cups chopped chicken breasts
1 cup sour cream
1 cup shredded Monterey Jack cheese
Salt to taste
Green onions to taste

Combine the beans with enough water to cover in a saucepan. Bring to a boil. Remove from heat. Let stand for 1 hour; drain. Combine the beans and broth in a stockpot. Bring to a boil. Reduce the heat. Simmer for 2 hours or until the beans are tender.

Sauté the onions, chiles and garlic in the olive oil in a skillet until tender. Add to the bean mixture. Cook for 20 minutes. Add the cumin, oregano, cayenne pepper and chicken. Simmer until chicken is cooked through. Stir in the sour cream, cheese and salt. Ladle into soup bowls. Top with green onions. Serve with corn or tortilla chips, sour cream, green onions, red onions, chopped tomatoes, salsa, cilantro, additional cheese or jalapeño chiles.

May substitute crawfish for the chicken. May be frozen before adding the sour cream and cheese.

Yield: 8 to 10 servings.

Friendship Bean Soup

1 cup Friendship Bean Soup Mix
4 cups water
1 slice bacon, chopped
1 onion, chopped
1 clove garlic
1 (10-ounce) can tomatoes with green chiles
8 ounces ham or smoked sausage, chopped
Salt and pepper to taste

Combine the Friendship Bean Soup Mix and water in a large saucepan. Soak for 8 to 12 hours. Add the bacon, onion and garlic. Cook for 1 1/2 hours. Stir in the tomatoes with green chiles and ham. Cook for 1 hour or until the beans are tender. Season with salt and pepper.

Yield: 4 to 6 servings.

Friendship Bean Soup Mix

1 (1-pound) package of 5 or 6 of the following:
Red kidney beans
Small white beans
Split green peas
Black-eyed peas
Pinto beans
Black beans
Lima beans
Navy beans

Combine the beans and peas in a large bowl and mix well. Fill pint jars with the bean mixture. Cover, tie on ribbons and give as a gifts to friends.

Black Bean Soup

2 (16-ounce) cans black beans
1 (16-ounce) can dark red kidney beans
4 carrots, peeled, chopped
1 onion, chopped
1 rib celery, chopped
1 clove garlic, minced
1 tablespoon vegetable oil
1 tablespoon chopped cilantro (optional)
2 bay leaves
1/4 teaspoon cayenne pepper
1 tablespoon salt
2 teaspoons ground cumin
1/2 teaspoon oregano
4 cups beef stock
1/2 to 1 cup water

⚷ Combine the black beans, kidney beans, carrots, onion, celery, garlic and oil in a blender container. Process at low speed until smooth. Pour into a Dutch oven. Add the cilantro, bay leaves, cayenne pepper, salt, cumin, oregano and stock and mix well. Add enough water to make of the desired consistency. Bring to a simmer. Simmer for 1 hour, adding additional water as needed.

Remove the bay leaves. Ladle into soup bowls. Garnish with cheese and sour cream.

Yield: 10 servings.

Baked Potato Soup

2 tablespoons margarine
1/3 cup chopped green onions
4 medium baking potatoes, baked,
    cut into bite-size pieces
1 (10-ounce) can cream of chicken soup
1 cup chicken broth
1 cup half-and-half
Salt and pepper to taste
1/2 cup shredded Cheddar cheese
6 slices bacon, crisp-cooked, crumbled
Sour cream
Chopped fresh chives or parsley

⚷ Heat the margarine over medium heat in a large saucepan until melted. Add the green onions. Sauté until translucent. Stir in the potatoes, soup, broth and half-and-half. Season with salt and pepper. Bring to a simmer. Simmer until hot; do not boil. Ladle into soup bowls. Top with the cheese, bacon, a dollop of sour cream and chives.

Yield: 4 servings.

To thicken soups use one tablespoon flour per cup of milk. If it's a potato soup use less flour.

Butternut Squash Soup with Ginger and Lime

1 cup finely chopped onion
1/2 tablespoon minced gingerroot
3 tablespoons butter
2 cups water
2 pounds butternut squash, peeled,
*   seeded, sliced*
2 cups chicken broth
3 cloves garlic
2 tablespoons fresh lime juice
Salt and freshly ground pepper to taste
1 piece of gingerroot, cut into fine slivers
1/3 cup vegetable oil
Ribbons of lime peel

Cook the onion and minced gingerroot in the butter in a stockpot over medium-low heat until onion is tender. Add the water, squash, broth and garlic. Bring to a boil. Reduce the heat. Simmer, covered, for 15 to 20 minutes or until squash is tender. Let stand until slightly cooled.

Purée the squash mixture in a blender in batches. Return to the stockpot. Add the lime juice, salt and pepper. Reheat over low heat.

Cook the gingerroot slivers in the hot oil in a small skillet until crisp. Drain on paper towels.

Ladle the soup into shallow soup bowls. Top with cooked gingerroot slivers and lime ribbons.

Yield: 4 to 6 servings.

Tomato Basil Cream Soup

2 shallots, chopped
1 rib celery, chopped
1 clove garlic, minced
2 tablespoons vegetable oil
4 cups fresh tomatoes, peeled, chopped, or
*   canned whole tomatoes, crushed*
4 cups unsalted tomato juice
6 to 8 fresh basil leaves, chopped
1 cup chicken broth
Salt to taste
1 cup heavy cream
1/2 cup (1 stick) unsalted butter, softened
1/4 teaspoon cracked pepper

Sauté the shallots, celery and garlic in the oil in a Dutch oven over low heat for 10 minutes or until tender; do not brown. Add the tomatoes, tomato juice and basil. Cook for 10 minutes over medium-low heat, stirring occasionally. Add the broth and salt. Bring to a boil. Reduce the heat. Simmer for 30 minutes, stirring occasionally. Cool slightly.

Process half the tomato mixture in batches in a food processor or blender until smooth. Return to the Dutch oven. May be frozen for up to 1 month at this point. Add the cream and butter, stirring until butter is melted. Stir in the pepper.

Ladle into soup bowls. Garnish with basil sprigs. Serve with crusty French bread.

Yield: 8 servings.

Deep South Tortilla Soup

2 (28-ounce) cans stewed tomatoes
2 tablespoons tomato paste
2 corn tortillas, coarsely chopped
1 large onion, coarsely chopped
4 cloves garlic, minced
1 tablespoon chopped fresh cilantro, or
     1 1/2 teaspoons dried cilantro
3 tablespoons vegetable oil
2 quarts chicken stock
1 teaspoon chili powder
1 tablespoon ground cumin
1/8 teaspoon ground red pepper, or to taste
2 bay leaves
Salt and black pepper to taste
4 corn tortillas
Vegetable oil
2 boneless skinless chicken breasts,
     cut into strips
1 avocado, chopped
1 cup shredded Cheddar cheese

Purée the tomatoes, tomato paste and chopped corn tortillas in a food processor or blender until smooth; set aside. Purée the onion in a food processor or blender until smooth.

Sauté the garlic and cilantro in 3 tablespoons hot oil in a stockpot over medium heat. Stir in the tomato purée and onion purée. Bring to a boil. Add the stock, chili powder, cumin, red pepper and bay leaves. Bring to a boil. Reduce the heat.

Simmer for 30 minutes. Discard the bay leaves. Season with salt and black pepper if desired. Keep warm.

Cut the 4 corn tortillas into strips. Pour oil 1 inch deep in a heavy skillet. Heat over medium-high heat. Cook the tortilla strips in the hot oil until brown. Remove and drain on paper towels, reserving 1/2 tablespoon oil in the skillet.

Cook the chicken strips in the hot oil for 10 minutes or until cooked through, turning once. Drain and cut into cubes.

Ladle the soup into bowls. Arrange the chicken, avocado and cheese over the soup. Top with the tortilla strips. Serve immediately.

Yield: 10 to 12 servings.

Ice cubes will eliminate the fat from soup and stew. Just drop a few into the pot, stir and remove with a slotted spoon. The fat will stick to the ice cubes.

Classic Caesar Salad

2 eggs
4 cloves garlic
4 anchovy fillets, or 2^1/$_2$ teaspoons
    anchovy paste
Salt to taste
Black pepper to taste
White pepper to taste
1 teaspoon Dijon mustard
Juice of 2 lemons
1 cup olive oil
2 teaspoons Worcestershire sauce
1 teaspoon Louisiana hot sauce
5 ounces grated Parmesan cheese
2 large heads of romaine, torn
12 ounces croutons

Bring a small amount of water to a boil in a medium saucepan. Remove from heat. Break the eggs into the water; do not break the yolks. Let stand for 1 minute; drain.

Rub the inside of a salad bowl with the garlic cloves. Mash the garlic, anchovies, salt, black pepper and white pepper in the salad bowl, forming a paste. Whisk in the eggs, mustard and lemon juice until smooth. Add the olive oil gradually, whisking constantly until dressing emulsifies. Whisk in the Worcestershire sauce and hot sauce. Add the Parmesan cheese, lettuce and croutons. Toss to coat.

Yield: 6 to 8 servings.

Greek Feta Salad

^{1}/$_2$ cup olive oil
^{1}/$_4$ cup lemon juice
1 clove garlic, minced
^{1}/$_4$ teaspoon salt
^{1}/$_4$ teaspoon pepper
^{1}/$_4$ teaspoon oregano
Green leaf lettuce
Black olives
Cherry tomatoes, cut into halves
Feta cheese, crumbled

Combine the olive oil, lemon juice, garlic, salt, pepper and oregano in a small bowl. Whisk until blended. Refrigerate, covered, until completely chilled.

Arrange the lettuce on individual salad plates. Arrange the olives and tomato halves over the lettuce. Sprinkle the feta cheese over the salads. Drizzle the dressing over the top.

Yield: 6 to 8 servings.

A tomato's skin should be smooth and firm with no cuts or blemishes. Slice it vertically to prevent moisture loss and add to the salad immediately before serving.

Spinach Salad

4 bunches fresh spinach, stemmed, torn into
    bite-size pieces
8 ounces fresh mushrooms, sliced
1 (8-ounce) can water chestnuts, drained,
    sliced (optional)
8 slices bacon, crisp-cooked, crumbled
4 hard-cooked eggs, sliced
Red Wine Vinegar Dressing

Combine the spinach, mushrooms, water chestnuts, bacon and eggs in a large salad bowl. Toss to combine. Just before serving, pour the Red Wine Vinegar Dressing over the salad, tossing to coat. Serve immediately.

Yield: 16 servings.

Red Wine Vinegar Dressing

1 cup vegetable oil
5 tablespoons red wine vinegar
1/4 cup sour cream
2 tablespoons sugar
1 1/2 teaspoons salt
1/4 teaspoon dry mustard
1/4 teaspoon pepper
2 teaspoons chopped fresh parsley
2 cloves garlic, crushed

Combine the oil, vinegar, sour cream, sugar, salt, dry mustard, pepper, parsley and garlic in a blender container. Process until smooth. Refrigerate until completely chilled or for up to 2 weeks.

Corn Bread Salad

5 cups cubed corn bread
3 cups chopped fresh Roma tomatoes
1 cup chopped cucumber
1 cup chopped sweet onion
1 cup chopped green bell pepper
1 pound bacon, crisp-cooked, crumbled
1/4 cup sweet pickle relish
1 cup mayonnaise or sour cream
1/4 cup sweet pickle juice
Shredded Parmesan cheese
1 bunch green onions, chopped

Place the corn bread cubes in a large salad bowl. Combine the tomatoes, cucumber, sweet onion, bell pepper, bacon and pickle relish in a separate bowl and mix well. Add to the corn bread.

Combine the mayonnaise and pickle juice in a small bowl and mix well. Pour over the corn bread mixture and toss to coat. Sprinkle with the Parmesan cheese and green onions. Refrigerate until ready to serve.

Yield: 10 to 12 servings.

Salt does not dissolve well in oil, so mix the salt with the vinegar first, then add the oil and the pepper to make your favorite salad dressing.

Pasteurizing Eggs

In order to avoid raw eggs that may contain salmonella, mix 1 egg yolk with 1 tablespoon lemon juice or vinegar and 1 tablespoon water in a small glass bowl. Microwave, covered, on High for 30 seconds or until the mixture begins to rise. Microwave for 5 seconds longer. Whisk until smooth. Microwave on High for 10 seconds or until the mixture rises again. Beat again. Mixture should be at 200 degrees. Cover the bowl and let stand for 1 minute before using.

Shoe Peg Corn Salad

4 (15-ounce) cans Shoe Peg corn, drained
1 (2-ounce) jar chopped pimentos
1 bunch green onions, chopped
6 ribs celery, chopped (optional)
1 bell pepper, chopped
³/₄ cup white vinegar
¹/₂ cup each vegetable oil and sugar
1 tablespoon water
1 teaspoon each salt and pepper
1 cup shredded Cheddar cheese

Mix the corn, pimentos, green onions, celery and bell pepper in a bowl.

Combine the vinegar, oil, sugar, water, salt and pepper in a saucepan. Cook until sugar is dissolved, stirring occasionally. Remove from heat. Let stand until cooled. Pour over the corn mixture and toss to coat. Chill, covered, for 24 hours or longer. Add the cheese and toss to combine.

Yield: 12 servings.

Creamy Broccoli Salad

6 ounces cream cheese, softened
1 egg
2 tablespoons vinegar
2 tablespoons sugar
2 tablespoons vegetable oil
1 teaspoon mustard
¹/₄ teaspoon garlic salt
6 cups chopped fresh broccoli
¹/₄ cup finely chopped onion
¹/₃ cup golden raisins (optional)
Lettuce leaves
6 slices bacon, crisp-cooked, crumbled
4 ounces sunflower seeds

Combine the cream cheese, egg, vinegar, sugar, oil, mustard and garlic salt in a blender container. Process for 2 minutes or until smooth.

Combine the broccoli, onion and raisins in a large bowl and toss to combine. Add the cream cheese mixture. Toss to coat. Refrigerate for 3 hours or longer.

Line a large salad bowl with lettuce leaves. Spoon the salad over the lettuce. Just before serving, sprinkle with the bacon and sunflower seeds. Serve immediately.

Yield: 6 servings.

Festive Cranberry Salad

1 (14-ounce) can sweetened condensed milk
1/4 cup lemon juice
1 (20-ounce) can crushed pineapple, drained
1 (16-ounce) can whole cranberry sauce
2 cups miniature marshmallows
1/2 cup chopped pecans
8 ounces nondairy whipped topping

Combine the condensed milk and lemon juice in a large bowl and mix well. Add the pineapple, cranberry sauce, marshmallows and pecans and mix well. Fold in the whipped topping. Spoon into a 9x13-inch dish.

Freeze for 4 hours or until firm. Cut into squares to serve.

Yield: 12 to 16 servings.

Baked Potato Salad

4 pounds red potatoes
8 ounces bacon, coarsely chopped
2 cups mayonnaise
16 ounces Cheddar cheese, shredded
1 bunch green onion tops, chopped
Salt and pepper to taste

Combine the potatoes with enough water to cover in a saucepan. Bring to a boil. Boil until tender; drain. Cut into quarters. Let stand until slightly cooled.

Cook the bacon in a skillet until crisp. Remove the bacon, reserving 1 tablespoon of the bacon drippings.

Combine the mayonnaise and reserved bacon drippings in a large bowl and mix well. Add the potatoes and mix well. Set aside a small amount of the bacon, cheese and green onions. Add the remaining bacon, cheese and green onions to the potato mixture and mix well. Season with salt and pepper.

Garnish with the reserved bacon, cheese and green onions. Serve at room temperature.

Yield: 20 to 25 servings.

Most families enjoy the ritual of decorating the Christmas tree–many times with homemade ornaments and garlands. There are two secrets you should know when making that popcorn garland. First, let the popcorn get stale before stringing it–this allows the needle to pass through without breaking it. Second, be sure to spray it with hair spray; this will keep the family dog from pulling over the Christmas tree while trying to sneak a quick snack. This event makes a great story–but a huge mess.

Roquefort Potato Salad

2 pounds new potatoes
Tarragon Vinegar Dressing
1/2 cup crumbled Roquefort cheese
1/2 cup cream or half-and-half
2 tablespoons minced chives
Lettuce leaves
10 slices bacon, crisp-cooked, crumbled

Combine the potatoes with enough water to cover in a saucepan. Bring to a boil. Boil until tender; drain. Peel and cut the warm potatoes into slices. Place the potatoes in a bowl. Pour one-third to one-half of the Tarragon Vinegar Dressing over the potatoes and mix well. Combine the Roquefort cheese, cream, chives and remaining dressing in a separate bowl and mix well.

Arrange the potato mixture over the lettuce leaves on a serving platter. Spoon the Roquefort dressing mixture over the top. Sprinkle with the bacon.

Yield: 10 to 12 servings.

Tarragon Vinegar Dressing

3 tablespoons tarragon vinegar
1/2 teaspoon pepper
3 chopped green onions
1 teaspoon Dijon mustard
9 tablespoons olive oil
2 tablespoons parsley

Combine the vinegar, pepper, green onions, mustard, olive oil and parsley in a bowl and mix well.

Poppy Seed Chicken Salad

1/4 cup sugar
1/4 cup vinegar
1 teaspoon salt
1/2 teaspoon pepper
1/2 cup vegetable oil
4 boneless skinless chicken breasts
3 green onions, finely chopped
5 ounces slivered almonds
2 tablespoons poppy seeds
3 ounces Chinese noodles

Combine the sugar, vinegar, salt, pepper and oil in a jar and cover. Shake until ingredients are well mixed. Refrigerate for 8 hours or longer, shaking every 4 to 6 hours.

Combine the chicken with enough water to cover in a saucepan. Bring to a boil. Reduce the heat. Simmer until cooked through; drain. Let stand until cooled. Shred into bite-size pieces.

Combine the cooled chicken, green onions, almonds and poppy seeds in a salad bowl and toss to combine. Shake the dressing to mix well. Pour over the chicken mixture. Toss to coat. Add the noodles and toss to combine. Serve immediately.

Yield: 4 to 6 servings.

Oriental Chicken Salad

1 1/2 pounds boneless skinless chicken breasts
Oriental Dressing
1 tablespoon vegetable oil
1 head of cabbage, shredded
1 (10-ounce) package frozen snow peas,
     thawed, drained
4 green onions, thinly sliced
1 red bell pepper, cut into 1-inch strips
1 package Ramen noodles, crushed

Cut the chicken into bite-size pieces. Place in a shallow dish. Pour half the Oriental Dressing over the chicken pieces. Marinate, covered, in the refrigerator for 1 hour; drain.

Sauté the chicken in the oil in a skillet until cooked through; drain. Combine the chicken, cabbage, snow peas, green onions and bell pepper in a bowl and mix well. Refrigerate, covered, for 1 hour. Add the noodles and mix well. Serve with the remaining Oriental Dressing.

Yield: 6 to 8 servings.

Oriental Dressing

2/3 cup vegetable oil
1/4 cup soy sauce
1/4 cup lemon juice
3 tablespoons rice salad vinegar
1 clove garlic, minced
1/4 teaspoon ginger
1/2 teaspoon salt
1/4 teaspoon pepper

Combine the oil, soy sauce, lemon juice, vinegar, garlic, ginger, salt and pepper in a jar and cover. Shake vigorously.

Bonnie and Clyde

Dining in Louisiana is always a memorable experience, even if you are quickly passing through, as Bonnie and Clyde did in May of 1934 en route to their final ambush in Arcadia, Louisiana. It is suspected that these notorious gangsters from the early part of the twentieth century had their last meal at Lea's, a small, well-known diner in Cheneyville, just south of Alexandria. Since then, Lea's has moved farther north to Lecompte, Louisiana. Still famous for it's delicious variety of homemade pies and dough-baked ham, Lea's is a favorite stop for a good country meal.

Basic Salad Dressing

1 part acid (lemon juice or vinegar)
plus 2 to 3 parts oil

Mix desired herbs with acid portion and then add to the oil. A dash of dry mustard or paprika added to the oil and vinegar slow separation. Vinegar and salt in a dressing wilt lettuce and reduce vitamin content. Add dressing immediately before serving.

Fried Crawfish Salad

1 pound crawfish tails
1/4 cup Louisiana hot sauce
1 cup flour
1/2 cup cornstarch
1/2 teaspoon each red pepper, white pepper
  and black pepper
Salt to taste
Vegetable oil for deep-frying
1 package spring lettuce mix
Andouille Dressing

Arrange the crawfish in a thin layer in a shallow dish. Pour the hot sauce over the crawfish. Marinate, covered, in the refrigerator.

Mix the flour and cornstarch in a shallow dish. Add the seasonings and mix well.

Drain the crawfish. Dredge in the flour mixture, shaking off the excess. Deep-fry in hot oil for 2 minutes or until golden brown. Drain on paper towels. Place the lettuce mix in a salad bowl. Add the Andouille Dressing and toss. Arrange the cooked crawfish over the top.

Yield: 4 to 6 servings.

Andouille Dressing

2 egg yolks
1 tablespoon Creole mustard
1 cup vegetable oil
1/3 cup red wine vinegar
1 slice bacon, chopped
1 cup chopped andouille
1/3 cup chopped onion
1 clove garlic, chopped
1 teaspoon brown sugar
1 tablespoon hot sauce
Salt and pepper to taste

Combine the egg yolks and mustard in a bowl and mix well. Whisk in the oil and vinegar alternately in a fine stream.

Cook the bacon in a skillet until crisp. Add the andouille. Cook for 2 minutes. Stir in the onion. Cook for 1 minute. Stir in the garlic and brown sugar. Stir in the hot sauce. Remove from heat. Whisk a small amount of the hot mixture into the eggs. Whisk the remaining hot mixture into the eggs. Season with salt and pepper.

When choosing salad leaves, choose lettuces that smell fresh and look slightly damp on the surface. Check that the heart is well formed. There should be no wilting or brown patches on the leaves.

Shrimp Pasta Salad with Artichoke Pesto

4 (12-ounce) packages small shell pasta
Olive oil
2 pounds shrimp, boiled, peeled
1 cup chopped celery
1 (2-ounce) can sliced black olives
1 cup chopped green onion tops
2 large packages cherry tomatoes, cut into
    quarters, seeded
3 (14-ounce) cans artichoke hearts, drained,
    coarsely chopped
3 tablespoons chopped cornichons
Artichoke Pesto Dressing
2 cups freshly grated Parmesan cheese

Cook the pasta in enough boiling water to cover until al dente; drain. Drizzle with a small amount of olive oil and toss to coat.

Combine the cooked pasta, shrimp, celery, olives, green onions, tomatoes, artichoke hearts and cornichons in a large bowl and mix well. Add the Artichoke Pesto Dressing and toss to mix well. Add the Parmesan cheese and mix well. Adjust the seasonings as desired. Sprinkle with additional cheese if desired. Serve at room temperature.

Yield: 12 servings.

Artichoke Pesto Dressing

2 cups mayonnaise
1 cup sour cream
1 cup artichoke pesto
1 teaspoon minced garlic
1 tablespoon Creole seasoning
1 tablespoon lemon juice
1 tablespoon lemon zest
Salt and black pepper to taste
Cayenne pepper to taste

Artichoke Pesto

1 cup tightly packed fresh spinach leaves
1/2 cup tightly packed fresh Italian
    parsley
1/4 cup tightly packed fresh basil leaves
1 teaspoon minced garlic
1/4 cup finely chopped walnuts
2 cups coarsely chopped artichokes,
    drained
1/3 cup (or more) olive oil
1 cup freshly grated Parmesan cheese
Salt and black pepper to taste
1/8 teaspoon cayenne pepper

Combine the spinach, parsley and basil in a food processor container fitted with a metal chopping blade. Add the garlic, walnuts and artichokes. Add the olive oil in a fine stream, processing constantly until smooth. Add additional olive oil as needed to make of the desired consistency. Pour into a bowl. Fold in the Parmesan cheese. Season with salt, black pepper and cayenne pepper.

Whisk the mayonnaise, sour cream, pesto, garlic, Creole seasoning, lemon juice, lemon zest, salt, black pepper and cayenne pepper in a bowl.

Shrimp Caesar Salad with Garlic Lemon Croutons

1/4 cup extra-virgin olive oil
2 tablespoons grated Parmesan cheese
2 tablespoons fresh lemon juice
2 teaspoons minced garlic
1 1/2 teaspoons minced anchovy fillets
1 teaspoon Dijon mustard
1 teaspoon Worcestershire sauce
2 large hearts romaine, cut into halves
    lengthwise
2 pounds medium shrimp, boiled, peeled
1/4 cup coarsely grated Parmesan cheese
Garlic Lemon Croutons

⚷— Purée the olive oil, 2 tablespoons Parmesan cheese, lemon juice, garlic, anchovies, mustard and Worcestershire sauce in a blender. Refrigerate until ready to use or for up to 1 day.

Place each lettuce half on a plate. Arrange the shrimp over the lettuce. Drizzle with the oil mixture. Top with 1/4 cup Parmesan cheese and Garlic Lemon Croutons.

Yield: 4 servings.

Garlic Lemon Croutons

1 tablespoon extra-virgin olive oil
1 tablespoon chopped garlic
1 tablespoon chopped fresh parsley
1 teaspoon lemon zest
12 thin French bread slices

⚷— Combine the olive oil, garlic, parsley and lemon zest in a small bowl and mix well. Spread over the bread slices. Cut into cubes. Arrange on a baking sheet. Bake at 425 degrees for 5 minutes or until crisp.

Asian Vinaigrette

1 teaspoon hot sesame oil
1 tablespoon soy sauce
1/4 cup rice wine vinegar
1/2 cup vegetable oil
1 teaspoon chopped gingerroot
1 clove garlic, minced
Salt and pepper to taste
Sugar to taste

⚷— Combine the sesame oil, soy sauce, vinegar, vegetable oil, gingerroot, garlic, salt, pepper and sugar in a jar with a tight-fitting lid. Cover and shake to mix well.

Yield: 4 servings.

Basil Honey Vinaigrette

1 cup apple cider vinegar
1 cup sugar
1 tablespoon dry mustard
$1/2$ teaspoon basil
1 teaspoon celery seeds
$1/8$ teaspoon crushed red pepper
4 cups mayonnaise
$1/4$ cup honey

Combine the vinegar, sugar, dry mustard, basil, celery seeds and red pepper in a saucepan and mix well. Bring to a simmer. Simmer until reduced by half. Refrigerate until completely chilled. Fold in the mayonnaise and honey.

Yield: 20 to 25 servings.

Creole Vinaigrette

1 cup extra-virgin olive oil
$1/4$ cup balsamic vinegar
$1/2$ teaspoon thyme
$1/2$ teaspoon basil
$1/2$ teaspoon oregano
$1/4$ teaspoon minced garlic
1 tablespoon fresh lime juice
2 tablespoons Creole mustard
2 tablespoons cane syrup
1 teaspoon Tabasco sauce
$1/8$ teaspoon Creole seasoning

Combine the olive oil, vinegar, thyme, basil, oregano, garlic, lime juice, mustard, syrup, Tabasco sauce and Creole seasoning in a food processor container. Pulse until smooth. Pour into a jar and cover. Shake to mix well.

Yield: 4 to 6 servings.

Oil and Vinegar Do Mix

The proportions for a classic vinaigrette are three parts oil to one part vinegar. A generous seasoning with salt and pepper is also included in the traditional recipe. There is some controversy over whether vinaigrette must contain vinegar to earn the name. If the vinegar is replaced by lemon juice, the dressing may still be called vinaigrette. (The proportions change, however, to half oil, half lemon juice). Many people prefer a lighter mixture and may use half oil and half vinegar, adding a bit of sugar to cut the tartness. Another trick to use when increasing the amount of vinegar is to substitute balsamic vinegar, which isn't quite as strong as regular vinegar.

Romano Dressing

6 ounces Romano cheese, grated
4 ounces bleu cheese, crumbled
$3/4$ cup lemon juice
$1/2$ cup olive oil
$1^{1}/2$ cups vegetable oil
1 teaspoon finely chopped garlic
$1/2$ teaspoon salt

Combine the Romano cheese, bleu cheese, lemon juice, olive oil, vegetable oil, garlic and salt in a jar and cover. Shake to mix well. Refrigerate until chilled.

Yield: 12 to 15 servings.

Accompaniments

One of the special ingredients that makes central Louisiana an attractive place to live is our small-town flavor. Although the metropolitan area is home to more than 50,000 people, friendship and family circles are far-reaching.

We never venture out without encountering friends along the way. A trip to the grocery store that is only five minutes away will likely take much longer if you factor in time for visiting with friends you meet in the aisles. Discussion could start with the quality of the produce and end with the recounting of last week's PTA meeting.

Churches and schools provide excellent opportunities for building community and nurturing friendships, quite often centered around a shared meal. We live in an area where our homes are open to neighbors and we know them by name. Block parties, play groups, progressive suppers, and cookouts are still prevalent in many neighborhoods.

In central Louisiana, we know one of the secrets to a happy life is found in the smile and imagination of a child. On a hot summer day, lemonade stands can be found throughout our town manned by young entrepreneurs. Magic marker signs entice customers to quench their thirst while bringing a smile to a child's face.

Many people have said that it takes an entire village to raise a child. In central Louisiana, we all look out for each other—children, adults, and senior citizens. Community spirit is alive and well in Alexandria. In fact, it's the secret that keeps people coming here to build their lives.

This small-town atmosphere complements our family life. We hope the recipes in this section complement your entrées, and offer you a taste of the flavors we enjoy.

We live in an area where our homes are open to neighbors and we know them by name. Block parties, play groups, progressive suppers, and cookouts are still prevalent in many neighborhoods.

Accompaniments Key Sponsor

Louisiana
Physical Therapy
Centers

Stuffed Artichoke Casserole

2 (16-ounce) cans wax beans, drained
2 (14-ounce) cans artichoke hearts, drained
1 cup seasoned bread crumbs
1 cup grated Parmesan cheese
1 large onion
5 cloves garlic
1/2 cup olive oil
1/2 teaspoon pepper

Chop the beans and artichoke hearts coarsely; place in a large bowl. Add the bread crumbs and Parmesan cheese and toss to combine.

Chop the onion and garlic finely. Heat the olive oil in a skillet. Add the onion and garlic. Sauté until the onion is tender. Add to the artichoke mixture. Add the pepper and mix well.

Spoon into a 9x13-inch baking dish. Bake at 350 degrees for 30 minutes.

Yield: 20 servings.

Asparagus with Red Pepper Butter

3 cups canned low-sodium chicken broth
1 1/2 pounds thin asparagus spears, trimmed
2 tablespoons olive oil, preferably extra-virgin
1 1/4 cups chopped green onions
1/3 cup minced shallots
1 teaspoon sugar
1 tablespoon minced garlic
1 1/2 tablespoons Dijon mustard
1 tablespoon fresh lemon juice
1 teaspoon minced fresh thyme
1/2 teaspoon lemon zest
Salt and pepper to taste
1/2 cup chopped red bell pepper

Bring the broth to a boil in a large pot. Add the asparagus. Cook for 4 minutes or until tender-crisp. Drain, reserving 1 cup of the broth. Place the asparagus in a large bowl of ice water. Drain and pat dry. May be wrapped in paper towels, sealed in a plastic bag and refrigerated for up to 1 day.

Heat 1 tablespoon of the olive oil in a medium nonstick skillet over medium heat. Add 1 cup of the green onions, shallots and sugar. Sauté for 5 minutes or until the green onions and shallots are tender. Add the garlic. Sauté for 2 minutes. Stir in the reserved broth, remaining 1 tablespoon olive oil, mustard, lemon juice, thyme and lemon zest. Simmer for 5 minutes or until the mixture is reduced to 1 1/4 cups. Season with salt and pepper. Remove from heat. Let stand until cooled to room temperature.

Arrange the asparagus on a serving platter. Spoon the sauce over the asparagus. Sprinkle with the remaining 1/4 cup green onions and bell pepper.

Yield: 8 servings.

Ranch-Style Baked Beans

2 pounds ground chuck
1 cup chopped onions
1 cup catsup
1/4 cup mustard
1/4 cup maple syrup
1/2 cup packed brown sugar
2 (22-ounce) cans ranch-style beans

Brown the ground chuck with the onions in a skillet, stirring until the ground chuck is crumbly; drain.

Combine the catsup, mustard, syrup and brown sugar in a large bowl and mix well. Add the cooked ground chuck mixture and the beans and mix well. Pour into a greased 3-quart baking dish.

Bake, covered, at 325 degrees for 1 1/2 hours.

Yield: 10 servings.

Carrot Soufflé

1 pound carrots, peeled, chopped
1/2 cup sugar
1 teaspoon baking powder
1 teaspoon vanilla extract
3 tablespoons flour
3 eggs, beaten
1/2 cup (1 stick) margarine, softened
Confectioners' sugar

Combine the carrots with enough water to cover. Bring to a boil. Boil until very tender; drain. Combine the hot cooked carrots, sugar, baking powder and vanilla in a mixer bowl. Beat until smooth. Add the flour and mix well. Add the eggs and mix well. Add the margarine and mix well. Pour into a 9x9-inch baking dish coated with nonstick cooking spray.

Bake at 350 degrees for 45 minutes or until top is a light golden brown; do not overbake. Sprinkle lightly with confectioners' sugar. Serve warm.

Yield: 6 servings.

Choose vegetables in season when they are at their freshest and most readily available; this is when they will taste their best and be at their most nutritious. Always look for crisp, fresh looking vegetables that have brightly colored leaves. Avoid any that have brown patches, wilted leaves, bruised, or pulpy flesh.

Crispy Cauliflower

3 tablespoons butter
4 cups cauliflowerets
1 cup sliced celery (optional)
1 tablespoon onion flakes or chopped onion
3/4 cup white wine
1/2 teaspoon MSG
Dash of cayenne pepper
2 tablespoons chicken stock base
1/2 cup slivered almonds (optional)
Salt to taste

Heat the butter in a large skillet until melted. Add the cauliflower, celery and onion flakes. Sauté for 2 to 3 minutes. Add the wine, MSG and cayenne pepper. Bring to a low boil. Add the chicken stock base, stirring until dissolved. Cook for 10 minutes or just until crispy. Stir in the almonds. Season with salt.

Yield: 6 servings.

Corn Maque Choux

2 slices bacon
1 (15-ounce) can tomatoes with green chiles
1 (15-ounce) can white cream-style corn
2 (15-ounce) cans white Shoe Peg corn

Cook the bacon in a heavy pan over medium-high heat until crisp and the bottom of the pan is brown. Add the tomatoes. Simmer until most of the liquid is evaporated, stirring and scraping the bottom of the pan constantly. Add the cream-style corn. Simmer until thickened and caramelized, stirring and scraping the bottom of the pan constantly. Stir in the Shoe Peg corn. Cook until heated through.

Yield: 12 to 15 servings.

Corn Pudding

10 to 12 ears of corn, such as Silver Queen
3 tablespoons butter, melted
2 1/2 cups milk, scalded
4 eggs, beaten
1 teaspoon sugar
1 tablespoon flour
1/2 teaspoon salt
1/4 teaspoon Tabasco sauce

Remove the tips from the corn. Scrape the kernels off the cobs. Place 4 cups of the kernels in a large bowl. Reserve any remaining kernels for another use.

Add the butter, milk, eggs, sugar, flour, salt and Tabasco sauce to the corn and mix well. Spoon into a buttered 2-quart baking dish.

Place the baking dish in a larger pan. Pour hot water into the large pan around the baking dish. Place in the oven. Bake at 350 degrees for 1 hour or until a knife inserted 2 inches from the center comes out clean. Let stand for 15 minutes.

May substitute 2 thawed 32-ounce packages frozen whole kernel corn for the fresh corn.

Yield: 10 servings.

Eggplant Josephine

1 large eggplant
Salt to taste
1/4 cup (1/2 stick) butter
1/2 cup sauterne
1 pound crab meat
1 (32-ounce) jar Italian spaghetti sauce
Flour
Vegetable oil
1 cup shredded mozzarella cheese
1 envelope hollandaise sauce mix

⚷ Peel and cut the eggplant into 3/4- to 1-inch-thick slices. Spread the slices in a single layer in a colander. Sprinkle salt evenly over the cut surfaces. Let stand for 30 minutes. Rinse under cold running water and pat dry.

Heat the butter in a saucepan until melted. Add the sauterne and crab meat and mix well. Bring to a boil. Boil for 6 minutes. Set aside.

Heat the spaghetti sauce in a saucepan until heated through. Dredge the eggplant slices in flour. Cook in a small amount of hot oil in a skillet until light brown on both sides.

Layer the eggplant, crab meat mixture, spaghetti sauce and cheese in a greased 9x9-inch baking dish. Bake at 450 degrees until the cheese is melted and bubbly.

Prepare the hollandaise sauce using the package directions. Pour over the hot eggplant mixture. Serve immediately.

Yield: 4 servings.

Salting Eggplant

For most dishes, eggplant does not need peeling. However, they can contain bitter juices, which are best extracted before cooking. This technique is called salting and is advisable if eggplant are to be fried in oil–it firms the flesh so that less oil is absorbed during cooking.

Slice the eggplant. Spread the slices in a single layer in a colander. Sprinkle salt evenly over the cut surfaces. Leave for about 30 minutes. Rinse under cold running water, then pat dry before cooking.

95

Eggplant Casserole

2 large eggplant
1 large onion, chopped
1¹/2 cups chopped celery
1 medium bell pepper, chopped
3 cups water
1 pound ground beef
1 cup Italian-style bread crumbs
¹/2 cup (1 stick) margarine, softened
8 ounces mild Cheddar cheese, shredded
2 eggs, lightly beaten
Salt and pepper to taste

Peel and cut the eggplant into bite-size pieces. Combine the eggplant, onion, celery, bell pepper and water in a saucepan. Bring to a boil. Boil until vegetables are tender; drain.

Brown the ground beef in a skillet, stirring until crumbly; drain.

Combine the eggplant mixture, ground beef, bread crumbs, margarine, half the cheese, eggs, salt and pepper in a large bowl and mix well. Spoon into a greased baking dish. Sprinkle with the remaining cheese. Bake at 350 degrees for 30 to 40 minutes.

Yield: 6 to 8 servings.

When selecting peas and beans, choose those with bright green pods that are full and plump.

Bean Bundles

2 to 3 (16-ounce) cans whole green beans,
    drained
1 pound bacon slices, cut into halves
1 (8-ounce) bottle French dressing
1 (2- or 3-ounce) jar pimentos

Arrange the green beans in bunches of 8. Wrap a half slice of bacon around each bunch. Place in a 9x13-inch baking dish. Pour the dressing over the beans. Refrigerate, covered, for 3 hours or longer.

Bake at 350 degrees for 40 minutes or until the bacon is cooked through, turning the bundles over after 20 minutes. Arrange the bean bundles on a serving platter. Arrange the pimentos around the bundles.

Yield: 6 to 10 servings.

Spanish Green Beans

2 slices bacon, chopped
¹/4 cup chopped onion
2 tablespoons chopped green bell pepper
2 tablespoons flour
2 (14-ounce) cans stewed tomatoes, drained
4 (14-ounce) cans green beans, drained
Salt and pepper to taste

Cook the bacon in a heavy skillet until crisp. Remove the bacon and crumble. Add the onion and bell pepper. Sauté until tender. Remove from heat. Stir in the flour and bacon. Add the tomatoes and green beans and mix well.

Season with salt and pepper. Spoon into a greased 3-quart baking dish. Bake at 350 degrees for 30 minutes.

Yield: 6 servings.

Braised Greens in Lime Sauce

2 tablespoons extra-virgin olive oil
1 medium onion, coarsely chopped
2 small shallots, minced
2 small cloves garlic, finely minced
2 tablespoons chicken stock or broth
2 pounds fresh mustard greens, rinsed, stems
    removed
2 teaspoons fresh lime juice
$1/2$ teaspoon salt
$1/4$ teaspoon freshly ground pepper

Heat the olive oil in a large saucepan over medium heat. Add the onion, shallots and garlic. Cook for 8 to 10 minutes or until golden brown, stirring frequently. Add the stock.

Arrange the greens over the onion mixture. Cook, covered, for 20 minutes or until tender, turning the greens frequently. Season with lime juice, salt and pepper. Toss and serve.

Yield: 6 servings.

No More Tears

Chopping onions (or garlic or shallots) releases a sulfuric compound. The chemical reacts with the saline in your eyes to create a mild sulfuric acid. Your eyes handle the attack by producing lots of tears to rinse the acid away.

The National Onion Association recommends refrigerating onions for an hour or so before cutting them to slow down the release of the irritating compound. Because the chemical is more concentrated in the base of the onion, don't cut the bottom (root end) off the onion before you start slicing. Cut off the top, and peel the skin from the sides of the onion. Cut a small slice off one side of the onion so that the onion can rest flat on the cutting surface. Slice until you get to the base, which you can then discard. If all else fails, you can wear protective goggles.

Glorious Grilled Onions

4 medium Vidalia onions
$1/4$ cup ($1/2$ stick) butter
4 bouillon cubes
White pepper to taste

Peel the onions. Cut off the tops and bottoms. Place each onion in the center of a foil square. Place 1 tablespoon of butter and a bouillon cube on top of each onion. Sprinkle with white pepper. Bring the edges of the foil together to enclose the onion. Fold edges over to seal tightly. Grill over hot coals for 30 minutes or bake at 375 degrees for 30 to 40 minutes.

Yield: 4 servings.

Vidalia French Onion Casserole

3 medium Vidalia or sweet onions
2 tablespoons butter
8 ounces fresh mushrooms, sliced
2 cups shredded Swiss cheese
1 (10-ounce) can cream of mushroom soup
1 (5-ounce) can evaporated milk
2 teaspoons soy sauce
6 ($\frac{1}{2}$-inch-thick) slices French bread
$\frac{1}{4}$ cup finely chopped parsley

Peel and slice the onions crosswise. Cut each slice into halves. Heat the butter in a skillet over medium-high heat until melted. Add the onions and mushrooms. Cook until tender, stirring constantly. Spoon into a greased 2-quart baking dish. Sprinkle with 1 cup of the cheese.

Combine the soup, evaporated milk and soy sauce in a bowl and mix well. Pour over the cheese. Arrange the bread slices over the layers. Sprinkle with the remaining 1 cup cheese and parsley. Refrigerate, covered, for 4 to 8 hours. Let stand at room temperature for 30 minutes.

Bake at 350 degrees for 15 to 20 minutes. Let stand for 5 minutes.

Yield: 6 to 8 servings.

Texas Caviar

2 (16-ounce) cans field or black-eyed peas, drained
1 small purple onion, chopped
1 medium tomato, seeded, chopped
1 bell pepper, chopped
1 rib celery, chopped
2 (11-ounce) cans Shoe Peg corn, drained
$\frac{1}{4}$ cup vegetable oil
1 clove garlic, minced
$\frac{1}{4}$ cup vinegar
2 tablespoons sugar, or to taste
Tabasco sauce to taste
2 teaspoons Worcestershire sauce, or to taste
Chopped fresh basil to taste

Combine the peas, onion, tomato, bell pepper, celery, corn, oil, garlic, vinegar, sugar, Tabasco sauce, Worcestershire sauce and basil in a large bowl and mix well. Refrigerate, covered, for 2 hours or longer.

Yield: 12 servings.

To use dried beans or peas in a recipe, boil for two minutes, remove from heat, soak for one hour, and then cook according to recipe directions.

Black-eyed peas (sometimes known as cowpeas) originated in Africa, though they've been fundamental to the southern diet for at least three centuries. Southerners believe that those who eat black-eyed peas on New Year's Day will have good luck throughout the coming year.

Ever Mashed
...oes

...tatoes
...ablespoons butter
...unces cream cheese, softened
...cup sour cream
...ablespoon prepared horseradish
...2 teaspoon seasoned salt
...2 teaspoon garlic salt
...2 teaspoon paprika

Combine the potatoes with enough ...to cover in a saucepan. Bring to a boil. Boil ...tender; drain. Peel and cut into pieces.

Combine the potatoes, butter, cream cheese, sour cream and horseradish in a mixer bowl. Beat at medium speed until smooth. Add the seasoned salt and garlic salt and mix well. Spoon into a greased baking dish. Sprinkle with the paprika.

Bake, covered with foil, at 350 degrees for 15 minutes. Remove the foil. Bake for an additional 15 minutes.

Yield: 8 to 10 servings.

Cottage Potatoes

12 potatoes
1 large onion, chopped
8 ounces Cheez Whiz or Velveeta
cheese, cubed
4 ounces chopped pimentos
Salt and pepper to taste
1/2 cup (1 stick) butter, melted
1/2 cup milk
1 cup seasoned bread crumbs

Combine the potatoes with enough water to cover in a large saucepan. Bring to a boil. Boil until tender; drain. Peel and cut into pieces.

Combine the potatoes, onion, Cheez Whiz and pimentos and mix well. Season with salt and pepper. Spoon into a greased 9x12-inch baking pan. Pour the butter over the potato mixture. Pour the milk over the potato mixture. Sprinkle the bread crumbs over the top.

Bake, covered, at 325 degrees for 45 minutes to 1 1/4 hours. Remove the cover. Bake for 15 minutes or until light brown.

Yield: 8 to 10 servings.

When selecting carrots, potatoes, beets, rutabagas, celery, and radishes, choose those that are firm, heavy, and have wrinkle-free skin. Avoid soft patches or sprouting.

Potato and Mushroom Gratin

3 tablespoons butter
1 1/2 pounds button mushrooms, coarsely
    chopped
2 tablespoons minced garlic
1 teaspoon dried thyme
1 teaspoon dried rosemary leaves, finely
    crushed
1 1/2 cups low-sodium chicken broth
Salt and pepper to taste
2/3 cup freshly grated Parmesan cheese
2/3 cup shredded mozzarella cheese
1 1/2 pounds Yukon Gold or russet potatoes,
    peeled, cut into 1/8-inch-thick slices
1 1/3 cups half-and-half
1 1/3 cups heavy cream
1 teaspoon salt
1 teaspoon pepper

 Heat the butter in a large saucepan over high heat until melted. Add the mushrooms. Sauté for 10 minutes or until the liquid is evaporated. Add the garlic, thyme and rosemary. Sauté for 1 minute. Add the chicken broth. Reduce the heat to medium. Cook for 20 minutes or until the liquid is evaporated, stirring frequently. Season with salt and pepper to taste. Let stand until cooled.

Combine the Parmesan cheese and mozzarella cheese in a bowl and mix well. Spray a 9x9-inch baking dish with nonstick cooking spray. Layer half the potato slices overlapping slightly, half the mushroom mixture, one-third of the cheese mixture, the remaining potato slices, the remaining mushroom mixture and half of the remaining cheese mixture in the prepared baking dish.

Whisk the half-and-half, heavy cream, 1 teaspoon salt and 1 teaspoon pepper in a bowl. Pour over the layers. Cover loosely with foil. Bake at 375 degrees for 1 1/4 hours or until the potatoes are tender and the sauce is thickened. Remove the foil. Press the layers to submerge in the sauce, using a metal spatula. Sprinkle with the remaining cheese mixture. Bake for an additional 15 minutes or until the cheese melts and the gratin is golden brown at the edges. Let stand for 10 minutes before serving.

Yield: 6 servings.

A leftover baked potato can be rebaked if you dip it in water and bake in a 350-degree oven for about 20 minutes.

Spinach and Crab Timbales

1/4 cup heavy cream
2 eggs
1 teaspoon fresh lemon juice
1/2 teaspoon Dijon mustard
1/8 teaspoon celery salt
1/8 teaspoon cayenne pepper
8 ounces lump crab meat
Salt and freshly ground black pepper to taste
2 pounds fresh spinach
3 tablespoons unsalted butter
2 tablespoons flour
3/4 cup milk
1/2 cup heavy cream
1/8 teaspoon nutmeg
3 eggs, beaten

Combine 1/4 cup cream, 2 eggs, lemon juice, mustard, celery salt, cayenne pepper and crab meat in a bowl and mix well. Season with salt and black pepper. Set aside.

Bring a small amount of water to a boil in a large saucepan. Add the spinach. Return to a boil; drain. Rinse the spinach with cold water. Drain, squeezing out the excess moisture. Chop the spinach finely.

Heat the butter in a heavy saucepan over medium heat until melted. Add the flour. Cook for 3 minutes, stirring constantly. Whisk in the milk, 1/2 cup cream and nutmeg. Season with salt and black pepper. Bring to a boil, stirring constantly. Cook for 2 minutes or until thickened, stirring constantly. Fold in the cooked spinach. Let stand for 10 minutes. Stir a small amount of the hot mixture into the beaten eggs. Stir the eggs into the hot mixture.

Fill eight 1/3-cup timbale molds or ramekins half full with the crab mixture. Spoon the spinach mixture over the crab mixture, filling the molds to the top.

Place the molds in a larger pan. Pour enough hot water into the pan to come halfway up the sides of the molds. Bake at 375 degrees for 50 minutes or until set. Invert onto plates. Serve with a beurre blanc sauce.

Yield: 8 servings.

Creamed Spinach

2 (10-ounce) packages frozen chopped
    spinach, thawed, drained
4 slices bacon, chopped
1/2 cup finely chopped onion
2 teaspoons chopped garlic
2 tablespoons flour
1 teaspoon seasoned salt
1/2 teaspoon pepper
1 cup milk
1 cup half-and-half

Process the spinach in a food processor until finely chopped.

Cook the bacon in a skillet until crisp. Stir in the onion and garlic. Remove from heat. Stir in the flour, seasoned salt and pepper. Add the milk and half-and-half gradually, stirring constantly. Cook until the mixture is thickened, stirring constantly. Stir in the spinach. Cook for 3 to 4 additional minutes.

Yield: 6 servings.

Stilton

Robust and aromatic, this grand English cheese is a popular choice for winter evenings, especially when paired with walnuts and a glass of vintage port. The firm cow's milk cheese should have lots of distinctive blue veins. Stilton is made in large cylindrical forms, and it can be served in a wedge or in a round. Such a sophisticated treat deserves a top-quality knife so that the blade is strong enough to make quick work of cutting even a hard Stilton, and pieces of cheese can be speared by the prong at the tip.

Squash Casserole

2¹/2 pounds yellow squash, cut into slices
1 cup chopped onion
1 cup water
1 cup shredded Cheddar cheese
1 (8-ounce) can water chestnuts
1 (2-ounce) jar dried pimentos
1 cup mayonnaise
¹/4 cup finely chopped green bell pepper
1 egg, lightly beaten
1 tablespoon sugar
Salt and pepper to taste
1 cup butter cracker crumbs
2 tablespoons margarine, softened

Combine the squash, onion and water in a saucepan. Bring to a boil. Reduce the heat. Simmer until the squash is tender; drain. Mash the squash mixture in a bowl. Add the cheese, water chestnuts, pimentos, mayonnaise, bell pepper, egg, sugar, salt and pepper and mix well. Spoon into a 3-quart baking dish. May be refrigerated, covered, at this point for up to 1 day.

Combine the cracker crumbs and margarine in a bowl and mix well. Sprinkle over the top. Bake at 350 degrees for 40 minutes or until heated through.

Yield: 12 servings.

Posh Squash

2 pounds yellow squash, cut into slices
or cubes
1 small onion, chopped
1/2 cup chopped green bell pepper
1 cup mayonnaise
2 eggs, beaten
1 cup grated Parmesan cheese
1 cup sour cream
Salt and pepper to taste
3/4 cup bread crumbs or crushed crackers

Bring enough water to cover the squash to a boil in a saucepan. Add the squash. Cook until tender-crisp; drain.

Combine the cooked squash, onion, bell pepper, mayonnaise, eggs, cheese and sour cream in a large bowl and mix well. Season with salt and pepper. Spoon into a 1-quart baking dish. Sprinkle with the bread crumbs. Bake at 350 degrees for 30 to 40 minutes or until heated through.

Yield: 6 servings.

Sweet Potato Soufflé

4 large sweet potatoes
1/2 cup sugar
1/2 cup (1 stick) butter, melted
2 eggs, beaten
1 teaspoon vanilla extract
1/3 cup milk
1/3 cup butter, melted
1 cup packed brown sugar
1/2 cup flour
1 cup chopped pecans

Combine the sweet potatoes with enough water to cover in a large pot. Bring to a boil. Boil until tender. Drain and peel the sweet potatoes. Beat the sweet potatoes, sugar, 1/2 cup butter, eggs, vanilla and milk in a mixer bowl until smooth. Spoon into a greased 9x13-inch baking dish.

Combine the melted butter, brown sugar, flour and pecans in a bowl and mix well. Sprinkle over the sweet potato mixture. Bake at 350 degrees for 25 minutes.

Yield: 10 to 12 servings.

It's no secret that central Louisiana enjoys the theatre. The Paramount Theatre no longer stands in downtown Alexandria, but in its heyday it hosted the same vaudeville shows that toured through New Orleans and other large cities. Nowadays our community enjoys great community theatre. There's nothing quite like small-town life with big-city culture.

Tomatoes Rockefeller

1 (10-ounce) package frozen chopped spinach
1/3 cup herb-seasoned stuffing mix, crushed
3 green onion tops, minced
1 egg, beaten
3 tablespoons unsalted butter, melted
2 tablespoons grated Parmesan cheese
1/4 teaspoon salt
1/4 teaspoon black pepper
6 thick tomato slices
Garlic salt to taste
Cayenne pepper to taste

Cook the spinach using the package directions; drain. Combine with the stuffing mix, green onions, egg, butter, cheese, salt and black pepper in a bowl and mix well.

Arrange the tomato slices in a greased baking dish. Sprinkle with the garlic salt. Spoon the spinach mixture over the tomato slices.

Bake at 350 degrees for 15 minutes or until the tomatoes are tender. Sprinkle with cayenne pepper.

Yield: 6 servings.

Tomato and Olive Tart

1 all ready pie pastry
1 egg white
4 ounces shredded mozzarella cheese
2 ounces grated Parmesan cheese
1 tablespoon chopped fresh basil, or 1 teaspoon dried basil
1/4 cup finely chopped drained water-pack artichokes
1/4 cup chopped drained Muffuletta Olive Mix
1 large tomato, thinly sliced
1/8 teaspoon garlic powder
Salt and pepper to taste
Olive oil

Line the bottom of a tart pan with parchment paper or use a nonstick tart pan. Fit the pie pastry into the prepared pan, trimming to fit. Brush with the egg white.

Combine the mozzarella cheese and Parmesan cheese in a bowl and mix well. Sprinkle over the pastry. Layer the basil, artichokes, olive mix and tomato slices over the pastry. Sprinkle with the garlic powder, salt and pepper. Drizzle with olive oil.

Bake at 400 degrees for 35 minutes. May substitute green olives with pimento for the Muffuletta Olive Mix but must also substitute marinated artichokes for the water-pack artichokes.

Yield: 6 servings.

Jalapeño Cheese Soufflé

1 cup milk
$1/4$ cup ($1/2$ stick) butter
$1/4$ cup flour
1 cup shredded Cheddar cheese
2 tablespoons chopped jalapeño chiles
$1/4$ cup chopped green onions
1 teaspoon salt
$1/2$ teaspoon black pepper
$1/2$ teaspoon white pepper
5 egg yolks, beaten
5 egg whites
$1/8$ teaspoon cream of tartar

Bring the milk to a boil in a saucepan; do not scorch. Remove from heat.

Heat the butter in a saucepan over low heat until melted. Add the flour, stirring until well blended. Whisk in $1/3$ of the hot milk. Whisk in the remaining milk. Cook for 5 minutes, stirring constantly. Stir in the cheese; do not boil. Stir in the chiles, green onions, salt, black pepper and white pepper. Remove from heat. Let stand for 5 minutes.

Stir a small amount of the hot mixture into the egg yolks. Stir the egg yolks into the hot mixture. Let stand until completely cool.

Beat the egg whites with the cream of tartar until stiff peaks form. Fold $1/3$ into the cheese mixture. Fold the remaining beaten egg whites into the cheese mixture. Pour into a buttered $1^1/2$-quart soufflé dish.

Place the soufflé dish in a large baking pan. Pour enough hot water into the pan to come halfway up the sides of the dish. Bake in a 375-degree oven for 5 minutes. Serve immediately, spooning from the middle of the dish to the outside.

Yield: 4 servings.

Zucchini Basilico

2 tablespoons olive oil
6 small zucchini, cut into $1/4$-inch diagonals
1 tablespoon fresh sliced basil
Salt and white pepper to taste

Heat the olive oil in a skillet until hot. Add the zucchini and basil. Cook until light brown, stirring constantly. Season with salt and white pepper. Cook, covered, until tender-crisp.

Yield: 6 servings.

If you can't find green tomatoes easily, don't despair. Just ask the produce manager at your grocery store. While it's not standard procedure for supermarkets to stock them, they often have some because 90 percent of all tomatoes are picked and shipped in the firm, green stage so they won't bruise easily. Then they're placed in rooms where ethylene gas (the gas all fruits release as they ripen) is piped in to encourage the ripening process. The leftover green ones are often thrown away.

Ripen green tomatoes by wrapping in newspaper and storing in a cool, dark place.

Baked Mushroom Rice

1/4 cup (1/2 stick) butter or margarine
1 cup long grain rice
1 (10-ounce) can condensed chicken broth
1 (10-ounce) can French onion soup
1 (3-ounce) can sliced mushrooms, drained
1 tablespoon finely chopped green onion tops

Spray a 2-quart baking dish with nonstick cooking spray. Place the butter in the dish. Heat in a 350-degree oven until the butter is melted. Add the rice, chicken broth, French onion soup and mushrooms and mix well.

Bake, covered, for 1 hour. Remove the cover. Sprinkle with the green onions. Turn off the oven. Let the rice stand in the oven for 10 minutes. Serve immediately.

Yield: 6 to 8 servings.

Spinach with Rice

1 bunch fresh spinach
1 medium onion, chopped
1/2 cup vegetable oil or margarine
2 1/3 cups water
Salt and pepper to taste
1 cup rice

Wash the spinach and chop coarsely. Sauté the onion in the oil in a skillet until light brown. Add the spinach. Cook, covered, until the spinach is slightly limp. Add the water, salt, pepper and rice; do not stir. Cook over medium-high heat for 10 minutes or until the mixture boils. Reduce the heat. Simmer for 15 minutes.

Place a platter over the skillet and turn upside down. Let stand for 5 minutes. Garnish with lemon. May add 8 ounces ground beef with the onion.

Yield: 4 servings.

To cook rice by the absorption method, combine water, rice and salt in a pan; bring to a boil. Stir, lower the heat and cover.

Simmer for 15 minutes, then let stand for 15 minutes. Fluff up the grains with a fork.

Roasted Garlic and Mushroom Risotto

2 large heads garlic, cloves separated
2 tablespoons olive oil
3/4 ounce dried porcini mushrooms
1 tablespoon olive oil
12 ounces mixed fresh wild mushrooms,
    cut into slices
Salt and pepper to taste
1 tablespoon olive oil
1 cup chopped shallots
2 tablespoons chopped fresh thyme or
    2 teaspoons dried thyme
1 1/2 cups arborio or medium-grain white rice
1/2 cup dry white wine
3 1/2 to 4 cups low-sodium chicken broth
2 cups thinly sliced fresh spinach leaves
1/3 cup freshly grated Parmesan cheese

 Combine the garlic and 2 tablespoons olive oil in a small baking dish. Bake at 400 degrees for 50 minutes or until the garlic is golden brown and tender, stirring occasionally. Let stand until slightly cooled; peel. Chop enough garlic to measure 1/4 cup packed.

Combine the porcini and enough hot water to cover in a bowl. Let stand for 30 minutes or until soft. Drain and squeeze to remove the excess moisture. Chop the porcini coarsely.

Heat 1 tablespoon olive oil over medium-high heat in a large nonstick skillet. Add the fresh mushrooms. Sauté for 7 minutes or until golden brown and the juices are evaporated. Add the porcini. Cook for 1 minute, stirring constantly. Season with salt and pepper. Set aside.

Heat 1 tablespoon olive oil in a heavy saucepan over medium-high heat. Add the shallots and thyme. Sauté for 4 minutes or until tender. Add the rice, stirring to coat. Add the wine. Cook until the liquid is almost evaporated. Stir in the roasted garlic and 3 1/2 cups of the broth. Bring to a boil. Reduce the heat to medium. Cook for 20 minutes or until the rice is tender and the mixture is creamy, stirring occasionally and adding additional broth as needed. Add the mushroom mixture and spinach. Cook until the spinach wilts, stirring constantly. Stir in the cheese. Season with salt and pepper.

Yield: 6 to 8 servings.

Roasting mellows and sweetens the flavor of garlic so that it can be used as a delicious accompaniment as well as a flavoring. Roast whole heads of garlic in their skins at the same time as a roast. If they are trimmed decoratively to form a flower, they also make very attractive garnishes.

Slice off the top of each head of garlic, cutting through the cloves. Place them cut side up in a baking dish. Brush with olive oil and roast at 350 degrees for about 50 minutes.

Preparing Eggplant for Baking

To ensure the pulp of halved eggplant cooks evenly, the cut surfaces are deeply scored. You can perfume the pulp by inserting razor-thin slices of garlic into the incisions before baking.

Remove the stalk and calyx (the cup around the base of the stalk) and cut the eggplant into halves lengthwise using a chef's knife. Cross-hatch the pulp deeply, using a sharp pointed knife, then sprinkle with salt.

Ebony Eggplant Dressing

1 or 2 large eggplant, peeled, cut into quarters
1 1/2 teaspoons salt
1 (16-ounce) package fresh hot pork sausage
1/4 cup (1/2 stick) margarine
2 pounds shrimp, peeled
1 cup chopped green bell pepper
3 cloves garlic, chopped
2 cups chopped celery
1 cup chopped onions
1 cup cooked rice
1 cup Italian bread crumbs
2 cups shredded mozzarella cheese

Combine the eggplant with enough water to cover in a saucepan. Add the salt. Bring to a boil. Boil for 20 minutes. Drain well and cut into bite-size pieces. Set aside.

Cook the sausage in a skillet, stirring until crumbly. Drain on paper towels. Heat the margarine in a skillet until melted. Add the shrimp, bell pepper, garlic, celery and onions. Sauté for 2 minutes. Stir in the cooked eggplant and sausage. Cook over medium heat for 10 minutes, stirring occasionally. Add the rice and bread crumbs gradually until eggplant mixture is of the desired consistency.

Spoon the eggplant mixture into a 3-quart baking dish. Bake at 350 degrees for 25 minutes. Sprinkle the cheese over the top. Bake for an additional 5 minutes.

Yield: 10 servings.

Corn Bread and Nut Stuffing

1 cup minced onions
1 cup minced celery
2 tablespoons minced parsley
1/2 cup (1 stick) margarine
1 cup chopped pecans
6 cups corn bread crumbs
3 cups soft bread crumbs
1 1/2 teaspoons salt
1/2 teaspoon each pepper, thyme and sage
1/2 cup cooking sherry
7 cups chicken or beef stock
5 green onions, chopped
4 eggs

Sauté the onions, celery and parsley in the margarine in a skillet for 8 minutes or until tender. Combine with the pecans, corn bread crumbs, soft bread crumbs, salt, pepper, thyme, sage, sherry, stock, green onions and eggs in a large bowl and mix well.

Spoon into a greased 9x13-inch baking dish. Bake at 350 degrees for 30 minutes or until light brown.

Yield: 10 to 12 servings.

To make nut butter, grind roasted nuts in a food processor fitted with a metal blade. Add twice as much butter as nuts and blend together using the pulse button. Turn out the nut butter and shape into a log on baking parchment, then wrap and refrigerate. Slice as required.

Toasting and Skinning Nuts

Hazelnuts and Brazil nuts are best toasted rather than blanched before skinning. Hazelnuts can be toasted in the oven or they can be toasted by dry-frying them on top of the stove. For dry-frying, place in a nonstick heavy frying pan over a low heat and stir until lightly toasted on all sides, two to four minutes.

For oven-toasting, spread the nuts evenly on a baking sheet and toast at 350 degrees for 10 minutes, shaking the baking sheet occasionally.

Then wrap the toasted nuts in a kitchen towel to steam for a few minutes. Rub to remove the skins.

Converted Rice

Converted rice is a name for parboiled rice; it is a trademark of Uncle Ben's brand rice.

Parboiling originated in India at least two thousand years ago. The whole rice grain is soaked and steamed under pressure, a technique that forces some of the nutrients from the hull (which includes the bran and the germ) into the heart of the kernel. Because those nutrients would normally be lost during milling, parboiled rice is more nutritious than regular white rice.

Parboiling also changes the structure of rice's starch coating; when it is cooked, the kernels do not stick together. Because parboiled rice is slightly tougher than regular rice, it can take a little longer to cook.

When cooking rice, remember that 1 cup uncooked rice will yield 3 cups of cooked rice.

Rice and Oyster Dressing

2 cups rice
1 pint oysters
8 ounces chicken livers, coarsely chopped
3 tablespoons vegetable oil
1 large onion, chopped
6 green onions, chopped
4 ribs celery, chopped
2 large eggs, lightly beaten
1 tablespoon sage
$1/3$ cup chopped parsley
2 teaspoons salt
$1/4$ teaspoon black pepper
$1/2$ teaspoon cayenne pepper
$1/4$ cup ($1/2$ stick) butter

Cook the rice using the package directions. Drain the oysters, reserving the liquid. Cut each oyster into thirds.

Sauté the livers in the oil in a skillet for 5 minutes. Add the onion, green onions and celery. Cook until tender. Combine with the cooked rice and eggs in a large bowl and mix well. Add the oysters, sage, parsley, salt, black pepper and cayenne pepper and mix well.

Heat the butter in a large heavy skillet until melted. Add the rice mixture. Cook until the eggs begin to set and the edges of the oysters begin to curl, stirring frequently and adding the reserved oyster liquid as needed. Spoon into a greased 3-quart baking dish. Bake at 350 degrees for 45 to 60 minutes or until brown.

Yield: 8 to 10 servings.

Buttons and Bows

1/4 cup (1/2 stick) butter
1/3 cup margarine
1 or 2 cloves garlic, minced
1 (4-ounce) can button mushrooms, drained
8 ounces small white fresh mushrooms
1/4 cup finely chopped red bell pepper
1/4 teaspoon pepper
4 cups farfalle
Salt to taste
1/2 cup chopped parsley
1 cup sour cream, at room temperature
1/3 cup milk or cream
1/2 cup grated Parmesan cheese
1/8 teaspoon oregano

⚲ Heat the butter and margarine in a skillet until melted. Add the garlic, button mushrooms, fresh mushrooms, bell pepper and pepper. Sauté until the mushrooms and bell pepper are tender.

Cook the farfalle in boiling salted water in a large pot until al dente; drain. Place in a 2-quart serving dish.

Add the parsley to the pasta and toss to mix. Add the mushroom mixture, sour cream and milk and toss to mix. Add the cheese and oregano and toss lightly. Serve immediately.

Yield: 4 to 6 servings.

Mint Orzo

2 tablespoons olive oil
1/2 cup finely chopped onion
1 tablespoon minced garlic
1 cup orzo
1 teaspoon salt
4 turns freshly ground pepper
1/4 cup chopped fresh mint
3 cups chicken stock
1 tablespoon unsalted butter, softened

⚲ Heat the olive oil in a saucepan over high heat. Add the onion, garlic, orzo, salt and pepper. Stir-fry for 2 minutes. Stir in the mint and stock. Bring to a boil.

Reduce the heat to medium. Cook for 20 minutes, stirring occasionally. Remove from the heat. Add the butter and stir until the butter is melted. Serve immediately.

Yield: 6 servings.

Entrées

It's no secret that Louisianians love the outdoors, and the residents of central Louisiana are certainly no exception. The secret to our love for nature stems from a climate that is great for outdoor activities any time of the year. Opportunities to enjoy nature and the environment abound.

Louisiana's only national forest surrounds Alexandria. Spring in Kisatchie provides opportunities for hiking, bird watching, and relaxation among the dogwoods and wild azaleas. Mountain biking has also become a popular sport on the trails surrounding Kincaid Lake. Within the city, the Garden District comes alive with varying shades of purple, pink, and white as azaleas display their majesty around Easter. Larkspur, daylilies, and irises are among the flora that decorate the lush backyard sanctuaries of Alexandria's oldest dwellings.

During summer months, water sports are particularly popular along central Louisiana's rivers, lakes, and bayous. Secret baits and locations of favorite fishing holes are guarded family secrets passed down from generation to generation. Swimming, skiing, and fishing provide hours of recreation for young and old alike. A stringer of crappie, bream, or bass is the perfect reason for a fish fry to celebrate friendship and a good day on the water. Nothing can rival the flavor of fish caught and cooked on the same afternoon with cherished family and friends.

The diverse and abundant wildlife in central Louisiana provides a challenge for hunters during fall and winter seasons. Hunting is a family tradition among male members of most families, and exaggerated hunting stories are the typical entertainment as the family enjoys an exceptional meal featuring wild game dishes.

Louisiana truly is a sportsman's paradise, and this outstanding natural environment is central to making our area special. We hope these entrées will share the nature of our unique flavor with your family.

The Garden District comes
alive with varying shades of purple,
pink, and white as azaleas display
their majesty around Easter.
Larkspur, daylilies, and irises
are among the flora that decorate
the lush backyard sanctuaries of
Alexandria's oldest dwellings.

Entrées Key Sponsor

JERRY CAMPO'S
FINE PRINT

Reserved

Beef Tenderloin with Roasted Shallots, Bacon and Port

12 ounces large shallots, peeled, cut into halves
    lengthwise
2 teaspoons olive oil
Salt and pepper to taste
1 (3- to 3¼-pound) beef tenderloin, trimmed
1 teaspoon thyme
4 slices bacon, chopped
3 cups beef broth
¾ cup port or cabernet
1½ teaspoons tomato paste
¼ cup (½ stick) butter, softened
2 tablespoons flour

∞—m Combine the shallots and olive oil in a 9-inch round baking pan, tossing the shallots to coat. Season with salt and pepper. Bake at 375 degrees for 30 minutes or until deep brown and very tender, stirring occasionally. Set aside.

Pat the beef dry. Sprinkle with thyme, salt and pepper. Cook the bacon in a large nonstick skillet over medium heat for 8 minutes or until golden brown. Remove the bacon and place on paper towels to drain. Place the beef in the skillet. Cook over medium-high heat for 7 minutes or until brown on all sides. Place the beef on a rack in a shallow roasting pan. Roast at 375 degrees for 25 minutes for medium-rare or to the desired degree of doneness. Place on a serving platter and tent loosely with foil. Let stand for 15 minutes. Cut into ½-inch-thick slices.

Combine the broth and port in a saucepan. Bring to a boil. Boil for 15 minutes or until reduced by half. Whisk in the tomato paste. Combine 2 tablespoons of the butter with the flour in a small bowl and mix to form a smooth paste. Whisk into the broth mixture. Cook for 2 minutes or until the sauce thickens, whisking constantly. Whisk in the remaining 2 tablespoons butter. Stir in the roasted shallots and bacon. Season with salt and pepper. Serve over the beef.

Yield: 6 servings.

Italian Pot Roast

1/2 teaspoon salt
1/4 teaspoon pepper
Flour to coat
1 (3- to 4-pound) boneless roast
2 tablespoons vegetable oil
2 medium onions, sliced
2 (4-ounce) cans sliced mushrooms, drained
1/4 cup water
1/4 cup catsup
1/4 cup dry sherry
1 clove garlic, crushed
1/4 teaspoon dry mustard
1/4 teaspoon dried whole rosemary
1/4 teaspoon dried whole thyme
1/4 teaspoon dried whole marjoram
1 bay leaf
1 tablespoon flour
1/4 cup cold water

Combine the salt, pepper and flour in a shallow dish and mix well. Dredge the roast in the flour mixture. Heat the oil in a Dutch oven. Add the roast and cook until brown on all sides. Place the onions over the roast.

Combine the mushrooms, 1/4 cup water, catsup, sherry, garlic, mustard, rosemary, thyme, marjoram and bay leaf in a bowl and mix well. Pour over the roast. Bake, covered, at 325 degrees for 2 1/2 to 3 hours or until tender.

Remove the roast and vegetables to a serving platter, reserving the pan drippings. Remove and discard the bay leaf. Combine 1 tablespoon flour and 1/4 cup cold water in a small bowl and whisk until smooth. Pour into the pan drippings. Cook until thickened and bubbly, stirring constantly. Serve with the roast.

Yield: 6 to 8 servings.

Camp Alpine

The great outdoors is open to all nature enthusiasts in the Alexandria area. Camping, canoeing, fishing, water sports, hunting, and hiking are all within fifteen minutes of our back door.

Taking advantage of these natural resources, the Junior League of Alexandria sponsored Camp Alpine, a summer camp for underprivileged girls, between 1945 and 1974. These girls were exposed to the great camping experiences and traditions that build friendships and memories that linger long after the campfire's smoldering embers burn out.

Boeuf à la Bourguignonne

6 slices bacon, cut into 1/2-inch strips
1 tablespoon olive oil
3 pounds lean beef, cut into 2-inch cubes
1 carrot, peeled, chopped
1 onion, sliced
Salt to taste
Black and white pepper to taste
2 tablespoons flour
3 cups red wine
3 cups beef stock
1 tablespoon tomato paste
2 cloves garlic, crushed
1 teaspoon fresh thyme, crushed
1 bay leaf
16 ounces mushrooms, cut into quarters
Butter

Combine the bacon with enough water to cover in a saucepan. Bring to a simmer. Simmer for 10 minutes. Drain and pat dry. Sauté in the olive oil in a Dutch oven until crisp. Remove the bacon and set aside.

Pat the beef dry. Sauté in the bacon drippings in batches until brown on all sides. Remove the beef and set aside. Sauté the carrot and onion in the bacon drippings until brown.

Return the bacon and beef to the Dutch oven. Season with salt and pepper. Sprinkle with the flour, tossing to coat evenly.

Pour in the wine and enough stock to just cover the beef. Add the tomato paste, garlic, thyme and bay leaf. Bring to a simmer. Bake, covered, in a 350-degree oven until the beef is tender.

Sauté the mushrooms in a small amount of butter in a skillet until tender. Add to the beef mixture. Skim the fat off the beef mixture.

Return the Dutch oven to the stove top. Bring to a simmer. Simmer until the sauce thickens, stirring occasionally. Adjust the seasonings as desired. Remove the bay leaf. Serve with hot cooked noodles or rice.

Yield: 6 servings.

BBQ Brisket

Brisket, trimmed
Onion salt
Celery salt
Garlic salt
Creole seasoning
2 tablespoons liquid smoke
Worcestershire sauce
1 (18-ounce) bottle barbecue sauce

Sprinkle both sides of the brisket with onion salt, celery salt, garlic salt and Creole seasoning. Drizzle 1 tablespoon of the liquid smoke over each side of the brisket. Place in a large foil-lined roasting pan. Marinate, covered, in the refrigerator for 8 to 10 hours.

Pour Worcestershire sauce over the brisket. Bake, covered, at 250 degrees for 5 hours. Pour the barbecue sauce over the brisket. Bake for 1 hour longer.

Yield: Variable.

Tortilla Torte

1 pound ground beef
1 small onion, chopped
Salt and pepper to taste
1 envelope taco seasoning mix
1 (15-ounce) can black beans, rinsed, drained
2 (15-ounce) cans diced Rotel tomatoes
4 (10-inch) flour tortillas
2 cups shredded Cheddar or Monterey Jack
    cheese
2 cups sour cream
1 bunch green onions, chopped
1/2 cup guacamole
Salsa

⚷—ⵜ Brown the ground beef with the onion in a skillet, stirring until the ground beef is crumbly; drain. Season with salt and pepper. Stir in the taco seasoning mix. Combine the cooked beef mixture, beans and tomatoes in a large bowl and mix well.

Layer the tortillas, beef mixture and cheese one-fourth at a time in a Dutch oven sprayed with nonstick cooking spray. Cook, covered, over medium-low heat for 15 to 20 minutes or until the cheese is melted and the torte is hot in the center. Serve with the sour cream, green onions, guacamole and salsa.

Yield: 6 servings.

Creole Seasoning Blend

3/4 to 1 cup salt
1/4 cup black pepper
2 tablespoons white pepper
2 tablespoons red pepper
2 tablespoons garlic powder
2 tablespoons onion powder
1/4 cup paprika
2 tablespoons sugar

Combine the salt, black pepper, white pepper, red pepper, garlic powder, onion powder, paprika and sugar in a bowl and mix well. Store in an airtight container. Use like salt for seasoning.

Tiny Lamb Riblets

Racks of New Zealand baby lamb (see Note)
1 tablespoon minced garlic
1 1/2 teaspoons thyme
1 1/2 teaspoons rosemary or oregano
1 teaspoon salt
1 teaspoon pepper
Mint Dipping Sauce

Cut the lamb away from the end of the rib so that part of the bone is exposed on each lamb chop. Trim any excess fat.

Combine the garlic, thyme, rosemary, salt and pepper in a small bowl and mix well. Sprinkle over the chops. Let stand for 2 hours.

Grill over hot coals for 3 to 4 minutes per side or to the desired degree of doneness. Serve with Mint Dipping Sauce.

Note: Have enough racks to yield 50 chops.

Yield: 25 servings.

Mint Dipping Sauce

1 cup white wine vinegar
1/2 cup sugar
1/2 cup minced fresh mint
Salt and pepper to taste

Combine the vinegar and sugar in a saucepan. Cook until the sugar is dissolved. Stir in the mint. Let stand until cool. Season with salt and pepper.

Stuffed Artichokes

1/2 cup pine nuts
Margarine or butter
1 pound lamb shoulder or beef, finely chopped
1 medium onion, finely chopped
1/8 teaspoon cinnamon
Salt and pepper to taste
6 to 8 young artichokes
1/2 cup lemon juice

Sauté the pine nuts in margarine until golden brown. Add the lamb. Sauté until tender. Add the onion, cinnamon, salt and pepper. Cook until the onion is tender. Set aside.

Rinse the artichokes. Peel and trim the outer leaves. Remove the prickly leaves and hairy choke from the center. Stuff each artichoke with an equal amount of lamb mixture. Arrange upright in a baking dish. Combine the lemon juice with enough water to fill the baking dish halfway up the artichokes. Bake, covered, at 400 degrees for 30 to 35 minutes.

Yield: 6 to 8 servings.

Lamb Shanks Braised in Wine Sauce

2 tablespoons Creole seasoning
8 (2¹/₂-inch-long) lamb shanks
2 tablespoons olive oil
1 cup chopped onion
1 cup chopped celery
1 cup chopped carrots
2 cups dry red wine
¹/₂ cup chopped, peeled seeded Italian
    plum tomatoes
¹/₄ cup minced garlic
4 bay leaves
4 teaspoons chopped fresh thyme
2 teaspoons salt
4 turns freshly ground black pepper
7 cups lamb stock or beef stock

  Sprinkle the Creole seasoning over the lamb shanks. Heat the olive oil in a large nonreactive skillet over high heat. Add the shanks. Sear for 4 minutes or until brown on all sides. Add the onion, celery and carrots. Sauté for 1 minute. Stir in the wine, tomatoes, garlic, bay leaves and thyme. Simmer for 3 minutes.

  Stir in the salt, pepper and stock. Bring to a boil. Reduce the heat to low. Simmer, covered, for 1 hour or until the lamb is tender and the sauce is syrupy, basting occasionally. Remove the bay leaves. Place 2 lamb shanks on each dinner plate. Drizzle with any remaining sauce in the skillet.

Yield: 4 servings.

Good Food and Good Times

Since men in the South have their hunting and golfing, etc., their women have created several outlets for themselves. The older generation of women enjoyed bridge clubs and garden clubs as ways to socialize and enjoy sharing a hobby. These were often fancy affairs complete with gloves and hats. Today's generation of women has traded bridge for other card games like pokeno and bonko, but still enjoys socializing and sharing. At all of these gatherings you're sure to find great food, and if you don't have a group to gather and giggle with, you're missing out on the stories and secrets that spill out when the men aren't around.

Stuffed Cabbage Leaves

1 (2-pound) head of cabbage
1 cup rice
1 pound lamb or beef, finely chopped
1/8 teaspoon cinnamon
1/4 teaspoon allspice
Salt and pepper to taste
1/2 cup (about) water
1 small head of cabbage, cored
1 large onion, sliced
2 tablespoons olive oil
1 tablespoon chopped garlic
2 tablespoons dry mint, or 1/4 cup
*   fresh mint*
1/4 cup lemon juice

Core the 2-pound head of cabbage. Bring a large pot of water to a boil. Add the cabbage and cook until the leaves are limp and easy to roll; drain. Separate the leaves. Slice each leaf into halves along the rib, removing or flattening part of the rib if it is large or coarse; the leaves should be a uniform size.

Combine the rice, lamb, cinnamon, allspice, salt, pepper and enough water to soften in a bowl and mix well. Place 1 teaspoon of the lamb mixture on each leaf. Spread the mixture lengthwise along the rib. Roll to enclose the filling. Gently press each rolled leaf.

Separate the leaves of the small head of cabbage. Sauté the cabbage leaves and onion in the olive oil in a skillet until tender. Arrange over the bottom of a 5- or 6-quart pot. Layer the rolled leaves in compact rows over the sautéed mixture, sprinkling garlic, salt and mint between the layers. Place a pottery plate over the layers so that the rolls will remain firm and intact. Add enough water to bring 1/2 inch above the layers.

Cook, covered, over medium heat for 15 to 18 minutes. Remove the plate. Pour the lemon juice over the top of the cabbage layers. Simmer for 20 minutes or until the rice is tender. Let stand for 5 to 6 minutes before serving.

Yield: 6 to 8 servings.

Stuffed Grape Leaves

1 pound lamb shoulder, finely chopped
1 cup rice, rinsed, drained
1/8 teaspoon cinnamon
1/8 teaspoon allspice
Salt and pepper to taste
55 to 65 (3- to 4-inch) grape leaves
1 tablespoon salt
1/4 cup lemon juice

Mix the lamb, rice, cinnamon, allspice, salt to taste and pepper in a bowl.

Wilt the grape leaves by rinsing in hot water a few at a time; drain. Arrange enough leaves over the bottom of a 2 1/2-quart saucepan to cover. Place 1 heaping teaspoon of the lamb mixture on the edge of the dull side of one of the remaining leaves. Roll over once to enclose the lamb mixture. Fold in thirds and finish rolling. Repeat the process until all the grape leaves and lamb mixture are used.

Arrange the rolled grape leaves close together in rows in the prepared saucepan. Add enough water to just cover. Sprinkle with the 1 tablespoon salt. Place a plate on top of the rolled grape leaves to keep them firm and intact. Cook, covered, over medium heat for 15 minutes. Add the lemon juice. Reduce the heat. Simmer for 15 minutes. Invert onto a serving plate. Serve with yogurt.

Yield: 6 to 8 servings.

Fried Kibbi Patties

3 cups plus 4 teaspoons burghul
1 large onion, grated
2 tablespoons salt
1/4 teaspoon pepper
1/8 teaspoon cinnamon
1/8 teaspoon allspice
2 pounds ground lean lamb

Combine the burghul with enough cold water to cover in a large bowl. Let stand for 10 minutes. Drain and press to remove excess water.

Combine the onion, salt, pepper, cinnamon and allspice in a bowl and mix well. Knead in the lamb. Knead in the burghul, dipping hands in ice water frequently to keep the mixture cold. May put the mixture through a meat grinder 1 to 3 times for a finer consistency.

Shape into patties. Fry in a skillet until cooked through and brown on both sides or bake in a greased baking dish at 400 degrees for 20 minutes.

Variation: Substitute beef for the lamb, reduce the burghul to 2 2/3 cups and add 1/4 teaspoon ground basil.

Yield: 8 to 12 servings.

Honeyed Pork Tenderloins

1/4 cup light soy sauce
1/4 cup honey
2 tablespoons light brown sugar
1 1/2 to 2 pounds pork tenderloins
Mustard Sauce

Combine the soy sauce, honey and brown sugar in a sealable plastic bag and mix well. Add the pork tenderloins, coating with the marinade. Seal the bag . Marinate in the refrigerator for 8 to 10 hours, turning occasionally. Drain the pork, discarding the marinade.

Place the pork on a rack in a shallow roasting pan. Bake at 350 degrees for 1 1/4 hours or until cooked through. Wrap in foil and let stand for 5 to 10 minutes.

Slice into 1/4-inch-thick medallions. Serve with Mustard Sauce.

Yield: 4 to 6 servings.

Mustard Sauce

2/3 cup sour cream
2/3 cup mayonnaise
2 tablespoons dry mustard
1/4 cup thinly sliced green onions

Combine the sour cream, mayonnaise, dry mustard and green onions in a bowl and mix well. Chill, covered, until ready to serve.

Jamaican Spice Blend

Jamaican jerk is a spice mixture, actually a way of cooking meat—usually pork. The technique was first developed by the Arawak Indians, who originally inhabited Jamaica. It involves grinding a combination of vegetables, herbs, and spices (such as green onions, chiles, allspice, garlic, thyme, cinnamon, and pepper) into a paste, which is then used to coat the meat. The actual ingredients vary from cook to cook. After marinating for at least one hour or overnight, the meat is barbecued.

Pork Medallions in Creole Mustard Sauce

1 (2-pound) pork tenderloin
1 teaspoon salt
1 teaspoon pepper
1/2 cup flour
1/2 cup (1 stick) butter
1 tablespoon minced garlic
2 tablespoons vermouth
1 to 2 tablespoons Creole mustard
1 cup half-and-half
4 to 5 slices Swiss cheese
16 ounces fettuccini or vermicelli

Cut the tenderloin into 1/4-inch-thick slices. Sprinkle with the salt and pepper. Dredge in the flour.

Heat 1/4 cup of the butter in a heavy skillet until melted. Add the pork. Cook until lightly browned on both sides. Remove from the skillet and keep warm.

Add the remaining 1/4 cup butter to the skillet and heat until melted. Add the garlic and sauté. Stir in the vermouth and mustard. Reduce the heat to low. Stir in the half-and-half. Add the cheese and cook until the cheese melts. Return the pork to the skillet. Bring to a simmer. Simmer for 10 to 15 minutes.

Cook the fettuccini using the package directions; drain. Place the fettuccini on a serving platter. Arrange the pork and sauce over the top.

Yield: 6 to 8 servings.

Pork Chops with Mushroom Bourbon Cream Sauce

2 tablespoons olive oil
16 ounces mushrooms, sliced
1/4 cup chopped shallots
2 large garlic cloves, chopped
1/2 cup dry white wine
1 cup chicken stock
1/2 cup heavy cream
1/4 cup bourbon
1 egg
2 tablespoons water
4 (6- to 7-ounce) center cut pork chops
Salt and pepper to taste
Flour
2 cups fresh French bread crumbs
3 tablespoons vegetable oil
2 tablespoons minced fresh basil
1 tablespoon bourbon

 Heat the olive oil in a heavy large skillet over medium heat. Add the mushrooms, shallots and garlic. Sauté for 15 minutes or until the mushrooms are brown. Add the wine. Bring to a boil. Boil for 4 minutes or until almost reduced to a glaze. Add the stock, cream and 1/4 cup bourbon. Simmer for 12 minutes or until thickened. May be refrigerated for up to 1 day.

Whisk the egg and water in a shallow dish. Sprinkle the pork chops with the salt and pepper. Dip into the flour, then the egg mixture and then the bread crumbs. Heat the vegetable oil in a large skillet. Add the pork chops. Cook for 4 minutes per side or until browned. Place in a baking dish. Bake at 400 degrees for 10 minutes or until cooked through.

Bring the sauce to a simmer. Stir in the basil and 1 tablespoon bourbon. Season with salt and pepper. Divide the sauce among 4 plates. Place the pork chops over the sauce.

Yield: 4 servings.

Searing exposes meat to a very high temperature to brown it on the surface. It was once thought that searing formed a waterproof crust through which the meat's juices and flavor could not escape. But, according to some food scientists, this is not true. Even so, there is one excellent reason to sear—flavor. While the brown crust that is formed by searing may not be waterproof, it is delicious.

Feta, Artichoke and Smoked Ham Casserole

2 cups milk
1/4 cup olive oil
8 cups (1-inch cubes) trimmed French bread
1 1/2 cups heavy cream
5 eggs
1 tablespoon chopped garlic
1/2 teaspoon salt
3/4 teaspoon pepper
1/2 teaspoon nutmeg
12 ounces feta cheese, crumbled
1 teaspoon sage
1 teaspoon thyme
1 1/2 teaspoons herbes de Provence
1 cup shredded mozzarella cheese
1 cup grated Parmesan cheese
12 ounces smoked ham, chopped
3 (7-ounce) jars marinated artichoke hearts,
*   drained, cut into quarters*

Whisk the milk and oil in a bowl. Add the bread, stirring to coat. Let stand for 10 minutes or until the liquid is absorbed.

Whisk the cream, eggs, garlic, salt, pepper and nutmeg in a bowl. Add the feta cheese and mix well.

Combine the sage, thyme and herbes de Provence in a small bowl and mix well. Combine the mozzarella cheese and Parmesan cheese in a small bowl and mix well.

Layer the bread mixture, ham, artichoke hearts, herbes de Provence mixture, cheese mixture and cream mixture one-half at a time in a buttered 9x13-inch glass baking dish. May be refrigerated for up to 1 day.

Bake in a preheated 350-degree oven for 1 hour or until the center is set and edges are brown.

Yield: 8 servings.

Sautéed Veal with Mushroom Cream Sauce

2 tablespoons olive oil
8 ounces veal scallops
Salt and pepper to taste
1 tablespoon butter
8 ounces mixed fresh wild mushrooms such as
*   oyster, crimini and stemmed shiitake,*
*   sliced*
1/3 cup finely chopped shallots
6 tablespoons Cognac or brandy of choice
6 tablespoons heavy cream
Chopped fresh parsley

Heat the olive oil in a large heavy skillet over high heat. Season the veal with salt and pepper. Add to the oil and sauté for 1 minute per side or just until cooked through. Remove to a platter. Tent with foil to keep warm.

Add the butter to the skillet. Heat over medium-high heat until melted. Add the mushrooms and shallots. Sauté for 5 minutes or until golden brown. Add the Cognac. Bring to a boil. Boil for 2 minutes. Add the cream. Boil for 2 minutes or until of the desired consistency, stirring occasionally. Season with salt and pepper. Spoon over the veal. Sprinkle with the parsley.

Yield: 2 servings.

Mediterranean Veal Chops

6 veal chops
Flour
Salt to taste
Lemon pepper to taste
Creole seasoning to taste
6 tablespoons vegetable oil
1/4 cup chopped onion
1 tablespoon minced garlic
1 cup smoked chopped chicken or turkey
1 tablespoon flour
1 cup chicken stock
1 cup green olives, pitted, blanched
16 ounces angel hair pasta or pasta of choice, cooked, hot

Dust the veal chops with flour. Season with salt, lemon pepper and Creole seasoning. Sauté in hot oil in a nonstick skillet until brown on both sides. Add the onion, garlic and chicken. Cook, covered, over low heat until the veal chops are tender, turning once. Remove the veal chops to a platter.

Add 1 tablespoon flour to the skillet, stirring to mix well. Stir in the stock and olives. Bring to a simmer. Simmer until thickened, stirring constantly. Combine with the hot pasta in a large bowl. Toss to coat the pasta. Place on a large platter. Top with the veal chops.

Yield: 6 servings.

Venison Delights

1 venison tenderloin or backstrap
1 (8-ounce) bottle Italian salad dressing, milk or marinade of choice
8 ounces cream cheese
1 (11-ounce) jar sliced jalapeño chiles
12 ounces bacon slices

Place the venison in a shallow dish. Pour the salad dressing over the venison. Marinate, covered, in the refrigerator for 8 hours; drain.

Cut the venison into 1- to 1½-inch cubes. Cut the cream cheese into 18 to 20 small pieces.

Wrap a venison cube, cream cheese piece and 1 or 2 chile slices in a bacon slice, covering the cream cheese completely with the bacon and securing with a wooden pick. Repeat the process until all ingredients are used. Grill cheese side up over hot coals for 30 minutes.

Variation: For Dove Delights, substitute dove for the venison and place the cream cheese, chile slices and bacon in the cavity of the dove.

Yield: 8 servings.

If you live in the South and your husband hunts, come hunting season you are commonly known as a hunting widow. During this time these ladies find themselves spouseless every weekend. He returns smiling, handing over his bounty—hopefully plucked, cleaned, or gutted. This phenomenon has prompted the southern woman to be creative with cooking up that wild game. That is so she doesn't have to convince the kids that it tastes "just like chicken."

Making a White Sauce

For a pouring sauce, use 1 tablespoon butter and 2 tablespoons flour to 1¹/4 cups milk; for a coating sauce use 1¹/2 tablespoons butter and 2¹/2 tablespoons flour. Cook the flour just enough to burst the starch grains and avoid a raw taste. To prevent lumps and give an even color, stir constantly over the entire base of the pan.

Step 1: Add flour to melted butter. Stir with a wooden spoon over a low heat for 1 to 2 minutes to create a white roux.

Step 2: Remove pan from heat. Gradually add hot milk, beating constantly to blend it with the roux.

Step 3: Bring to a boil, stirring constantly. Lower the heat and simmer until the sauce reaches the desired thickness.

Greek Chicken Casserole

8 chicken breasts
Salt to taste
1/4 cup (1/2 stick) margarine
1 large bell pepper, chopped
2 ribs celery, chopped
1 large onion, chopped
12 ounces elbow pasta
1 (7-ounce) jar chopped pimentos
4 (10-ounce) cans cream of mushroom soup
1 tablespoon Cavender's Greek seasoning, or to taste
1 teaspoon white pepper
1 teaspoon MSG
1 cup broth (optional)
2 cups grated sharp cheese
Seasoned bread crumbs

Combine the chicken with enough water to cover in a large pot. Season with salt. Bring to a boil. Reduce the heat. Simmer until cooked through. Remove the chicken, reserving the broth.

Remove the meat from the chicken, discarding the skin and bones. Cut into bite-size pieces.

Heat the margarine in a skillet until melted. Add the bell pepper, celery and onion. Sauté until tender.

Bring the reserved chicken broth to a boil. Add the pasta. Boil until tender; drain.

Combine the chicken, sautéed vegetables, pimentos, soup and pasta in a large bowl and mix well. Add the Greek seasoning, white pepper and MSG and mix well. Add the broth and mix well.

Spoon into two 8x10-inch baking dishes. Sprinkle the cheese and bread crumbs over the tops. May be frozen at this point.

Bake at 350 degrees for 30 to 45 minutes or until bubbly.

Yield: 12 to 16 servings.

Chicken Artichoke Casserole

6 tablespoons butter
Flour for coating
Salt and pepper to taste
10 boneless skinless chicken breasts
2 tablespoons butter
2 tablespoons flour
3/4 cup chicken broth
3/4 cup white wine
1/4 cup chopped green onions
1 (4-ounce) can mushrooms
1 (6-ounce) jar marinated artichoke hearts

☌━━ Place the 6 tablespoons butter in a 9x12-inch baking dish. Heat in a 375-degree oven until the butter is melted.

Combine the flour for coating, salt and pepper in a sealable plastic bag. Add the chicken and shake to coat. Remove the chicken from the bag, shaking to remove excess flour. Dip in the melted butter and place butter side up in the baking dish.

Bake, covered with foil, for 45 to 60 minutes or until cooked through.

Heat the 2 tablespoons butter in a saucepan until melted. Stir in 2 tablespoons flour. Whisk in the chicken broth and wine gradually. Cook until thickened, stirring constantly. Add the green onions, undrained mushrooms and undrained artichoke hearts and mix well. Spoon over the chicken.

Bake, covered, at 325 degrees for 15 to 20 minutes. Bake, uncovered, for 10 minutes.

Yield: 10 servings.

Chicken Broccoli Casserole

2 (10-ounce) packages frozen broccoli spears
6 boneless skinless chicken breasts
Salt to taste
1/2 cup (1 stick) margarine
1 medium onion, chopped
6 tablespoons flour
2 1/2 cups milk
8 ounces sharp Cheddar cheese, cut into cubes
1 1/2 teaspoons salt
1/2 teaspoon white pepper
2 teaspoons soy sauce
1/4 teaspoon Tabasco sauce
1 teaspoon MSG
1 (4-ounce) jar sliced pimentos, drained

☌━━ Cook the broccoli using the package directions; drain.

Combine the chicken with enough salted water to cover in a saucepan. Bring to a boil. Reduce the heat. Simmer until the chicken is cooked through; drain. Cut into bite-size pieces.

Heat 2 tablespoons of the margarine in a skillet until melted. Add the onion and sauté until tender.

Heat the remaining 6 tablespoons margarine in a saucepan until melted. Stir in the flour. Cook for 1 minute, stirring constantly. Whisk in the milk gradually. Cook over low heat until thickened, stirring constantly. Add the cheese. Cook until smooth, stirring constantly. Stir in the cooked onion, 1 1/2 teaspoons salt, white pepper, soy sauce, Tabasco sauce, MSG and pimentos. Remove from heat.

Layer the chicken, broccoli and sauce one-half at a time in a 9x13-inch baking dish. Bake at 350 degrees for 30 minutes or until bubbly.

Yield: 12 servings.

Chicken Lasagna with Cream Sauce

3 boneless skinless chicken breasts
2 tablespoons minced garlic
1 teaspoon white pepper
1/2 teaspoon salt
2 tablespoons butter
16 ounces mushrooms, sliced
1/2 cup minced onion
1/4 cup white wine
1 (14-ounce) can water-pack artichokes,
*   drained, coarsely chopped*
Cream Sauce
1 (26-ounce) jar marinara sauce (see Note)
1 cup ricotta cheese
3/4 teaspoon cayenne pepper, or to taste
8 ounces lasagna noodles, cooked
1 pound mozzarella cheese, shredded

Combine the chicken with enough water to cover in a saucepan. Add 1 tablespoon of the garlic, 1/2 teaspoon of the white pepper and salt. Bring to a boil over medium-high heat. Reduce the heat. Simmer, covered, for 15 minutes; drain. Shred the chicken and set aside.

Heat the butter in a large skillet over medium heat until melted. Add the mushrooms, onion, remaining 1 tablespoon garlic, remaining 1/2 teaspoon white pepper and the wine. Sauté until the mushrooms and onion are partially cooked. Stir in the artichokes and set aside.

Set aside 1 1/4 cups of the Cream Sauce. Combine the remaining Cream Sauce with the marinara sauce and ricotta cheese in a bowl and mix well. Add the cayenne pepper, stirring until smooth. Spread a thin layer over the bottom of a 9x13-inch baking pan sprayed with nonstick cooking spray. Combine the remaining marinara mixture, the chicken and mushroom mixture in a bowl and mix well.

Layer the noodles, chicken mixture and mozzarella cheese one-third at a time in the prepared baking dish. Pour the reserved Cream Sauce over the top.

Spray a piece of heavy-duty foil with nonstick cooking spray. Place over the layers. Bake at 350 degrees for 45 minutes or until heated through and bubbly. Remove the foil. Bake for an additional 10 minutes or until browned. Let stand for 10 to 15 minutes.

Note: Choose a marinara sauce with seasonings only and not meat, mushrooms or other additions.

Yield: 10 servings.

Cream Sauce

2 shallots, minced
1/4 cup (1/2 stick) butter
2 tablespoons white wine
3/4 cup flour
1 1/2 cups milk
1 1/2 cups heavy cream
1/2 teaspoon nutmeg
1/4 teaspoon white pepper
1/8 teaspoon salt

Sauté the shallots in the butter in a skillet over medium heat until tender. Stir in the wine. Whisk in the flour gradually. Whisk in the milk and cream. Cook until the mixture begins to thicken, whisking constantly. Reduce the heat. Add the nutmeg, white pepper and salt and mix well.

Chicken Bundles

12 boneless skinless chicken breasts
1/4 cup lemon juice
1 cup molasses
1/2 teaspoon ginger
1/4 teaspoon garlic powder
2 tablespoons Worcestershire sauce
1/4 cup soy sauce
1/4 cup olive oil
2 pounds mushrooms, sliced
20 green onions, sliced
1/2 cup (1 stick) butter, melted
3/4 teaspoon salt
3/4 teaspoon pepper
24 slices bacon

Pound each chicken breast to a 1/4-inch thickness between sheets of waxed paper. Place in a large shallow container. Combine the lemon juice, molasses, ginger, garlic powder, Worcestershire sauce, soy sauce and olive oil in a bowl and mix well. Pour over the chicken. Marinate, covered, in the refrigerator for 8 hours. Drain, reserving the marinade.

Sauté the mushrooms and green onions in the butter in a skillet until tender. Sprinkle with the salt and pepper. Cook until all of the liquid is evaporated, stirring constantly.

Lay 2 slices of the bacon in a crosswise pattern on a flat work surface. Place 1 chicken breast in the center of the bacon. Place 3 tablespoons of the mushroom mixture in the center of the chicken. Fold over the sides of the chicken, forming a bundle. Bring the bacon ends up over the bundle and secure with a wooden pick. Repeat the process with the remaining chicken, bacon and mushroom mixture.

Pour the reserved marinade in a small saucepan. Bring to a boil. Boil for 2 minutes. Grill the chicken bundles over hot coals for 55 to 60 minutes or until cooked through, turning and basting with the cooked marinade every 15 minutes.

Yield: 12 servings.

Chicken Spaghetti

10 to 12 boneless chicken breasts
3 quarts water
1 teaspoon salt
16 ounces spaghetti or vermicelli
1 cup (2 sticks) butter
1 (8-ounce) can mushrooms
1 onion, chopped
1 bell pepper, chopped
2 cups chopped celery
2 cloves garlic, minced
1 cup flour
1 cup half-and-half
2 (16-ounce) cans chicken broth
2 tablespoons chili powder
1/4 teaspoon cayenne pepper
Salt and white pepper to taste
1 tablespoon Worcestershire sauce
1 pound Cheddar cheese, shredded

Place the chicken, water and 1 teaspoon salt in a large pot. Bring to a boil. Reduce the heat. Simmer until the chicken is cooked through. Remove the chicken, reserving the liquid. Cut the chicken into bite-size pieces. Add the spaghetti to the reserved liquid and cook until al dente. Drain and set aside.

Heat the butter in a large skillet until melted. Add the undrained mushrooms, onion, bell pepper, celery and garlic. Sauté for 10 minutes or until the vegetables are tender. Stir in the flour. Add the half-and-half and broth gradually. Cook over low heat until the sauce thickens, stirring constantly. Add the chili powder, cayenne pepper, salt and white pepper to taste and Worcestershire sauce and mix well.

Combine the sauce, chicken and spaghetti in a large bowl and mix well. Divide evenly among two 9x13-inch baking dishes. Sprinkle the Cheddar cheese over the top. Bake at 250 degrees for 1 hour.

Yield: 12 servings.

Whether it is boiled or baked, pasta should be cooked until it is what Italians call al dente, which means "firm to bite." If it is overcooked, it will be mushy.

Just before the end of the recommended cooking time, lift a piece of pasta out of the water with tongs and test it by biting into it. When it is perfectly cooked, the pasta should feel tender, without any hint of rawness, but there should be just a touch of resistance to the bite. If the pasta is done, take it off the heat and drain it immediately. If not, continue testing every 30 to 60 seconds until it is.

Chicken Florentine

4 (10-ounce) packages frozen spinach,
  thawed, drained
2 (15-ounce) cans artichokes, drained, cut into
  quarters
Salt to taste
Red pepper to taste
Black pepper to taste
Garlic powder to taste
6 boneless skinless chicken breasts
1 cup flour
1 cup (2 sticks) butter, melted
2 cups half-and-half
1 cup grated Parmesan or Romano cheese
Paprika to taste

Press the spinach between paper
towels to remove the excess moisture. Arrange
evenly over the bottom of a buttered 11x14-inch
baking dish, pressing to compact. Sprinkle the
artichoke quarters over the spinach. Sprinkle
with the salt, red pepper, black pepper and
garlic powder.

Season the chicken lightly with the salt, red
pepper, black pepper and garlic powder. Dredge
in the flour. Dip in the butter. Place over the
artichokes. Pour the half-and-half over the layers.
Sprinkle with the cheese and paprika. Bake at
325 degrees for 1 to 1¹/2 hours or until the
chicken is cooked through.

Variation: Substitute margarine for the butter
and skim milk for the half-and-half. Bake at 375
degrees for 45 to 60 minutes or until the chicken is
cooked through.

Yield: 6 servings.

Green Chile Chicken Enchiladas

1 cup chopped onion
2 tablespoons olive oil
3 (4-ounce) cans chopped green chiles
2 cloves garlic, minced
1¹/2 cups chicken broth
¹/2 teaspoon oregano
¹/2 teaspoon salt
1 (6-ounce) can evaporated milk
3 fresh chopped tomatoes, or 2 (15-ounce)
  cans diced tomatoes
16 ounces Monterey Jack cheese, diced
2 cups chopped cooked chicken or turkey
¹/2 cup water
12 corn tortillas
1 cup light sour cream

Sauté the onion in the olive oil in a
skillet. Add the chiles and garlic. Cook for
2 minutes. Add ¹/2 cup of the chicken broth,
oregano, salt, evaporated milk and tomatoes and
mix well. Simmer for 30 minutes. Add the cheese;
do not overheat. Add the chicken. Remove from
heat. Stir in ¹/2 cup of the remaining broth.

Combine the remaining ¹/2 cup broth with
the water in a shallow dish and mix well. Dip the
tortillas in the broth mixture to soften. Spread
1 spoonful of the chicken mixture down the center
of each tortilla. Roll up and place in a 9x13-inch
baking dish. Spread any remaining chicken
mixture over the tortillas. Spread the sour cream
over the top. Bake at 350 degrees for 30 minutes.

Yield: 6 servings.

Curing an Iron Skillet

Those of us who were not lucky enough to have that well-seasoned cast-iron skillet passed down to us from a generation of experienced family cooks need not be afraid to buy a new one and season it ourselves.

Here's how we do it . . .

Wipe the skillet with a thin coat of vegetable shortening. Do not use butter or margarine. Using a cloth or paper towel, cover the entire surface. Place the skillet in a 300- to 350-degree oven for 45 to 60 minutes. Remove it from the oven and dry with a paper towel. Use only mild detergents to clean and never use a scouring pad. Wipe it with vegetable shortening after each use and cleaning before storing. I remember my mom's secret of allowing the skillet to air dry on top of the stove after cleaning. Your well-seasoned skillet will turn black and develop a thin crust that will seal the surface of the iron and prevent rust or sticking.

Chicken, Andouille and Shrimp Jambalaya

1 bay leaf
$1/4$ teaspoon cayenne pepper
$1^1/2$ teaspoons salt
$3/4$ teaspoon white pepper
1 teaspoon thyme
$1/4$ teaspoon black pepper
2 tablespoons unsalted butter
8 ounces andouille, chopped
12 ounces boneless skinless chicken, cut into
    bite-size pieces
1 cup chopped onion
1 cup chopped celery
1 cup chopped green bell pepper
1 tablespoon minced garlic
1 (8-ounce) can tomato sauce
1 (15-ounce) can diced tomatoes
$2^1/2$ cups chicken broth
$1^1/2$ cups rice
8 ounces shrimp, cut into halves

Combine the bay leaf, cayenne pepper, salt, white pepper, thyme and black pepper in a bowl and mix well.

Heat the butter in a 2-quart saucepan over high heat until melted. Add the sausage. Cook for 3 minutes. Add the chicken and cook for 3 to 5 minutes, stirring often. Add the pepper mixture, onion, celery, green pepper and garlic. Cook for 5 to 8 minutes or until the vegetables are tender, stirring and scraping the bottom of the pan often. Stir in the tomato sauce. Cook for 1 minute. Add the undrained tomatoes. Remove from heat. May be refrigerated for up to 1 day at this point.

Stir in the broth, rice and shrimp. Spoon into a 9x13-inch baking dish. Bake at 350 degrees for 1 hour or until the rice is tender. Remove the bay leaf and stir. Serve immediately.

Yield: 6 servings.

Ducks à la Luna

2 domestic ducks, frozen, thawed
2 tablespoons sage
2 tablespoons thyme
1 tablespoon Cavender's Greek seasoning
2 onions, cut into quarters, separated
2 ribs celery, cut into halves
4 cloves garlic, minced
1/4 cup soy sauce
1 tablespoon Cavender's Greek seasoning
1 cup water
6 chicken bouillon cubes
1 (10-ounce) jar seedless blackberry,
    raspberry or cranberry preserves, or
    10 ounces fresh blackberries, raspberries
    or cranberries
1 cup sugar
2 teaspoons water
1/4 cup vinegar

Remove and reserve the excess skin and the neck, liver, heart and gizzard from the ducks. Chop the heart and gizzard finely and set aside. Combine the sage, thyme and 1 tablespoon Greek seasoning in a small bowl and mix well. Coat the cavities of the ducks generously with the sage mixture. Stuff the cavities of the ducks tightly with the onions and celery. Combine the garlic, soy sauce and 1 tablespoon Greek seasoning in a bowl and mix well. Coat the ducks with the soy sauce mixture. Place the ducks on a rack in a roasting pan. Bake at 325 degrees for 2 1/2 hours, covering with foil if ducks become too brown.

Cook the excess skin in a skillet over medium-high heat until 1/4-inch of oil is rendered. Remove and discard the skin. Add the liver and neck. Cook until both begin to brown and the liver sticks to the pan; drain. Remove and discard the liver. Add the 1 cup water, chopped gizzard, chopped heart and bouillon cubes to the neck in the skillet. Cook over medium-high heat for 20 to 30 minutes, adding water as needed and ending with 1 to 1 1/2 cups stock; strain. Combine the strained stock and preserves in a saucepan. Cook over low heat until used in the next step.

Moisten the sugar with 2 teaspoons water in a saucepan. Cook over medium heat until the mixture turns brown; do not stir. Add the vinegar and cover immediately. Remove the cover after 30 seconds. Stir in the stock mixture. Cook over low heat for 5 minutes.

Separate the breasts, thighs and legs of the ducks and place on a baking sheet with sides. Spoon the sauce over the duck pieces. Broil for 5 minutes.

Yield: 4 to 6 servings.

Wild Duck Supreme

6 teal, dressed, drawn
Creole seasoning to taste
18 oysters
1/2 cup (1 stick) butter
2 teaspoons grated onion
2 slices bacon
1 (10-ounce) can chicken broth
1/2 cup burgundy
1 (4-ounce) can mushrooms
1 tablespoon flour
1/2 cup chopped green onion tops and parsley
2 tablespoons currant jelly
Salt and pepper to taste
Garlic powder to taste

⌇ Season the teal inside and out with Creole seasoning. Stuff each with 3 oysters, 2 teaspoons of butter and 1 teaspoon grated onion. Place a wooden pick through each end of the duck openings. Sew with thread in a crisscross fashion from one wooden pick to the other, closing the openings.

Melt the remaining 1/4 cup butter in a Dutch oven over medium-high-heat. Add the teal and brown on all sides. Arrange the teal breast sides up with the bacon slices over the top. Pour in the broth and burgundy. Bake, covered, at 300 degrees for 2 hours or until tender, turning the ducks over after 1 hour. Remove the ducks to a platter and keep warm, reserving the pan juices.

Drain the mushrooms, reserving the liquid. Combine the flour and reserved mushroom liquid in a small bowl and stir until smooth. Add the green onion tops and parsley, mushrooms, currant jelly, salt, pepper, garlic powder and liquid mixture to the reserved pan juices. Cook until thickened, stirring constantly. Spoon over the teal. Serve the remaining gravy with the teal over hot cooked rice.

Yield: 6 servings.

Grilled Teriyaki Salmon

1 1/2 pounds fresh salmon fillets
2/3 cup low-sodium soy sauce
1/4 cup white wine
1 teaspoon (heaping) brown sugar
1 teaspoon dry mustard
1 teaspoon freshly grated gingerroot or ginger
    powder
2 cloves garlic, minced

⌇ Place the salmon in a shallow dish. Whisk the soy sauce, wine, brown sugar, mustard, ginger and garlic in a bowl. Pour over the salmon. Marinate, covered, in the refrigerator for 2 to 8 hours. Drain, reserving the marinade. Bring the marinade to a boil in a saucepan. Boil for 2 minutes.

Place the salmon skin side down on a grill over hot coals. Cook for 6 to 8 minutes. Turn and baste with the cooked marinade. Cook for 6 to 8 minutes or until the fish flakes easily.

You may brush the fish with a small amount of olive oil or butter and may vary the amount of spices used if desired.

Yield: 4 to 6 servings.

The Hunting and Fishing Widow's Calendar

September:

Labor Day is the opening of dove season. Don't count on family time for the long weekend.

October:

Tricks and Treats begin early for our hunter, with dove season continuing and the opening of squirrel and deer bow-hunting. Camouflage is Dad's choice of the Halloween costume.

November:

Regular deer season and quail season open. The long-awaited duck season officially begins. Wild game will be your bounty for your Thanksgiving table.

December:

Deer and duck season is in full swing. Santa must be careful when flying low over Louisiana skies.

January:

Duck and quail season continues. If Dad's a wingman he'll be out all month, or at least until the Super Bowl.

February:

Duck season ends. This may be the month to plan a romantic weekend, especially around Valentine's Day; after all, Cupid was a hunter too.

March:

Turkey season begins in late March. Spring cleaning duties may be possible at the beginning of the month.

April:

You are a fool if you believe that Dad will stay home during this prime turkey season.

May:

This is the month Dad trades his shotgun for a rod and reel. Bream start bedding in area lakes and fishing in coastal waters warm up.

June:

Send the kids along with Dad to his secret fishing holes. Freshwater and saltwater fishing are great all month. Take advantage of this time for you–plan a facial.

July:

Summer heat slows freshwater fishing. Saltwater fishing continues in full swing. Plan that family picnic and outing onboard the family boat.

August:

Too hot to move, but if Dad can't stand still, he will still be wetting a line.

Sautéed Bass with Artichoke and Mushroom Sauce

5 tablespoons butter or margarine
8 bass fillets
1 cup coarsely chopped artichokes
1¼ cups sliced mushrooms
½ teaspoon salt
⅛ teaspoon pepper
½ teaspoon Creole seasoning
1 cup Brown Sauce
2 tablespoons lemon juice
½ cup (1 stick) butter, melted

Heat 5 tablespoons butter in a large heavy skillet until melted. Add the bass, artichokes and mushrooms. Sprinkle with the salt, pepper and Creole seasoning. Cook for 10 minutes or until the bass flakes easily. Remove the bass and vegetables to a heated platter and keep warm.

Add the Brown Sauce, lemon juice and melted butter to the skillet and mix well. Cook over low heat until heated through, whisking constantly. Spoon the sauce over the bass fillets.

Yield: 8 servings.

Brown Sauce

1½ tablespoons butter
1½ tablespoons flour
2 cups beef broth

Heat the butter in a saucepan until melted. Whisk in the flour. Whisk in the broth. Bring to a boil. Boil for 3 to 5 minutes, stirring occasionally. Reduce the heat. Simmer for 30 minutes or until reduced to 1 cup, stirring occasionally.

Catfish Fingers

1½ pounds catfish fillets
3 tablespoons Creole mustard
2 tablespoons white wine
½ teaspoon salt
¼ teaspoon pepper
1 cup yellow cornmeal
½ cup corn flour or unseasoned fish fry mix
⅓ cup cornstarch
1 tablespoon Creole seasoning
Peanut oil for deep-frying
Hush Puppies (page 139)
Thompson's Tartar Sauce (page 139)

Cut the catfish into ½x2-inch pieces. Place in a shallow dish. Combine the mustard, wine, salt and pepper in a bowl and mix well. Pour over the catfish. Marinate, covered, in the refrigerator for 1 hour; drain.

Combine the cornmeal, corn flour, cornstarch and Creole seasoning in a shallow dish and mix well. Dredge the catfish in the cornmeal mixture.

Pour peanut oil into a heavy pan to a depth of 2 inches and heat. Drop the coated catfish into the hot oil a few at a time. Cook for 4 minutes. Remove and drain on paper towels. Serve with Hush Puppies and Thompson's Tartar Sauce.

Yield: 6 servings.

Hush Puppies

1 cup cornmeal
2 tablespoons baking powder
$1/2$ teaspoon salt
$1/4$ teaspoon black pepper
$1/8$ teaspoon white pepper
$1/3$ cup minced onion
1 egg, beaten
$1/4$ cup milk
Vegetable oil

Combine the cornmeal, baking powder, salt, black pepper, white pepper and onion in a bowl and mix well. Combine the egg and milk in a bowl and mix well. Whisk into the cornmeal mixture. Drop by spoonfuls into hot oil. Cook until golden brown.

Yield: 6 servings.

Thompson's Tartar Sauce

$1/2$ to 1 small onion, grated or finely chopped
1 tablespoon lemon juice
2 tablespoons vinegar
1 cup mayonnaise
2 tablespoons dill relish
1 tablespoon sweet pickle relish

Combine the onion, lemon juice, vinegar, mayonnaise, dill relish and sweet pickle relish in a bowl and mix well. Chill, covered, for 1 hour before serving.

Yield: 1 cup.

The History of Hush Puppies

What would a Louisiana Fish Fry be without freshly caught catfish and our legendary Hush Puppies? The tradition of the hush puppy begins as its name suggests. During those good ole-fashion fish fries, the dogs would howl at the smell of the cooking fish. The cook would roll up some cornmeal in the fish batter and toss it into the deep fryer. Once it was golden brown, he took it out and threw it over to the howling dogs, followed with the expression "Hush Puppies!"

Infusing Milk

A classic béchamel sauce is simply a white sauce made with milk that has been infused with flavorings. To be absolutely correct, the flavorings should be onion, cloves, bay leaves, freshly grated nutmeg, salt and pepper. There are, however, many variations on the basic sauce.

Step 1: Heat the milk and flavorings, stirring occasionally. Remove from heat. Cover with a plate and let stand for 10 minutes.

Step 2: Strain the infused milk through a sieve. Discard the flavorings. Add hot infused milk to roux.

Bayou Trout with Crab Meat and Crawfish

4 (8-ounce) trout fillets
Salt and white pepper to taste
6 tablespoons olive oil
8 ounces fresh peeled crawfish tails
5 ounces white wine
8 ounces jumbo lump crab meat
Juice of 1 lemon
1/4 cup finely chopped green onions
1/4 cup finely chopped parsley

Season the trout with the salt and white pepper. Sauté the trout in 2 tablespoons of the olive oil in a hot skillet for 4 minutes per side or until golden brown on both sides. Remove to a serving platter and set aside, keeping warm.

Heat the remaining 4 tablespoons olive oil in the skillet. Add the crawfish. Sauté for 2 minutes. Add the wine and cook for 2 minutes. Add the crab meat, lemon juice, green onions and chopped parsley. Adjust the seasonings as needed. Cook for 4 minutes. Spoon over the cooked trout. Garnish with a wedge of lemon and whole parsley.

Yield: 4 servings.

Trout Mein

6 trout fillets
Salt to taste
Pepper to taste
Louisiana hot sauce to taste
Flour
1/2 cup (1 stick) butter
Juice of 2 small lemons
1/4 cup water
Chopped parsley (optional)

Pat the trout dry. Season with salt, pepper and Louisiana hot sauce. Dust the trout with flour.

Heat the butter in a skillet over high heat until melted. Add the trout. Cook until the trout flakes easily, turning once. Remove to a warm plate and cover.

Add the lemon juice and water to the skillet and deglaze, scraping the bottom well. Pour over the fish. Top with chopped parsley.

Yield: 6 servings.

Crab Meat Caroline

2 tablespoons butter
2 tablespoons flour
1/4 cup minced green onions
1/4 cup minced green bell pepper
1 clove garlic, minced
1/8 teaspoon rosemary
1 tomato, peeled, chopped
1/4 cup dry white wine
1 cup heavy cream
1 teaspoon salt
1/4 teaspoon Tabasco sauce
1/3 cup grated Gruyère cheese
1/8 teaspoon dry mustard
1 pound lump crab meat
3 tablespoons shredded mozzarella cheese
3 tablespoons grated Parmesan cheese

Heat the butter in a large skillet until melted. Whisk in the flour gradually. Cook over low heat for 2 minutes, stirring constantly. Add the green onions, bell pepper, garlic, rosemary and tomato. Sauté for 2 to 3 minutes. Add the wine. Cook until the vegetables are tender-crisp.

Reduce the heat. Add the cream, salt and Tabasco sauce gradually, mixing well after each addition. Remove from heat. Stir in the Gruyère cheese and mustard. Fold in the crab meat. Spoon into 4 buttered ramekins.

Combine the mozzarella cheese and Parmesan cheese in a small bowl and mix well. Sprinkle over the crab meat mixture. Bake at 350 degrees for 10 to 15 minutes or until browned and bubbly.

Yield: 4 servings.

How Can I Make Crème Fraîche?

Crème fraîche is fermented cream thickened by acid-producing bacteria. Its nutty, slightly sour flavor and smooth consistency make it especially good for enriching sauces and for using as a garnish for desserts, canapés, soups, and caviar.

It is simple to make crème fraîche at home. In a small saucepan, warm two cups of heavy cream (avoid ultrapasteurized cream if you can because of the processing; it doesn't ferment as well) to 100 degrees. If you don't have a thermometer, you can test the temperature with your finger—the cream should feel slightly warmer than body temperature. Stir in 1/4 cup store-bought buttermilk (use the freshest buttermilk possible to ensure souring and thickening) and then transfer the mixture to a clean glass or plastic container with a cover. Set the cream in a warm spot that's about 70 degrees to 80 degrees (such as the top of a gas stove, providing the pilot is lit, or near a heater) and let it stand for at least 24 hours. Chill the crème fraîche in the refrigerator for at least four hours to let it thicken further. Crème fraîche will keep well under refrigeration for about ten days.

Crawfish Enchiladas

1/4 cup (1/2 stick) butter
1 tablespoon chopped garlic
3/4 cup chopped onion
1/4 cup chopped parsley
1/4 cup green or red bell pepper
2 ribs celery, chopped
1 tablespoon lemon juice
2 tablespoons flour
1 pound crawfish tails
8 ounces jalapeño cheese
5 ounces tomatoes with mild green chiles
1 1/2 cups half-and-half
12 flour tortillas
1 cup shredded Cheddar cheese

Heat the butter in a skillet until melted. Add the garlic, onion, parsley, bell pepper and celery. Sauté until the vegetables are tender-crisp. Add the lemon juice, flour and crawfish tails and mix well. Add the jalapeño cheese, tomatoes and half-and-half. Cook until the cheese is melted, stirring constantly. Reduce the heat. Simmer for 10 minutes.

Spread 2 to 3 tablespoons of the crawfish mixture down the center of each tortilla. Roll up the tortillas to enclose the filling. Arrange in a 10x14-inch baking pan. Spoon any remaining crawfish mixture over the enchiladas. Sprinkle the Cheddar cheese over the top. Cover loosely with foil sprayed with nonstick cooking spray. Bake at 350 degrees for 20 minutes.

Variation: For Crawfish Dip, reduce the half-and-half to 1/2 cup and omit the tortillas and Cheddar cheese.

Yield: 6 servings.

Crawfish Fettuccini

1 1/2 cups (3 sticks) butter
3 onions, chopped
2 bell peppers, chopped
3 ribs celery, chopped
3 cloves garlic, chopped
2 tablespoons chopped parsley
2 pounds crawfish
1/2 cup flour
2 cups half-and-half
16 ounces jalapeño cheese, shredded
18 ounces fettuccini, cooked, hot
3/4 cup grated Parmesan cheese

⚷ Heat the butter in a large saucepan until melted. Add the onions, bell peppers, celery, garlic and parsley. Sauté until the vegetables are tender. Stir in the crawfish and flour. Add the half-and-half and jalapeño cheese. Cook until the cheese is melted and the sauce is thickened, stirring constantly.

Combine the crawfish mixture and the fettuccini in a large bowl and toss to combine. Spoon into an 11x16-inch baking dish. Sprinkle with the Parmesan cheese. Bake at 350 degrees for 30 minutes.

Yield: 8 to 10 servings.

Crawfish and Crab Étouffée

1/2 cup (1 stick) margarine
2 cups chopped onions
1 cup chopped green bell pepper
1/2 cup chopped celery
2 cloves garlic, finely chopped
1 cup chicken broth
1/3 cup cream sherry
1 pound crawfish tails
1 pound crab meat
1 to 2 tablespoons Creole seasoning
1 teaspoon garlic powder
1 teaspoon pepper
1 tablespoon cornstarch
3 cups hot cooked rice
1/2 cup chopped green onions

⚷ Heat the margarine in a heavy cast-iron skillet over medium heat until melted. Add the onions, green pepper, celery and garlic. Sauté until tender-crisp. Stir in the broth and sherry. Bring to a low boil.

Season the crawfish tails and crab meat with the Creole seasoning, garlic powder and pepper. Add to the sauce. Simmer for 5 minutes.

Combine the cornstarch with a small amount of cold water and mix until smooth. Add to the crawfish mixture. Simmer for 5 minutes or until the crawfish are cooked through; do not overcook. Place the rice on a serving plate. Spoon the crawfish mixture over the rice. Sprinkle with the green onions.

Yield: 6 servings.

Crawfish Étouffée

2 large onions, chopped
1 rib celery, chopped
2 medium green bell peppers, chopped
2 cloves garlic, minced
1/2 cup (1 stick) butter
1 tablespoon flour
1 pound fresh mushrooms, sliced
1 (2-ounce) jar diced pimentos
1 (10-ounce) can golden mushroom soup
2 pounds crawfish tails
Creole seasoning to taste
Cayenne pepper to taste
1/2 to 1 cup hot water
2 tablespoons chopped parsley
2 tablespoons chopped green onion tops

Sauté the onions, celery, green peppers and garlic in the butter in a skillet until tender. Stir in the flour. Stir in the mushrooms and pimentos. Add the soup and crawfish tails and mix well. Season with the Creole seasoning and cayenne pepper.

Add enough hot water to make of the desired thickness. Simmer, covered, until the crawfish tails are tender. Sprinkle with the parsley and onion tops. Serve over hot cooked rice.

Yield: 4 to 6 servings.

Crawfish Pie

1 pound crawfish tails
1/4 cup (1/2 stick) butter
1 bunch green onions, chopped
1/2 cup chopped parsley
1/2 cup (1 stick) butter
3 tablespoons flour
2 cups half-and-half
1/4 cup sherry
Salt to taste
Black pepper to taste
Red pepper to taste
1 baked (9-inch) pie shell

Sauté the crawfish tails in 1/4 cup butter in a skillet for 10 minutes.

Sauté the green onions and parsley in 1/2 cup butter in a separate skillet until tender. Add the flour and mix until well blended. Add the half-and-half gradually, stirring constantly. Cook until the sauce is thickened, stirring constantly. Stir in the sherry.

Add the crawfish mixture to the cream sauce. Season with salt, black pepper and red pepper. Spoon into the pie shell. Bake at 350 degrees for 20 minutes.

Yield: 4 to 6 servings.

Oysters Rockefeller Casserole

5 dozen oysters
4 (10-ounce) packages frozen chopped spinach
2 cups (4 sticks) butter
1 1/4 teaspoons thyme
1 3/4 cups chopped green onions
1 1/3 cups chopped celery
2 cloves garlic, minced
4 teaspoons Worcestershire sauce
1 1/4 teaspoons anchovy paste
2 cups seasoned bread crumbs
1 cup chopped parsley
3/4 cup grated Parmesan cheese
2 tablespoons Pernod or anise liquor
3/4 teaspoon salt
1/2 teaspoon black pepper
1/4 teaspoon white pepper
1/4 teaspoon red pepper

Drain the oysters, reserving the liquid. Cook the spinach using the package directions; drain.

Heat the butter in a large skillet over medium heat until melted. Add the thyme, green onions, celery and garlic. Sauté for 5 minutes. Add the Worcestershire sauce, anchovy paste and bread crumbs and mix well. Cook for 5 minutes or until the bread crumbs are toasted, stirring frequently.

Add the oysters, 1/2 cup of the reserved oyster liquid, parsley, Parmesan cheese and Pernod and stir gently. Cook for 3 minutes or until the edges of the oysters begin to curl. Stir in the cooked spinach. Season with salt, black pepper, white pepper and red pepper.

Spoon the oyster mixture into a 3-quart baking dish. Bake at 375 degrees for 20 to 25 minutes.

Yield: 10 servings.

Corn and Oysters

3 eggs
2/3 cup milk
10 (or more) soda crackers, crushed
1 pint oysters
1 (17-ounce) can cream-style corn
1/4 teaspoon sugar
Salt to taste
Pepper to taste

Beat the eggs lightly in a mixer bowl. Add the milk and crushed crackers and mix well. Cut the oysters into halves if they are large. Stir the oysters and corn into the egg mixture. Add the sugar, salt and pepper and mix well. Add enough additional crushed crackers to make a thick mixture.

Spoon into a buttered baking dish. Bake at 375 degrees for 45 minutes.

Yield: 4 servings.

Grilled Scallops with Garlic Butter Sauce

3 tablespoons vinegar
3 tablespoons white wine
1 tablespoon minced garlic
1 teaspoon salt
1/2 cup heavy cream
1/2 cup (1 stick) butter
1 pound fresh sea scallops
Olive oil

Combine the vinegar, wine, garlic and salt in a saucepan. Cook over medium heat until reduced by half. Add the cream. Continue to cook until reduced by half. Let stand until cooled slightly.

Cut the butter into pieces. Whisk into the cream sauce until smooth and thickened. Set aside and keep warm.

Brush the scallops with olive oil. Grill over medium-high heat for 4 to 5 minutes per side or until cooked through.

Divide among 4 warm plates. Pour the cream sauce over the scallops. Garnish with herbs or edible flowers.

Yield: 4 servings.

Barbecued Shrimp
Cajun Style

2 pounds medium shrimp
2 tablespoons Creole seasoning
1/4 teaspoon pepper
3 tablespoons olive oil
1/4 cup chopped onion
2 tablespoons minced garlic
3 bay leaves
2 tablespoons fresh lemon juice
2 cups water
1/2 cup Worcestershire sauce
1/4 cup white wine
1/4 teaspoon salt
2 cups heavy cream
2 tablespoons unsalted butter, cut into pieces

⚷ Peel the shrimp, leaving the tail and first joint of the shell intact. Sprinkle with 1 tablespoon of the Creole seasoning and half the pepper. Place on a baking sheet. Refrigerate, uncovered, until completely chilled.

Heat 1 tablespoon of the olive oil in a skillet over medium-high heat until hot. Add the onion and garlic. Sauté for 1 minute. Add the remaining 1 tablespoon Creole seasoning, bay leaves, lemon juice, water, Worcestershire sauce, wine, salt and remaining 1/8 teaspoon pepper and mix well. Bring to a boil. Reduce the heat. Simmer for 30 minutes. Remove from heat and let stand for 15 minutes. Strain through a fine sieve into a small saucepan. Bring to a boil. Boil for 12 to 15 minutes. Remove from heat.

Heat 1 tablespoon of the remaining olive oil in a skillet over medium-high heat until hot. Sear half the shrimp for 1 minute on each side, stirring occasionally. Remove to a bowl. Repeat the process with the remaining olive oil and shrimp.

Add the cream and strained sauce to the skillet. Bring to a simmer. Simmer for 8 to 10 minutes, stirring occasionally. Stir in the shrimp. Simmer for 1 minute or until the shrimp are heated through. Add the butter. Cook until melted, stirring constantly.

Spoon the sauce onto 4 plates. Arrange the shrimp over the sauce. Garnish with chives.

Yield: 4 servings.

Frank Lloyd Wright once said, "Dining is and always was a great artistic opportunity." It certainly can be, especially if you go one step farther and decorate your food with flowers, leaves, and herbs, thus making the entire experience so much more beautiful and enticing. In addition, each small edible blossom is filled with flavor, a pleasure that in the past has often been underrated!

Seared Gulf Shrimp with Roasted Corn Salsa

Kernels of 2 ears of corn
4 tablespoons olive oil
1 small red onion, chopped
Juice of 1 lime
1 tablespoon chopped cilantro
1 minced jalapeño chile
Salt and pepper to taste
20 medium shrimp, peeled, deveined
2 tablespoons Creole seasoning

⚬—ᴍ Sauté the corn in 1 tablespoon of the hot olive oil in a skillet for $1^1/2$ minutes. Remove from heat. Add the onion, lime juice, cilantro and chile. Season with salt and pepper. Add 1 tablespoon of the remaining olive oil and mix well.

Sprinkle both sides of the shrimp with the Creole seasoning. Heat the remaining 2 tablespoons olive oil in a skillet until hot. Add the shrimp and sear on both sides until pink. Divide the shrimp among 4 serving plates. Arrange the corn mixture next to the shrimp.

Yield: 4 servings.

Coconut Beer-Battered Shrimp

$1/2$ cup Creole mustard
$1/2$ cup honey
$1^1/2$ cups flour
1 teaspoon salt
$1/2$ teaspoon pepper
4 large eggs, lightly beaten
$3/4$ cup beer
3 pounds large fresh shrimp, peeled, deveined
1 (14-ounce) package flaked coconut
Vegetable oil for frying

⚬—ᴍ Combine the mustard and honey in a small bowl and mix well. Set aside.

Combine the flour, salt and pepper in a shallow dish and mix well. Combine the eggs and beer in a shallow dish and mix well. Dredge the shrimp in the flour mixture. Dip in the egg mixture. Dredge in the coconut, pressing firmly to coat well.

Pour oil to a depth of $1/2$ inch in a skillet. Heat to 350 degrees. Fry the shrimp a few at a time in the hot oil for 1 to 2 minutes on each side or until golden brown. Drain on paper towels. Serve with the honey mixture. Garnish with fresh Italian parsley sprigs.

Yield: 6 to 8 servings.

To keep shrimp straight during cooking, insert a long wooden pick through the center of each shrimp before cooking. Remove the picks before serving.

Shrimp Creole

1/3 cup canola oil
1/4 cup flour
1/2 cup finely chopped white onion
1/2 cup finely chopped celery
1/2 cup finely chopped bell pepper
1 clove garlic, minced
1 (6-ounce) can tomato paste
1 1/2 cups (about) hot water
2 bay leaves
Salt and pepper to taste
4 to 6 drops of Tabasco sauce, or to taste
2 to 3 teaspoons Worcestershire sauce
2 to 3 pounds shrimp, peeled, deveined
Hot cooked rice

☉⎯ Combine the canola oil and flour in a skillet. Cook until golden brown, stirring constantly. Stir in the onion, celery, bell pepper and garlic. Cook over low heat for 5 minutes. Add the tomato paste and stir until well blended. Add enough hot water gradually to make of the desired consistency, mixing well after each addition.

Add the bay leaves, salt, pepper, Tabasco sauce and Worcestershire sauce. Cook until well blended, stirring constantly. Add the shrimp. Bring to a boil. Reduce the heat. Simmer, covered, for 10 minutes, stirring occasionally. Adjust seasonings as desired. Remove the bay leaves. Spoon over hot cooked rice. May be prepared 1 day ahead and reheated.

Yield: 6 servings.

Shrimp Supreme

1 pound shrimp, peeled, deveined
3/4 cup (1 1/2 sticks) butter
1 small bunch green onions, finely chopped
1/2 cup finely chopped parsley
3 tablespoons flour
2 cups half-and-half
3 tablespoons cooking sherry
Dash of Worcestershire sauce
1 (4-ounce) can mushrooms, drained, sliced
Salt to taste
Black pepper to taste
Red pepper to taste

☉⎯ Cook the shrimp in 1/4 cup of the butter in a skillet until pink; drain.

Sauté the green onions and parsley in the remaining 1/2 cup butter in a separate skillet until tender. Add the flour, stirring until well blended. Add the half-and-half gradually, stirring constantly. Cook until thickened, stirring constantly. Stir in the sherry, Worcestershire sauce and mushrooms. Stir in the cooked shrimp. Season with salt, black pepper and red pepper.

Serve over rice, pasta or in seafood shells. May be used as a cocktail dip on melba toast.

Variation: For Crawfish Supreme, substitute 1 pound crawfish for the shrimp.

Yield: 4 to 6 servings.

Shrimp and Vegetable Pasta

1¹/₂ cups (3 sticks) butter
1¹/₂ cups chopped green onions
3 to 4 garlic cloves, minced
³/₄ teaspoon each salt, red pepper, black pepper, basil, oregano and thyme
3 pounds medium shrimp
1¹/₂ pounds mushrooms, sliced
1 cup white wine
2 (12-ounce) packages vermicelli
1 (8-ounce) bottle Italian salad dressing
1 medium green bell pepper, chopped
1 medium red bell pepper, chopped
2 medium yellow bell peppers, chopped
3 medium yellow squash, cut into thin strips
3 cups sliced fresh mushrooms
1 medium onion, sliced
1¹/₂ cups chopped green onions
³/₄ cup sliced ripe olives
¹/₂ teaspoon salt
Parmesan cheese

Heat the butter in a large skillet until melted. Add 1¹/₂ cups green onions, garlic, ³/₄ teaspoon salt, red pepper, black pepper, basil, oregano and thyme. Sauté until the green onions are tender. Stir in the shrimp, mushrooms and wine. Cook for 3 to 4 minutes or until the shrimp turn pink, stirring occasionally.

Cook the vermicelli using the package directions. Drain and keep warm.

Combine the salad dressing, bell peppers, squash, mushrooms, onion, 1¹/₂ cups green onions, olives and ¹/₂ teaspoon salt in a large skillet. Cook over medium heat until tender-crisp.

Combine the squash mixture, cooked vermicelli and shrimp mixture in a bowl. Sprinkle with Parmesan cheese and toss to combine.

Yield: 10 to 12 servings.

Seafood Croquettes with Louisiana Hot Sauce Beurre Blanc

8 ounces salmon, cooked, flaked
8 ounces shrimp, cooked, chopped
8 ounces crawfish, cooked, chopped
3 tablespoons chopped green onions
1 teaspoon Old Bay seasoning or liquid crab boil
1 tablespoon lemon juice
1 tablespoon Worcestershire sauce
2 eggs, beaten
Salt to taste
Red pepper to taste
Black pepper to taste
White pepper to taste
²/₃ cup (about) bread crumbs
2 tablespoons vegetable oil
3 tablespoons chopped shallots
¹/₂ cup Louisiana hot sauce
1 cup (2 sticks) butter

Combine the salmon, shrimp, crawfish, green onions, Old Bay seasoning, lemon juice, Worcestershire sauce, eggs, salt, red pepper, black pepper and white pepper in a bowl and mix well. Add bread crumbs just until the mixture forms a ball.

Shape the seafood mixture by 2 heaping tablespoonfuls at a time into oval patties. Cook in hot oil in an ovenproof skillet until brown on both sides. Keep warm by placing in a warm oven.

Combine the shallots and hot sauce in a saucepan. Cook over medium heat until reduced by half. Reduce the heat to low. Whisk in the butter 1 tablespoon at a time. Arrange the croquettes on a serving platter. Spoon the sauce over the croquettes. Serve immediately.

Yield: 4 to 6 servings.

Seafood Gumbo

6 tablespoons (or more) vegetable oil
2 pounds okra, thinly sliced
1 tablespoon flour
2 cups finely chopped onions
2 ribs celery, chopped
1/2 cup finely chopped green bell pepper
1 cup finely chopped green onions
2 cloves garlic, pressed
1 (6-ounce) can tomato paste
3 large bay leaves
1/4 teaspoon thyme
1 tablespoon salt
1/2 teaspoon Tabasco sauce
1/4 teaspoon cayenne pepper
1/2 teaspoon black pepper
1 tablespoon Worcestershire sauce
1 (16-ounce) can whole tomatoes, chopped
7 cups (or more) water
2 1/2 pounds shrimp, peeled, deveined
1 pound crab meat
2 tablespoons chopped parsley
4 to 5 cups hot steamed rice

Heat 4 tablespoons of the oil in a large heavy skillet that is not cast iron. Add the okra. Cook for 40 to 50 minutes or until stringing stops, stirring frequently and adding additional oil if needed to prevent burning.

Heat the remaining 2 tablespoons oil in a 5-quart soup pot. Add the flour gradually, stirring constantly and cooking until the roux is dark brown. Add the onions and celery. Cook until tender. Add the bell pepper, green onions and garlic. Cook for 3 minutes. Stir in the tomato paste, bay leaves, thyme, salt, Tabasco sauce, cayenne pepper, black pepper and Worcestershire sauce.

Stir in the undrained tomatoes. Stir in the cooked okra. Add the water gradually, stirring constantly.

Bring to a boil. Simmer, covered, for 30 minutes. Add the shrimp and crab meat. Simmer, covered, for 10 minutes. Stir in the parsley. Cook for 10 minutes, adding additional water if needed to make of the desired consistency. Remove bay leaves.

Place the hot rice on a large platter. Spoon the gumbo over the rice.

Yield: 8 to 10 servings.

Fixing Hollandaise and Béarnaise Sauces

These butter sauces separate or curdle if the pan is too hot, the butter is added too quickly, or the finished sauce is left to stand too long. Here are two remedies:

· With the pan off the heat, add an ice cube and whisk quickly, drawing in the sauce as it melts.

· Whisk 1 egg yolk and 1 tablespoon hot water in a bowl over a bain marie; slowly whisk in the curdled hollandaise sauce.

Orecchiette con Broccoli

1 (8-ounce) package orecchiette pasta, or
    9 ounces fettuccini
2 to 3 garlic cloves, minced
1/2 teaspoon crushed red pepper (optional)
1/2 cup olive oil
1 (10-ounce) package frozen chopped
    broccoli, thawed
1 cup water
1 cup grated Parmesan cheese

Cook the orecchiette using the package directions; drain.

Sauté the garlic and red pepper in hot olive oil in a cast-iron skillet.

Drain the excess water from the thawed broccoli. Add the broccoli and 1 cup water to the garlic mixture. Cook until the broccoli is tender-crisp and the water is evaporated.

Combine the cooked pasta and broccoli mixture in a large bowl and toss to combine.

Yield: 4 servings.

Pasta Milanese

4 cups small seashell pasta
1 medium onion, chopped
3 cloves garlic
2 (2-ounce) cans oil-pack flat fillets of anchovies
1 tablespoon olive oil
2 (15-ounce) cans peeled whole tomatoes
1 (6-ounce) can tomato paste
1 tomato paste can water
1/2 teaspoon rosemary
1/2 teaspoon thyme
3 sprigs of fresh fennel, or 1/2 teaspoon dried
    crushed fennel
1/2 teaspoon basil
1 tablespoon chopped parsley
Salt and pepper to taste
1 1/2 cups bread crumbs
1/2 cup grated Parmesan cheese, or to taste
1/3 cup pine nuts

Cook the pasta using the package directions until al dente; drain.

Sauté the onion, garlic and anchovies with oil in the olive oil in a saucepan until the anchovies are dissolved. Purée the tomatoes with liquid in a food processor or food mill. Add to the anchovy mixture. Stir in the tomato paste and water. Bring to a simmer. Stir in the rosemary, thyme, fennel, basil and parsley. Cook for 15 minutes, adding additional water if the sauce is too thick. Season with salt and pepper.

Set aside a small amount of the bread crumbs and Parmesan cheese. Layer the tomato sauce, cooked pasta, remaining bread crumbs, pine nuts and remaining Parmesan cheese one-third at a time in a 2-quart baking dish. Sprinkle the reserved bread crumbs and Parmesan cheese over the layers. Bake at 350 degrees for 30 minutes or until the top is light brown and bubbly.

Yield: 4 to 6 servings.

Portobello Burgers

2 portobello mushrooms, about 4 inches
    in diameter
2 teaspoons olive oil
1 teaspoon basil
3/4 teaspoon garlic salt
1/8 teaspoon salt
Freshly ground pepper
2 slices mozzarella cheese, or 2 ounces goat
    cheese, sliced
2 tablespoons butter
2 sesame seed buns, split

    Remove the stems from the
mushrooms. Brush with the olive oil. Sprinkle
the basil, garlic salt, salt and pepper over the
mushrooms. Grill over hot coals or sear in a heavy
cast-iron skillet until the mushrooms are tender.
Place a cheese slice over each mushroom. Cook
until the cheese begins to melt.

    Spread the butter over the inside of each bun
half. Place the buns butter side up on a baking
sheet. Heat in the oven until the butter melts. Place
each cheese-topped mushroom between two bun
halves. Serve immediately.

    Yield: 2 servings.

    For a juicier hamburger, add cold water
to the ground beef before grilling (1/2 cup
water to 1 pound of ground beef).

Portobello Mushroom Fajitas

3 tablespoons water
3 tablespoons lime juice
1 tablespoon olive oil or vegetable oil
2 large cloves garlic, minced
1/2 teaspoon ground cumin
1/4 teaspoon oregano
10 ounces portobello mushrooms, thinly sliced
1 medium red, green or yellow bell pepper,
    cut into thin strips
4 green onions, cut into 1 1/2-inch pieces
6 (7-inch) flour tortillas
Lime wedges (optional)

    Combine the water, lime juice, olive
oil, garlic, cumin and oregano in a large sealable
plastic bag. Add the mushrooms, bell pepper
and green onions. Seal the bag and turn to coat
the vegetables. Marinate at room temperature for
15 to 30 minutes.

    Wrap the tortillas in foil. Bake at 350 degrees
for 10 minutes or until softened.

    Cook the vegetables and marinade in a
large nonstick skillet over medium-high heat for
5 minutes or until the bell pepper is tender and
most of the liquid is evaporated, stirring
occasionally.

    Spoon 1/6 of the mushroom mixture down
the center of each tortilla. Roll up to enclose the
filling. Place on a serving platter. Serve with the
lime wedges.

    Yield: 3 servings.

Desserts

Central Louisiana's food and traditions are influenced by a rich heritage
that is uniquely southern. The area is home to numerous historical sites and plantations,
some dating back hundreds of years.

Kent House is the oldest remaining structure in central Louisiana.
Visitors to this plantation can peek into the secrets of years gone by as they meander through
the four-acre complex that includes a kitchen, slave cabins, barn, carriage house, milk house,
blacksmith shop, and sugar mill. Even today, visitors can often observe the heritage of
open-hearth cooking and sugar making at Kent House.

History abounds throughout central Louisiana, sharing her stories through
our area plantations with Walnut Grove, Tyrone, Inglewood, Hard Times, and Ashton.
The southern traditions of our community began on working plantations as people traveled
along rivers and bayous settling the territory. Just south of Alexandria, Loyd Hall Plantation
has been in continuous operation since the early 1800s. It is believed to have been used
by both Union and Confederate troops during the Civil War. Guests who stay
in the bed-and-breakfast at this plantation get a hands-on look at Louisiana
agriculture and possibly a glimpse of one of the four ghosts believed
to secretly haunt the main house.

Along the Red River in downtown Alexandria, the Hotel Bentley,
built in 1908, has hosted many famous characters throughout history, including
General Patton and John Wayne.

The beautiful architecture of the Bentley and the stained glass windows in
the St. Francis Xavier Cathedral, built in 1898, proudly reflect the beauty and
tradition of the past that continues to exist throughout our community.

Folks in central Louisiana take great pride in the history of our community.
Many families have traditions and recipes they have passed down
for generations. We hope these selections from the kitchens of our friends
and families satisfy your sweet tooth for years to come.

Folks in central Louisiana take great pride in the history of our community. Many families have traditions and recipes they have passed down for generations.

Apple Cake with Praline Icing

2¹/2 cups flour
2 teaspoons baking powder
¹/2 teaspoon salt
1 teaspoon baking soda
1¹/2 teaspoons cinnamon
1 teaspoon ground nutmeg
1 cup vegetable oil
2 cups sugar
3 eggs, beaten
1 teaspoon vanilla extract
3 cups chopped peeled apples
1 cup chopped pecans
Praline Icing

Sift the flour, baking powder, salt, baking soda, cinnamon and nutmeg together. Beat the oil and sugar at high speed in a mixer bowl for several minutes. Add the eggs 1 at a time, mixing well after each addition.

Beat in the sifted dry ingredients. Add the vanilla and mix well. Stir in the apples and pecans. Pour into a greased bundt pan.

Bake at 350 degrees for 50 to 60 minutes or until a wooden pick inserted in the center comes out clean. Cool in the pan for 10 minutes. Invert onto a serving plate. Let stand until completely cooled. Drizzle with Praline Icing.

Yield: 12 servings.

Praline Icing

1¹/2 cups packed light brown sugar
¹/4 cup (¹/2 stick) margarine
¹/4 cup evaporated milk
1 teaspoon vanilla extract

Combine the brown sugar, margarine and milk in a saucepan. Bring to a boil, stirring constantly. Remove from heat. Stir in the vanilla. Let stand until slightly cooled. Beat until mixture is of spreading consistency.

Fresh Apple Cake

3 cups flour
1 teaspoon each baking soda, baking powder
    and salt
1 teaspoon cinnamon
³/4 teaspoon each nutmeg and mace
2 cups sugar
1 cup vegetable oil
3 eggs, beaten
2 teaspoons vanilla extract
3 cups chopped apples or pears
1 cup chopped pecans

Combine the flour, baking soda, baking powder, salt, cinnamon, nutmeg and mace in a bowl and mix well. Beat the sugar and oil together in a bowl. Add the eggs 1 at a time, mixing well after each addition. Stir in the vanilla. Add the flour mixture and mix well. Stir in the apples and pecans; batter will be stiff. Pour into a greased and floured bundt pan.

Bake in a preheated 350-degree oven for 1 hour or until a wooden pick inserted in the center comes out clean. Cool in the pan for 5 minutes. Invert onto a serving plate.

Yield: 12 servings.

Bourbon Pecan Pound Cake

3 cups flour
2 teaspoons baking powder
$1/2$ teaspoon salt
$1/2$ teaspoon nutmeg
1 cup sour cream
$1/2$ cup bourbon
1 cup shortening
$2^1/2$ cups sugar
6 eggs
1 cup finely chopped pecans
Bourbon Glaze

Combine the flour, baking powder, salt and nutmeg in a bowl and mix well. Combine the sour cream and bourbon in a small bowl and mix well.

Beat the shortening in a mixer bowl until light. Add the sugar gradually, beating until fluffy. Add the eggs 1 at a time, mixing well after each addition. Add the flour mixture and sour cream mixture alternately, beginning and ending with the flour mixture, mixing well after each addition. Stir in the pecans.

Spoon into a greased and floured 10-inch tube pan. Bake at 325 degrees for 70 to 75 minutes or until a wooden pick inserted in the center comes out clean. Cool in the pan for 10 to 15 minutes. Invert onto a serving plate. Let stand until cooled completely. Brush with the Bourbon Glaze.

Yield: 12 servings.

Bourbon Glaze

$2^1/4$ cups sifted confectioners' sugar
2 tablespoons bourbon
2 tablespoons water

Beat the confectioners' sugar, bourbon and water in a mixer bowl until well blended.

The History of King Cakes

King Cakes were initiated to celebrate "Kings Day." They are oval in shape and decorated with the colors green, yellow, and purple. These colors represent the gifts presented by the Wise Men. A small baby is placed in each cake as a symbol of "Find the Baby Jesus."

As the King Cake is cut, each person looks to see if his or her piece contains the baby. If it contains the baby, they become the Honored Guest, and designated King or Queen for that day. That person will then bring a King Cake to the next celebration or the next day, giving someone else the chance to become King or Queen.

Decadent Fudge Cake

1 cup (2 sticks) butter or margarine, softened
1½ cups sugar
4 eggs
1 cup buttermilk
½ teaspoon baking soda
2½ cups flour
2 (4-ounce) bars sweet baking chocolate,
    melted, cooled
1 cup chocolate syrup
2 teaspoons vanilla extract
4 ounces white chocolate, chopped
2 tablespoons shortening
½ cup milk chocolate miniature morsels
2 teaspoons shortening

Cream the butter in a large mixer bowl. Beat in the sugar gradually at medium speed. Add the eggs 1 at a time, mixing well after each addition. Combine the buttermilk and baking soda in a small bowl and mix well. Add to the creamed mixture alternately with the flour, beginning and ending with the flour. Add the melted chocolate, chocolate syrup and vanilla and mix well.

Spoon into a greased and floured 10-inch bundt pan. Bake at 300 degrees for 1 hour and 20 minutes or until a wooden pick inserted in the center comes out clean. Invert immediately onto a serving platter. Let stand until completely cooled. Heat the white chocolate and 2 tablespoons shortening in a double boiler over simmering water until melted, stirring occasionally. Remove from heat. Drizzle over the cooled cake. Heat the morsels and 2 teaspoons shortening in a small saucepan over low heat, stirring until smooth. Remove from heat. Let stand until cooled. Drizzle over the white chocolate.

Yield: 12 servings.

Ganny's Cake

1 (2-layer) package golden butter cake mix
4 eggs
½ cup vegetable oil
1 (11-ounce) can mandarin oranges
12 ounces nondairy whipped topping
1 (20-ounce) can juice-pack crushed pineapple
1 (4-ounce) package French vanilla instant
    pudding

Beat the cake mix, eggs and oil in a mixer bowl for 4 minutes. Add the oranges. Beat at low speed for 2 minutes or until smooth. Pour into a 9x12-inch baking pan. Bake at 325 degrees for 35 minutes or until a wooden pick inserted in the center comes out clean. Let stand until completely cooled.

Combine the whipped topping, pineapple and pudding mix in a bowl and mix well. Refrigerate until partially set. Spread over the cooled cake.

Yield: 12 servings.

Eggs at room temperature separate more easily and beat to their greatest volume. Egg whites will not beat as well with any yolk moisture or grease in the bowl. Always beat in stainless steel, glass, porcelain enamel, or copper bowls. Aluminum bowls will darken the eggs.

Flourless Chocolate Cake with Kahlúa Sauce

14 ounces semisweet chocolate, broken into
   small pieces
1$^{3}/_{4}$ cups (3$^{1}/_{2}$ sticks) butter, softened
1$^{3}/_{4}$ cups sugar
10 egg yolks, beaten
1 tablespoon Kahlúa
1 tablespoon vanilla extract
10 egg whites
$^{1}/_{2}$ cup sugar
6 ounces semisweet chocolate, chopped
$^{1}/_{4}$ cup ($^{1}/_{2}$ stick) butter
1 cup heavy cream
Kahlúa Sauce

    Preheat the oven to 250 degrees. Dust a 12-inch springform pan with flour. Heat the 14 ounces chocolate and 1$^{3}/_{4}$ cups butter in a saucepan until melted, stirring constantly. Add 1$^{3}/_{4}$ cups sugar, stirring until dissolved. Stir a small amount of the chocolate mixture into the egg yolks. Stir the egg yolks into the chocolate mixture. Cook until slightly thickened, stirring constantly. Stir in the Kahlúa and vanilla. Remove from heat.

    Beat the egg whites in a mixer bowl until soft peaks form. Add $^{1}/_{2}$ cup sugar gradually, beating until stiff peaks form. Fold into the chocolate mixture. Spoon into the prepared pan. Place the pan into a larger baking pan. Pour enough hot water into the baking pan to come halfway up the side of the springform pan. Bake at 250 degrees for 3 hours. Let stand until cooled to room temperature. Refrigerate until chilled completely. Unmold onto a flat serving plate.

    Heat 6 ounces chocolate with $^{1}/_{4}$ cup butter in a saucepan until melted, stirring constantly. Whisk in the cream gradually. Pour over the chilled cake and drip over the edges. Refrigerate until chilled completely.

    Cut the cake into serving pieces. Spoon the Kahlúa Sauce over the cake. Garnish with a dollop of whipped cream.

    Yield: 12 servings.

Kahlúa Sauce

8 ounces semisweet chocolate, chopped
$^{1}/_{2}$ cup Kahlúa

    Heat the chocolate in a saucepan until melted. Whisk in the Kahlúa until smooth.

Edible Flowers

Frost flowers, small berries, and fruits with sugar to give a shimmering look to compotes, cakes, and desserts like ice cream and sorbet. It's an easy task requiring only egg whites and sugar.

Decorating the tops of cakes with blossoms can be attractive, particularly for special occasions like weddings, birthdays, and teas. Use brightly colored pansies, blue borage flowers with vivid orange zest, or else try flowers in monochromatic tones, such as pale blush to bright pink roses. Coordinate the flowers with the color scheme of the table, room, or theme of the event, and these cakes will end up being much more than just dessert.

Creating attractive gifts for the kitchen can also be fun and economical. Edible blossoms and herbs can be made into delicious jams, jellies, vinegars, infused oils, and teas.

Chocolate Sheet Cake

2 cups flour
2 cups sugar
1/2 teaspoon salt
1/2 cup (1 stick) butter
1/4 cup baking cocoa
1/2 cup shortening
1 cup water
1/2 cup buttermilk
1 teaspoon baking soda
2 eggs
1 teaspoon vanilla extract
Chocolate Icing

Sift the flour, sugar and salt into a large bowl. Combine the butter, baking cocoa, shortening and water in a saucepan. Bring to a boil. Pour over the sifted dry ingredients and mix well. Add the buttermilk, baking soda, eggs and vanilla and mix well. Pour into a 10x15-inch baking pan sprayed with nonstick cooking spray.

Bake at 350 degrees for 20 minutes or until cake springs back when touched lightly on top. Spread the Chocolate Icing over the top of the cooled cake.

Yield: 20 servings.

Chocolate Icing

1 (1-pound) package confectioners' sugar
1/2 cup (1 stick) butter
1/4 cup baking cocoa
6 tablespoons milk
1 teaspoon vanilla extract
1 cup pecan halves, finely chopped

Place the confectioners' sugar in a bowl. Combine the butter, baking cocoa and milk in a saucepan. Bring to a boil. Pour over the sugar and mix well. Stir in the vanilla and pecans.

Pineapple-Filled Layer Cake

3 cups sifted cake flour
2¼ teaspoons baking powder
¾ teaspoon salt
1 cup shortening
2 cups sugar
½ teaspoon almond extract
4 eggs
1 cup milk
Pineapple Filling
Fluffy Frosting
Grated fresh coconut (optional)

Line the bottoms of three 9-inch round cake pans with waxed paper. Grease the pans and waxed paper.

Sift the flour, baking powder and salt together. Cream the shortening in a bowl until light. Add the sugar gradually, beating until fluffy. Beat in the almond extract. Add the eggs 1 at a time, mixing well after each addition. Add the sifted dry ingredients alternately with the milk, mixing well after each addition. Pour the batter into the prepared pans. Bake at 375 degrees for 25 minutes or until a wooden pick inserted in the center comes out clean. Cool in the pan for 5 minutes. Remove to a wire rack to cool completely.

Place one cake layer on a cake plate. Spread half the Pineapple Filling over the layer. Place a cake layer over the filling. Spread with the remaining Pineapple Filling. Place the remaining cake layer over the filling. Spread the Fluffy Frosting over the top and side of the cake. Sprinkle with coconut.

Yield: 14 to 16 servings.

Pineapple Filling

½ cup sifted cake flour
1 cup sugar
¼ teaspoon salt
¼ cup water
1 (20-ounce) can crushed pineapple
¼ cup lemon juice
4 egg yolks, lightly beaten

Combine the flour, sugar and salt in a heavy saucepan and mix well. Add the water and whisk until smooth. Drain the pineapple, reserving the juice. Add enough water to the juice to measure 1¼ cups. Add the pineapple juice and lemon juice to the flour mixture. Cook over low heat until mixture thickens and is almost transparent. Stir a small amount of the hot mixture into the egg yolks. Stir the egg yolks into the hot mixture. Add the drained pineapple. Cook for 5 minutes or until mixture thickens, stirring constantly. Let stand until cooled.

Fluffy Frosting

1½ cups sugar
½ teaspoon cream of tartar
⅛ teaspoon salt
½ cup hot water
4 egg whites
¼ teaspoon vanilla extract

Combine the sugar, cream of tartar, salt and hot water in a saucepan. Cook over high heat to 234 to 240 degrees on a candy thermometer, soft-ball stage; do not stir.

Beat the egg whites in a mixer bowl until stiff peaks form. Add the hot sugar mixture in a thin stream, beating at high speed constantly. Beat in the vanilla.

Pumpkin Upside-Down Cake

1 (16-ounce) can pumpkin
1 (12-ounce) can evaporated milk
1 cup sugar
3 eggs
2 teaspoons cinnamon
1 (2-layer) package yellow cake mix
1 cup pecan halves, chopped
1 cup (2 sticks) butter, melted
8 ounces cream cheese, softened
1 cup sugar
12 ounces nondairy whipped topping

Line a 9x13-inch baking pan with waxed paper. Combine the pumpkin, evaporated milk, 1 cup sugar, eggs and cinnamon in a bowl and mix well. Pour into the prepared pan. Sprinkle the cake mix over the pumpkin mixture. Sprinkle the pecans over the cake mix. Drizzle the butter over the layers. Bake at 350 degrees for 1 hour. Cool in the pan. Invert onto a flat plate.

Combine the cream cheese, 1 cup sugar and whipped topping in a bowl and mix well. Spread over the top of the cake. Chill for 1 to 2 hours or longer. Cut into 1-inch squares.

Yield: 24 servings.

Foolproof Pie Pastry

4 cups flour
1 tablespoon sugar
2 teaspoons salt
$1^3/4$ cups ($3^1/2$ sticks) margarine
1 tablespoon vinegar
1 egg
$^1/2$ cup water

Combine the flour, sugar and salt in a bowl. Cut in the margarine until crumbly. Combine the vinegar, egg and water in a separate bowl and mix well. Add to the flour mixture, mixing until moistened. Shape into a ball. Chill, wrapped in plastic wrap, for 15 minutes or for up to three days.

Divide into six equal portions. Roll each portion into the desired shape on a lightly floured surface.

Yield: 6 pastry shells.

Pierce airholes in the top of double-crusted pies to allow the steam to be released during baking. This keeps the fruit from overcooking and helps the liquid evaporate, preventing spillage from the fruit juices.

164

Coconut Pie

1¾ cups milk
¾ cup sugar
½ cup baking mix
4 eggs
¼ cup (½ stick) margarine, softened
1½ teaspoons vanilla extract
1 cup sweetened flaked coconut

⚷— Combine the milk, sugar, baking mix, eggs, margarine and vanilla in a blender container. Process on low speed for 3 minutes. Pour into a greased 9-inch pie plate. Sprinkle the coconut over the top. Let stand for 5 minutes. Bake at 350 degrees for 30 minutes.

Yield: 6 to 8 servings.

Hershey Bar Pie

8 ounces cream cheese
3 (1½-ounce) Hershey's candy bars
½ cup sugar
8 ounces nondairy whipped topping
1 (9-inch) chocolate graham cracker pie crust

⚷— Heat the cream cheese and candy bars in a saucepan until melted. Add the sugar and half of the whipped topping and mix well. Spoon into the pie crust. Spread the remaining whipped topping over the top. Chill until ready to serve.

Yield: 8 to 10 servings.

Mile-High Lime Pie

1 (12-ounce) can frozen limeade, thawed
1 (14-ounce) can sweetened condensed milk
12 ounces nondairy whipped topping
2 to 4 drops green food coloring
1 (9-inch) chocolate graham cracker pie crust
1 (10-ounce) package frozen strawberries, thawed

⚷— Combine the limeade and condensed milk in a bowl and mix well. Add the whipping topping and mix well. Add enough food coloring to make of the desired color and mix well. Pour into the pie crust. Freeze, covered, until firm. Cut into individual servings. Top with the strawberries.

Yield: 6 to 8 servings.

Fruit Pies

After baking, fruit pies must stand several hours to allow the juices to reabsorb into the fruit. Then they will cut like a charm. If a fruit pie is cut too soon, the filling will be soupy; the pie will be difficult to slice and will have a soggy bottom crust.

Leftover fruit pies always taste better when they are reheated. The crust will re-crisp and warm fruit is more flavorful.

Best Peanut Butter Pie

1/3 cup butter or margarine
1 cup chocolate chips
2 1/2 cups toasted rice cereal
8 ounces cream cheese, softened
1 (14-ounce) can sweetened condensed milk
3/4 cup peanut butter
3 tablespoons lemon juice
2 teaspoons vanilla extract
1 cup whipping cream, whipped
2 teaspoons chocolate syrup

Heat the butter and chocolate chips in a medium saucepan until melted, stirring occasionally. Remove from the heat. Stir in the rice cereal. Press over the bottom and up the side of a greased 9-inch pie plate. Chill for 30 minutes.

Beat the cream cheese in a mixer bowl until fluffy. Beat in the condensed milk, peanut butter, lemon juice and vanilla until smooth. Fold in the whipped cream. Pour into the prepared pie crust.

Drizzle with the chocolate syrup. Swirl the chocolate syrup with a spoon. Chill for 4 hours.

Yield: 6 to 8 servings.

Peach Praline Pie

1 teaspoon flour
1 unbaked (9-inch) deep-dish pie shell
1/3 cup flour
1/4 cup sugar
1/4 teaspoon salt
1/4 teaspoon nutmeg or cinnamon
1/2 cup light corn syrup
3 eggs
3 cups fresh peaches, peeled, cut into
    1-inch pieces
1/4 cup (1/2 stick) butter, melted
1/4 cup packed dark brown sugar
2 tablespoons butter, softened
1/2 cup coarsely chopped pecans

Sprinkle 1 teaspoon flour over the pie shell. Beat 3 tablespoons of the flour, sugar, salt, nutmeg, corn syrup and eggs in a mixer bowl for 1 minute. Stir in the peaches and the melted butter. Spoon into the prepared pie shell.

Combine the remaining flour and brown sugar in a bowl and mix well. Cut in 2 tablespoons butter until crumbly. Stir in the pecans. Sprinkle evenly over the peach mixture.

Bake at 375 degrees for 45 minutes or until set, covering the edge with foil as needed to prevent burning. Serve with ice cream.

Yield: 5 or 6 servings.

Meringue toppings should be dropped by spoonfuls around the edge of the pie or tart first, and then spooned into the center. The topping should be spread from the outside to the center.

Chocolate Pecan Pie

2 ounces unsweetened chocolate
2 1/2 tablespoons butter
3 eggs
2/3 cup sugar
2/3 cup dark corn syrup
1 1/2 cups chopped pecans
1 unbaked (9-inch) pie shell

Heat the chocolate and butter in a saucepan until melted, stirring occasionally. Let stand until cool.

Beat the eggs in a bowl. Add the eggs, sugar and corn syrup to the chocolate mixture and mix well. Stir in the pecans. Pour into the pie shell. Bake at 375 degrees for 40 to 45 minutes.

Yield: 6 servings.

When making a meringue, add the sugar gradually to the beaten egg white, about 1 tablespoon at a time. It should be added when the egg whites begin to stand in firm peaks.

Meringue will become firmer and have more body if it is beaten for 45 to 60 seconds after all of the sugar has been added. Conversely, beating meringue too long will result in a loss of volume.

Sugared Pecans

2 cups sugar
3/4 cup milk
1 tablespoon butter
Pinch of salt
4 cups pecan halves
1 teaspoon vanilla extract

Combine the sugar, milk, butter and salt in a large saucepan. Cook, uncovered, over medium heat to 235 degrees on a candy thermometer, soft-ball stage, stirring constantly. Stir in the pecans and vanilla. Spread the mixture on a large platter or waxed paper. Separate the pecans as they cool. Store in an airtight container.

Different Pecan Pie

1 unbaked (8-inch) pie shell
1 egg, beaten
1 cup sugar
1 tablespoon butter, melted
1/4 cup milk
1/2 teaspoon vanilla extract
1 cup pecan halves, finely chopped

Bake the pie shell at 325 degrees for 5 minutes. Combine the egg, sugar, butter, milk and vanilla in a bowl and mix well. Stir in the pecans. Spoon into the partially baked pie crust.

Bake for 45 minutes or until set, covering the edge with foil if needed. Let stand until cooled. Serve with whipped cream or whipped topping.

Yield: 4 to 6 servings.

Raspberry Cheese Pie

2 cups pecan halves, lightly toasted
1/3 cup packed brown sugar
1/4 teaspoon cinnamon
1/8 teaspoon ground cloves
1/4 cup (1/2 stick) unsalted butter, melted
16 ounces cream cheese, softened
1/2 cup heavy cream
1/2 cup sugar
1 teaspoon vanilla extract
1 tablespoon cornstarch
1/4 cup plus 2 teaspoons water
1/2 cup sugar
4 cups fresh raspberries

Process the pecans, brown sugar, cinnamon and cloves in a food processor until crumbly. Combine with the melted butter in a bowl and mix well. Press over the bottom and up the side of a 9-inch springform pan.

Chill for 30 minutes. Bake at 350 degrees for 20 minutes or until golden brown. Cool completely on a wire rack.

Beat the cream cheese, cream, 1/2 cup sugar and vanilla in a mixer bowl until smooth, scraping down the side of the bowl occasionally. Pour into the prepared crust. Chill, covered, for 4 hours or until firm.

Dissolve the cornstarch in 2 teaspoons of the water in a small bowl. Combine the remaining 1/4 cup water, 1/2 cup sugar and 2 1/2 cups of the raspberries in a heavy saucepan.

Cook over medium heat until the sugar is dissolved, stirring occasionally. Bring to a boil. Boil for 5 minutes or until berries are crushed. Stir in the cornstarch mixture. Boil for 1 minute or until mixture thickens, stirring constantly. Strain through a sieve set over a bowl, pressing on solids with the back of a spoon. Let stand until cooled.

Refrigerate, covered, until completely chilled. Stir the remaining 1 1/2 cups raspberries into the chilled sauce.

Loosen and remove the side of the pan. Cut into wedges and place on dessert plates. Spoon the raspberry sauce over each wedge.

Yield: 6 to 8 servings.

Chocolate
Macadamia Tarts

1¹/2 cups macadamia nuts, finely ground
³/4 cup flour
¹/3 cup sugar
¹/2 teaspoon cinnamon
2 tablespoons butter, melted
3 ounces semisweet chocolate, finely chopped
¹/2 cup heavy cream
8 ounces cream cheese, softened
¹/3 cup sugar
2 eggs
2 tablespoons heavy cream
2 tablespoons Kahlúa
¹/2 cup heavy cream
¹/3 cup milk
3 tablespoons sugar
2 egg yolks
1 teaspoon vanilla extract

Combine the macadamia nuts, flour, ¹/3 cup sugar and cinnamon in a bowl and mix well. Add the melted butter and mix well. Press over the bottoms and up the sides of six nonstick fluted 4-inch tart pans.

Place the chocolate in a small bowl. Bring ¹/2 cup cream to a boil over medium heat. Pour over the chocolate, stirring constantly until the chocolate is melted and the mixture is smooth.

Beat the cream cheese in a mixer bowl until smooth. Add ¹/3 cup sugar and beat for 3 minutes. Add the eggs 1 at a time, mixing well after each addition. Beat in 2 tablespoons cream and Kahlúa. Beat in the chocolate mixture just until blended. Pour into the prepared tart pans. Bake at 325 degrees for 25 to 30 minutes or until filling is set. Cool completely on a wire rack. Chill, covered, until ready to serve.

Combine ¹/2 cup cream and milk in a heavy saucepan. Cook over medium heat just until bubbles form around the edge of the saucepan. Remove from heat. Combine 3 tablespoons sugar and egg yolks in a bowl and mix well. Stir a small amount of the hot mixture into the egg yolk mixture. Stir the egg yolk mixture into the hot mixture. Cook over low heat until mixture thickens, stirring constantly; do not boil. Strain over a bowl. Stir the vanilla into the strained mixture. Refrigerate, covered, until ready to serve. Place each tart on a dessert plate. Spoon the sauce over the tarts.

Yield: 6 servings.

Roasted Salted Pecans

4 cups pecan halves
¹/4 cup (¹/2 stick) butter, melted
1 tablespoon salt

Spread the pecans on a heavy baking pan. Bake in a preheated 325-degree oven for 30 minutes. Drizzle with the butter, stirring to evenly coat the pecans. Bake for 15 minutes longer. Sprinkle with the salt, stirring to coat. Bake for 15 to 20 minutes longer. Let stand until cool. Store in an airtight container.

About Tarts

· If the top of a tart is browning too quickly, lay a strip of aluminum foil loosely over the top.

· To tell if a fruit tart is done, watch for the juices to bubble.

· Glaze the top of the baked tart while it is still hot. This will seal the surface.

· Fruit for tart shells should be cut according to its contour. Because pears are tapered, slice them lengthwise, starting from the stem end. Apples and most other round fruit fit better in the shell if sliced the opposite way.

· Fruit used for open tarts is rarely cut thick because it would take too long to soften during baking.

· Less fruit is used for tarts than for pies because most tarts are baked in shallow pans without a top crust.

· When arranging fruit in a tart shell, use the ends and irregular pieces for the bottom layer. Save the more uniform pieces for the top layer.

· Unlike pies, most fruit tarts can be served soon after baking.

Lemon Tart

2 egg yolks
$1/4$ cup heavy cream
2 cups flour
6 tablespoons sugar
$1/4$ cup confectioners' sugar
$1/8$ teaspoon salt
$1/2$ cup (1 stick) unsalted butter, chilled
1 cup heavy cream
$1/2$ cup fresh lemon juice
$3/4$ cup plus 2 tablespoons sugar
4 eggs
2 tablespoons flour
2 teaspoons lemon zest

Whisk the egg yolks and $1/4$ cup cream in a small bowl. Process 2 cups flour, 6 tablespoons sugar, confectioners' sugar and salt in a food processor until mixed. Add the butter in $1/2$-inch pieces and process until crumbly. Add the cream mixture and process just until moistened. Shape into a disk. Chill, wrapped in plastic wrap, for 1 hour or for up to 3 days.

Press the dough over the bottom and up the side of a buttered 11-inch tart pan with a removable bottom. Freeze for 15 minutes. Line with foil and fill with pie weights. Bake at 400 degrees for 15 minutes or until side is set. Remove the foil and weights. Bake for 8 minutes or until golden brown. Cool completely on a wire rack. Reduce the oven temperature to 325 degrees.

Whisk 1 cup cream, lemon juice, eggs, $3/4$ cup plus 2 tablespoons sugar, 2 tablespoons flour and zest together in a bowl. Pour into the prepared tart crust. Bake for 50 minute or until set. Cool on a wire rack. Refrigerate for 4 hours or until completely chilled. Remove the side of the pan. Cut into wedges. Serve with whipped cream.

Yield: 12 servings.

Almond Cream Confections

¹/2 cup (1 stick) butter
¹/4 cup sugar
2 tablespoons baking cocoa
2 teaspoons vanilla extract
¹/4 teaspoon salt
1 egg, lightly beaten
1 cup slivered almonds, toasted, chopped
1³/4 cups vanilla wafer crumbs
¹/2 cup flaked coconut
¹/3 cup butter, softened
1 egg
¹/2 teaspoon vanilla extract
2¹/2 to 3 cups sifted confectioners' sugar
2 ounces semisweet chocolate

Combine ¹/2 cup butter, sugar, baking cocoa, 2 teaspoons vanilla, salt and beaten egg in a heavy saucepan. Cook over low heat until the butter melts and mixture begins to thicken, stirring constantly. Remove from heat. Stir in the almonds, wafer crumbs and coconut. Press firmly over the bottom of a 9-inch square pan. Refrigerate, covered, until completely chilled.

Beat ¹/3 cup butter in a mixer bowl until light and fluffy. Beat in the egg and ¹/2 teaspoon vanilla. Add the confectioners' sugar gradually, mixing until smooth. Spread over the almond mixture. Refrigerate, covered, until completely chilled.

Cut into squares and place ¹/2 inch apart on a baking sheet. Place the chocolate in a sealable plastic bag. Submerge in hot water until melted. Snip a small hole in the end of the bag. Drizzle the chocolate over the squares.

Yield: 3 dozen.

White Chocolate Bread Pudding

6 cups heavy cream
2 cups milk
1 cup sugar
20 ounces white chocolate, chopped
9 eggs
1 large loaf stale French bread, sliced
³/4 cup heavy cream
8 ounces white chocolate, chopped

Heat the 6 cups cream, milk and sugar in a heavy saucepan until very hot. Remove from heat. Add 20 ounces white chocolate, stirring until melted.

Beat the eggs in a large bowl. Pour the hot cream mixture into the beaten eggs in a steady stream, beating constantly. Arrange the bread in a 9x13-inch baking pan. Pour the hot mixture over the bread so that all of the bread is moistened.

Bake, covered, at 350 degrees for 1 hour. Remove the cover. Bake for 30 minutes longer or until set and golden.

Bring ³/4 cup cream to a boil in a heavy saucepan. Remove from heat. Add 8 ounces white chocolate, stirring until melted and mixture is smooth. Cut the bread pudding into individual servings and place on dessert plates. Spoon the sauce over the pudding.

Yield: 12 to 16 servings.

Bread Pudding with Vanilla Sauce

3 eggs, lightly beaten
1 1/2 cups sugar
2 tablespoons brown sugar
1/2 teaspoon nutmeg
2 3/4 cups heavy cream
1/4 cup (1/2 stick) butter, melted
3/4 cup raisins
4 cups cubed French bread
Vanilla Sauce

Combine the eggs, sugar, brown sugar and nutmeg in a bowl and mix well. Stir in the heavy cream and melted butter. Fold in the raisins and bread cubes. Pour into a greased 2-quart baking dish.

Bake at 375 degrees for 25 minutes. Cover the top with foil and bake for an additional 30 minutes. Let stand for 15 minutes. Cut the bread pudding into individual servings and place on dessert plates. Serve with Vanilla Sauce.

Yield: 8 servings.

Vanilla Sauce

1/2 cup sugar
3 tablespoons brown sugar
Dash of nutmeg
1 egg
2 tablespoons butter
1 1/4 cups heavy cream
1 tablespoon flour
3 tablespoons heavy cream
1 tablespoon vanilla extract

Combine the sugar, brown sugar, nutmeg, egg and butter in a heavy saucepan. Cook over medium heat, whisking constantly until butter has melted.

Whisk in 1 1/4 cups cream. Mix the flour and 3 tablespoons cream in a bowl. Whisk into the hot cream mixture gradually.

Cook for 15 minutes or until thickened, whisking constantly. Remove from heat. Stir in the vanilla. Serve warm or at room temperature.

Buy edible flowers on the day you'll be using them, or gather them from the garden early that morning. Wash them thoroughly, then gently blot dry. Store everything, flower heads and petals, in a plastic bag in the refrigerator until you are ready to use them.

Godiva Marble Cheesecake

1 1/2 cups chocolate cookie crumbs
1/2 teaspoon cinnamon
1/4 cup (1/2 stick) butter, melted
12 ounces cream cheese, softened
1/2 cup sugar
1 teaspoon lemon zest
2 eggs
1 1/2 cups sour cream
4 ounces Godiva dark chocolate,
* melted, cooled*

Combine the cookie crumbs, cinnamon and butter in a bowl and mix well. Press over the bottom and up the side of a buttered 9-inch springform pan. Refrigerate, covered, until chilled.

Combine the cream cheese, sugar and zest in a mixer bowl and beat until well blended. Beat in the eggs and sour cream until smooth. Add the chocolate and mix with a fork just until batter is marbleized.

Pour into the prepared crust. Bake at 350 degrees for 35 to 40 minutes or until set. Let stand on a wire rack until cooled to room temperature. Chill, covered, for 2 hours or longer.

Yield: 10 to 12 servings.

Making Chocolate Curls

Leave block or square of white or semisweet chocolate in a warm place (80 to 85 degrees) for several hours or heat repeatedly in microwave oven 7 to 8 seconds (just enough to soften chocolate slightly). Place softened square or block against paper towel in one hand; using a sharp vegetable peeler, dig one blade into edge or side of chocolate (depending on how wide you want your curls) and bring peeler toward you; chocolate should come off in curls. If chocolate is too cold it may splinter; if it is too warm it will not curl.

Edible flowers can take many forms, some examples are:

· Chives–The mauve blossoms have a subtle onion flavor and are tasty on egg dishes and salads.

· Lavender–The bright purple flowers have a lemony taste and can be used for teas and to subtly scent sugar and honey.

· Marigolds–Use the bright orange petals for a saffron flavor in vegetables, poultry, eggs, rice, and salads.

· Nasturtiums–Use the whole yellow-orange blossoms and green leaves for a peppery flavor in soups and salads.

· Pansies–Use the petals for a subtle floral flavor in desserts and in drinks like iced tea, Champagne, and rose hip tea.

Sour Cream Cheesecake

3 cups graham cracker crumbs
1/2 cup (1 stick) butter, melted
1/4 cup sugar
1 teaspoon cinnamon
1/2 cup chopped nuts (optional)
24 ounces cream cheese, softened
4 eggs, beaten
2 teaspoons lemon juice
1 cup sugar
2 cups sour cream
1/4 cup sugar
2 teaspoons vanilla extract

⚷— Combine the graham cracker crumbs, butter, 1/4 cup sugar, cinnamon and nuts in a bowl and mix well. Press over the bottom and up the side of a 10-inch springform pan. Refrigerate until chilled.

Beat the cream cheese in a mixer bowl until light and fluffy. Add the eggs 1 at a time, mixing well after each addition. Add the lemon juice and mix well. Add 1 cup sugar and mix until smooth. Pour into the prepared crust. Bake at 350 degrees for 50 to 60 minutes or until set. Cool on a wire rack for 10 minutes.

Combine the sour cream, 1/4 cup sugar and vanilla in a bowl and mix well. Spread over the cheesecake. Bake for an additional 5 minutes. Let stand on a wire rack until cooled to room temperature. Refrigerate until completely chilled. Serve with fresh fruit.

Yield: 8 to 10 servings.

Raspberry Cheesecake

16 ounces cream cheese, softened
1/2 cup sugar
2 eggs
1/2 teaspoon vanilla extract
1 (9-inch) chocolate crumb pie shell
1 1/2 teaspoons unflavored gelatin
2 tablespoons cold water
10 tablespoons seedless raspberry preserves
1 teaspoon fresh lemon juice
1/4 cup whipping cream
2 tablespoons sugar

⚷— Combine the cream cheese, 1/2 cup sugar, eggs and vanilla in a mixer bowl and beat until smooth. Pour into the pie shell.

Bake at 325 degrees for 35 to 40 minutes or until set. Cool on a wire rack for 30 minutes. Chill for 1 1/2 hours.

Sprinkle the gelatin over the cold water in a microwave-safe bowl. Let stand for 2 minutes. Microwave on High for 40 seconds. Stir until gelatin has dissolved. Whisk in the preserves gradually. Stir in the lemon juice. Chill for 10 minutes or until cold.

Whip the cream and 2 tablespoons sugar in a mixer bowl until stiff peaks form. Fold into the gelatin mixture. Spread over the cheesecake. Chill for 1 hour or until set.

Yield: 8 servings.

White Chocolate Cheesecake with Raspberry Sauce

1/2 cup (1 stick) butter, melted
1 1/2 cups graham cracker crumbs
8 ounces white chocolate, chopped
32 ounces cream cheese, softened
1 cup sugar
4 eggs
1 tablespoon vanilla extract
2 cups raspberries
1 cup sugar
1/2 cup raspberry liqueur (optional)

Combine the butter and graham cracker crumbs in a bowl and mix well. Press over the bottom of a greased springform pan. Bake at 350 degrees for 10 minutes. Reduce oven temperature to 250 degrees.

Heat the white chocolate in a double boiler until melted, stirring frequently. Set aside.

Beat the cream cheese in a mixer bowl until light and fluffy. Add 1 cup sugar and mix well. Add the eggs 1 at a time, mixing well after each addition. Stir in the vanilla. Add the melted white chocolate and mix well. Pour into the prepared crust.

Place the springform pan in a larger baking pan. Pour hot water into the baking pan 1/4 inch deep. Bake at 250 degrees for 1 1/2 to 2 hours or until set. Cool in the pan for 5 minutes. Loosen the cheesecake from the side of the pan with a knife. Remove the side of the pan. Let stand on a wire rack until cooled to room temperature.

Purée the raspberries, 1 cup sugar and liqueur in a blender. Strain to remove the seeds. Drizzle over the top of the cheesecake before serving or serve with the cheesecake.

Yield: 10 to 12 servings.

Peach Cobbler

6 to 8 fresh peaches, peeled, sliced
3 tablespoons sugar
1/2 cup water
1/2 cup (1 stick) margarine
1 cup flour
1 cup sugar
2 teaspoons baking powder
1 cup milk

Combine the peaches, 3 tablespoons sugar and water in a saucepan. Cook until heated through. Heat the margarine in a 9-inch square pan in a 375-degree oven until melted. Pour the peach mixture over the melted margarine, arranging the peaches evenly.

Combine the flour, 1 cup sugar, baking powder and milk in a bowl and mix well. Pour evenly over the peach mixture; do not stir. Bake at 375 degrees for 45 minutes.

May substitute one 16-ounce can of syrup-pack peaches for the fresh peaches, 3 tablespoons sugar and water.

Yield: 8 servings.

Blackberries

Blackberries are found along roadsides throughout central Louisiana from mid-May through June depending on our spring weather. Picking them is truly a labor of love. After a weekend of blackberry picking, I am conscious of the purple stains and scratches on my hands when I return to work on Monday morning.

The secret ingredient in my Blackberry Crisp and blackberry jelly recipes is the love that goes into picking fresh blackberries. It is truly wonderful on a cold, frosty February morning to slather blackberry jelly on hot toast and remember a warm beautiful Saturday in May spent picking blackberries with someone you love. Blackberries freeze well in a ziplock storage bag. I do not rinse before freezing– just be sure to pick out any leaves or twigs.

Blackberry Crisp

1 cup flour
1 cup sugar
1 teaspoon baking powder
1 egg, beaten
4 to 5 cups blackberries
3/4 cup sugar
2 tablespoons flour
1/2 cup (1 stick) unsalted butter, melted

Combine the flour, 1 cup sugar and baking powder in a bowl and mix well. Make a well in the center. Add the egg and mix until crumbly. Set aside.

Place the blackberries in a large bowl. Combine 3/4 cup sugar and flour in a small bowl and mix well. Pour over the blackberries, tossing gently to coat.

Spoon into a buttered 9-inch square baking pan. Sprinkle the flour-egg mixture over the blackberry mixture. Drizzle the melted butter over the top.

Place the pan on a baking sheet. Bake at 375 degrees for 45 minutes.

Yield: 6 to 8 servings.

Crème Brûlée

2 cups heavy cream
1/2 cup milk
1/2 vanilla bean, or 2 teaspoons vanilla
    extract
5 egg yolks
1/2 cup sugar
1/8 teaspoon salt
4 cups (about) boiling water
5 tablespoons superfine sugar

Combine the cream and milk in a saucepan. Scrape the vanilla seed into the cream mixture and add the bean pod. Bring to a simmer. Remove from heat. Steep, covered, for 20 minutes.

Combine the egg yolks, sugar and salt in a bowl and mix well. Stir into the cream mixture; do not whisk or beat. Strain through a sieve into a bowl. Pour evenly into 6 ramekins. Place the ramekins in a 9x13-inch baking pan. Pour enough boiling water into the pan to come halfway up the sides of the ramekins. Bake at 325 degrees for 45 to 50 minutes or until sides are firm but center is not set. Remove to a wire rack to cool. Refrigerate, covered, until chilled.

Preheat the broiler. Blot the top of each custard dry with paper towel. Set the ramekins on a baking sheet. Sprinkle the superfine sugar over the top of each custard. Broil 4 inches from the heat source until the sugar is melted and caramelized, rotating the baking sheet every minute. Serve within 1 hour.

Variations: For Eggnog Crème Brûlée, substitute 1 1/2 cups eggnog and 1 cup heavy cream for the 2 cups heavy cream and 1/2 cup milk. For Coconut Lime Crème Brûlée, add the zest of 2 limes and 1 teaspoon coconut flavoring to the cream mixture.

Yield: 6 servings.

About Custards and Creams

Pastry cream and custard fillings are easy to make, but there are a few tricks that will help to guarantee your success.

· Avoid high oven temperatures because they cause custards to become watery.

· To prevent a soggy bottom crust, prebake the pastry shell before filling, or bake the pie or tart on a preheated pizza stone or baking sheet, preferably one made of dark metal, or brush the pastry shell with an egg wash or other sealer.

· Custards can be baked with or without a pastry shell.

· Don't use cookie crumbs or finely chopped nuts as a sealer for a bottom crust when baking custard pies; they will float to the top.

· Place larger, heavier ingredients–such as fresh or dried fruits, coarsely chopped nuts, or sautéed vegetables and meats for savories– on the bottom of the pastry shell before adding the custard.

· When making pastry cream, always use a heavy nonreactive saucepan, such as stainless steel or heavy-bottomed enamel.

· To prevent a skin from forming on the surface of a cooked filling as it cools, cover it with a sheet of buttered plastic wrap.

· Baked meringue topping can be substituted for whipped cream on most pies made with ordinary pastry cream fillings.

· Many baked custard pies and tarts have a short life. The sooner they are eaten the better. This also applies to meringue toppings.

Caramel Apple Crêpes

4 eggs
2 cups milk
6 tablespoons butter, melted
1/2 teaspoon salt
1 cup sifted flour
Butter or vegetable oil
2 cups cream cheese
2 cups apple pie filling
1/2 cup confectioners' sugar
Caramel Sauce
Sweetened whipped cream, vanilla ice cream
    or cinnamon ice cream
Thinly sliced apples

Combine the eggs, milk, melted butter, salt and flour in a blender. Process until smooth. Chill for 3 hours. Heat a crêpe pan. Brush lightly with butter or oil. Spoon 2 tablespoons of the batter in the pan and swirl to coat the pan evenly. Cook for 1 minute or until light brown. Turn and brown the other side. Stack with waxed paper between crêpes.

Combine the cream cheese, pie filling and confectioners' sugar in a bowl and mix well. Spread over each crêpe and roll up.

Spoon a small amount of warm Caramel Sauce onto a dessert plate. Place 2 filled crêpes over the Caramel Sauce. Place a dollop of whipped cream over the crêpes. Drizzle a small amount of Caramel Sauce over the whipped cream. Arrange 3 or 4 apples slices in a fan on the side of the plate. Repeat for remaining crêpes.

Yield: 6 to 8 servings.

Caramel Sauce

6 cups sugar
1 1/2 cups (3 sticks) unsalted butter, melted
3 cups heavy cream.

Heat the sugar in a heavy saucepan over medium heat, gently shaking the pan until the sugar is a caramel color. Whisk in the butter until almost blended. Whisk in the cream. Bring to a boil. Remove from heat. Stir with a wooden spoon until all of the sugar is dissolved. Let stand until completely cooled. Store in an airtight container in the refrigerator.

Reheat 2 tablespoons per serving in the top of a double boiler or in a microwave-safe bowl in the microwave.

Don't have time to prepare a complicated dessert? These quick dessert ideas make it easy to satisfy your sweet tooth.

   · Melt chocolate-covered mint patties in the microwave and serve over ice cream or baked pears.

   · Layer angel food cake or sponge cake with sliced strawberries or peaches and vanilla yogurt.

   · Fill cantaloupe halves with vanilla ice cream and top with fresh berries.

Homemade Vanilla Ice Cream

Egg substitute equivalent to 6 medium eggs
2 cups plus 6 tablespoons sugar
4 cups milk
2 cups half-and-half
3 cups heavy cream
1/4 teaspoon salt
6 3/4 teaspoons vanilla extract

⚭ Beat the egg substitute and sugar in a large bowl. Add the milk, half-and-half, heavy cream, salt and vanilla and beat well. Pour into an ice cream freezer container. Freeze according to the manufacturer's instructions.

Yield: 12 servings.

Hot Fudge Sundae Syrup

1/2 cup baking cocoa
1 cup sugar
1 cup light corn syrup
1/2 cup milk
3 tablespoons butter
1/4 teaspoon salt
2 tablespoons vanilla extract

⚭ Combine the baking cocoa, sugar, corn syrup, milk, butter and salt in a saucepan. Bring to a boil, stirring occasionally. Boil for 5 minutes. Remove from heat. Stir in the vanilla. Store in the refrigerator.

Yield: 3 cups.

A Secret Tip to the Rookie Mardi Gras Parade Watcher

Never reach for a thrown prize that has fallen to the street with your hands without first securing it with a good old-fashioned foot stomp. Do not lift your foot until you're ready to pick up your trinket to add to the rest of your treasures. Once you find yourself caught up in the festivities, and you have your growing collection, you ask yourself as all of us do, "What am I going to do with all of these beads?"

Homemade Peach Ice Cream

6 cups mashed peeled peaches
1/4 cup lemon juice
2 1/2 cups sugar
1/2 teaspoon salt
4 cups heavy cream
1 (14-ounce) can sweetened condensed milk
1 teaspoon almond extract
1 tablespoon vanilla extract

⚬—ᵐ Process the peaches in a food processor until almost puréed. Combine the peaches, lemon juice, sugar and salt in a bowl and mix well. Add the cream, condensed milk, almond extract and vanilla and mix well.

Pour into a 1-gallon ice cream freezer container. Freeze according to manufacturer's instructions.

Yield: 16 servings.

Oreo Delight

1/2 cup (1 stick) butter
1 cup sugar
1 cup evaporated milk
1 ounce German's sweet chocolate
1/2 cup (1 stick) butter, melted
30 Oreo cookies, crushed
1/2 gallon vanilla ice cream, softened
12 ounces nondairy whipped topping
Pecan halves

⚬—ᵐ Combine 1/2 cup butter, sugar, evaporated milk and chocolate in a heavy saucepan. Bring to a boil over medium heat, stirring constantly. Boil until mixture has thickened. Refrigerate until completely cooled.

Combine the melted butter and Oreos in a bowl and mix well. Press over the bottom of a 9x13-inch dish. Spread the ice cream over the Oreo layer. Spread the chilled chocolate mixture over the ice cream. Spread the whipped topping over the layers. Sprinkle the pecans over the top. Freeze, covered, for 8 to 12 hours.

Yield: 20 servings.

Midnight Delights

1³/4 cups flour
1/3 cup baking cocoa
1/4 cup sugar
1/8 teaspoon salt
3/4 cup (1¹/2 sticks) butter, chilled, cut into
    small pieces
1/3 to 1/2 cup strong-brewed coffee, chilled
12 ounces semisweet chocolate chips, melted
2/3 cup sugar
2 tablespoons butter, melted
2 tablespoons milk
2 teaspoons coffee liqueur
2 eggs, room temperature
1/2 cup toasted finely chopped walnuts

Sift the flour, baking cocoa, 1/4 cup sugar and salt into a food processor container. Add 3/4 cup butter and process until crumbly. Add the coffee gradually, processing until the mixture forms a ball. Knead on a lightly floured surface 4 to 6 times. Shape into a log. Chill, wrapped in plastic wrap, for 6 hours or longer.

Divide the chilled dough into 4 portions. Roll one portion into a 14- to 15-inch circle 1/8 inch thick on a lightly floured surface, keeping the remaining portions refrigerated. Cut into 3-inch circles. Press each circle into a greased miniature muffin cup. Repeat with remaining dough.

Combine the melted chips, 2/3 cup sugar, 2 tablespoons butter, milk and coffee liqueur in a bowl and mix well. Add the eggs and beat until smooth. Stir in the walnuts. Place 1 rounded teaspoonful into each prepared muffin cup. Bake at 350 degrees for 20 to 25 minutes or until filling is set. Cool in the pan for 15 minutes. Remove to a wire rack to cool completely.

Yield: 4 dozen.

Tiramisu

5 egg yolks
1/2 cup sugar
8 ounces cream cheese, softened
8 ounces mascarpone cheese or cream cheese,
    softened
1/4 cup marsala
2 cups whipping cream, whipped
36 ladyfingers, separated
2 cups strong-brewed coffee, cooled
Baking cocoa

Beat the egg yolks and sugar in a mixer bowl until foamy. Beat in the cream cheese and mascarpone cheese until smooth. Beat in the marsala. Fold in the whipped cream.

Dip the ladyfingers into the coffee. Layer the ladyfingers and cheese mixture half at a time in a 9x13-inch dish. Sprinkle baking cocoa over the top. Refrigerate, covered, until firm.

Yield: 16 servings.

Chocolate Trifle

1 (22-ounce) package fudge brownie mix
1/4 cup Kahlúa or other coffee-flavored liqueur
    (optional)
3 (4-ounce) packages chocolate instant
    pudding mix
12 ounces nondairy whipped topping
6 (1 1/2-ounce) Heath candy bars, crushed

⊶ Prepare and bake the brownie mix using package directions for a 9x13-inch baking pan. Prick the top of the warm brownies and drizzle with the Kahlúa. Let the brownies stand until cool; crumble.

Prepare the pudding mixes using package directions; do not chill.

Layer the crumbled brownies, pudding, whipped topping and candy bars one-third at a time in a 3-quart trifle dish. Chill until ready to serve.

Yield: 16 to 18 servings.

Plan a cookie exchange as an easy way to get friends together. Each guest should bring one or more batches of cookies made from her favorite recipes, along with copies of the recipes and a container in which to take home the leftovers. The hostess should provide a choice of drinks.

Praline Thumbprint Cookies

1 cup (2 sticks) butter, softened
1 cup sifted confectioners' sugar
2 cups flour
1 tablespoon vanilla extract
1 cup finely chopped pecans
Praline Filling

⊶ Beat the butter in a mixer bowl until light and fluffy. Add the confectioners' sugar gradually, beating at medium speed. Add the flour and mix well. Add the vanilla and mix well. Stir in the pecans.

Shape into 1-inch balls. Place 2 inches apart on a cookie sheet. Make an indentation in the center of each cookie using your thumb. Bake at 375 degrees for 15 to 17 minutes; do not brown. Cool on a wire rack. Spoon 1/2 teaspoon of Praline Filling into each cookie indentation.

Yield: 3 dozen.

Praline Filling

1/2 cup (1 stick) butter
1 cup packed brown sugar
Dash of salt
1/2 cup evaporated milk
2 cups sifted confectioners' sugar
1/2 teaspoon vanilla extract

⊶ Heat the butter in a saucepan until melted. Add the brown sugar and salt. Bring to a boil. Boil for 2 minutes, stirring constantly. Remove from heat. Stir in the evaporated milk. Return to the heat. Bring to a boil. Boil for 2 minutes. Remove from heat and cool to lukewarm. Stir in the confectioners' sugar and vanilla. Beat with a wooden spoon until smooth.

Iced Pumpkin Cookies

2 cups flour
2 teaspoons baking powder
1/2 teaspoon salt
2 teaspoons cinnamon
1/2 teaspoon nutmeg
1/4 teaspoon ginger
1/2 cup (1 stick) margarine, softened
1 cup sugar
2 eggs
1 cup pumpkin
1 cup raisins
Lemon Icing

Sift the flour, baking powder, salt, cinnamon, nutmeg and ginger together. Beat the margarine, sugar and eggs in a mixer bowl at medium speed until fluffy. Beat in the pumpkin at low speed. Add the flour mixture, beating just until combined. Stir in the raisins.

Drop by heaping teaspoonfuls onto a greased cookie sheet. Bake at 350 degrees for 12 to 15 minutes. Remove to a wire rack to cool. Frost warm cookies with Lemon Icing.

Yield: 3 dozen.

Lemon Icing

1 (1-pound) package confectioners' sugar
1 tablespoon lemon juice
Water

Combine the confectioners' sugar and lemon juice in a bowl and mix well. Add enough water to make of a spreading consistency.

Storing a Stash

· *Cool cookies completely before packing in tins or other containers so they don't stick together, become misshapen, or get soggy.*

· *Tuck treats into self-sealing bags with air squeezed out, metal tins (coffee cans work well), or sturdy plastic containers. Bar cookies can be stored in their baking pan, cut or uncut, covered with a layer of plastic wrap and foil.*

· *Keep goodies at room temperature for 1 to 2 weeks, or freeze for up to 2 to 3 months, or as recipe directs. To defrost, just unwrap and thaw at room temperature.*

· *Store soft cookies with a wedge of apple or a slice of white bread to keep them moist; replace the fruit or bread every couple of days.*

Toffee Crunch Cookies

1/2 cup (1 stick) margarine, softened
1 (2-layer) package yellow butter cake mix
with pudding
2 eggs, lightly beaten
1 1/2 cups almond butter chips or Heath candy
pieces
1/2 cup chopped pecans

Combine the margarine, cake mix and eggs in a bowl and mix well. Stir in the butter chips and pecans.

Drop by rounded teaspoonfuls on a greased cookie sheet. Bake at 350 degrees for 8 to 10 minutes. Remove to a wire rack to cool.

Yield: 5 dozen.

Chocolate Caramel Oat Squares

1 1/2 cups flour
1 1/2 cups old-fashioned oats
1 1/2 cups packed light brown sugar
1/2 teaspoon baking soda
1/4 teaspoon salt
3/4 cup (1 1/2 sticks) unsalted butter, chilled,
cut into pieces
1 cup milk chocolate chips
1 cup semisweet chocolate chips
1/2 cup heavy cream
1 (14-ounce) package caramels

Combine the flour, oats, brown sugar, baking soda and salt in a food processor container. Add the butter and pulse until mixture sticks together; set aside 2 cups. Press remaining mixture over the bottom of a greased 9x13-inch baking pan. Sprinkle with the milk chocolate and semisweet chocolate chips.

Combine the cream and caramels in a microwave-safe container. Microwave for 2 1/2 minutes or until caramels are melted, stirring at 1 minute intervals. Pour over the chocolate chips. Sprinkle with the reserved oat mixture. Bake at 350 degrees for 20 minutes. Cool completely before cutting into squares.

Yield: 2 1/2 dozen.

Pack homemade refrigerator cookie dough into clean 6-ounce frozen juice cans. Freeze until needed. Thaw for about 15 minutes, remove the bottom of the can and push dough up, using the top edge as a cutting guide.

Magic Cookie Bars

¹/₂ cup (1 stick) margarine or butter
1¹/₂ cups graham cracker crumbs
1 (14-ounce) can sweetened condensed milk
8 ounces milk chocolate chips
8 ounces white chocolate chips
¹/₂ cup pecan halves, chopped

☙— Place the margarine in a 9x13-inch baking pan. Heat in a 350-degree oven until melted. Sprinkle the crumbs over the melted margarine. Pour the condensed milk over the crumbs. Sprinkle the milk chocolate chips, then the white chocolate chips and then the pecans over the layers. Press down firmly.

Bake for 30 minutes or until light brown. Cool on a wire rack. Cut into bars. May substitute semisweet chocolate chips and peanut butter chips for the milk chocolate chips and white chocolate chips.

Yield: 2 to 3 dozen.

Cream Cheese Brownies

1 (2-layer) package yellow cake mix
1 cup chopped pecans
¹/₂ cup (1 stick) butter, melted
1 egg, beaten
2 eggs
8 ounces cream cheese, softened
1 (1-pound) package confectioners' sugar

☙— Combine the cake mix, pecans, butter and 1 egg in a bowl and mix well. Press over the bottom of a greased 9x13-inch baking pan.

Beat 2 eggs in a mixer bowl until fluffy. Add the cream cheese and confectioners' sugar. Beat until smooth. Spread over the cake layer.

Bake at 325 degrees for 40 to 50 minutes or until brownies pull away from the sides of the pan.

Yield: 3 dozen.

Burned Cookie Bottoms

There are several causes for this problem, one of which is dark cookie sheets. If your pans are dark, decrease your oven temperature by 25 degrees. Make sure the oven rack is in the middle position, and cook only one sheet of cookies at a time to ensure proper air circulation. Finally, check your oven temperature periodically with an oven thermometer. Many ovens have hot spots or heat to a temperature higher than they are set for. If the temperature is inaccurate, adjust the dial accordingly.

Praline Brownies

¹/3 cup packed light brown sugar
5¹/3 tablespoons butter
²/3 cup flour
¹/4 cup chopped pecans or walnuts
2 ounces unsweetened chocolate
¹/4 cup shortening
¹/4 cup (¹/2 stick) butter
¹/4 cup sugar
¹/2 cup packed light brown sugar
1 teaspoon vanilla extract
2 eggs
¹/4 cup Kahlúa
¹/2 cup flour
¹/4 teaspoon salt
¹/2 cup chopped pecans or walnuts
Kahlúa Butter Cream Frosting

⚷ Combine ¹/3 cup brown sugar,
5¹/3 tablespoons butter, ²/3 cup flour and ¹/4 cup
pecans in a bowl and mix well. Press over the
bottom of a 9x9-inch baking pan.

Heat the chocolate, shortening and ¹/4 cup
butter in a saucepan over low heat until melted,
stirring occasionally. Remove from heat. Let stand
for 5 minutes. Add the sugar, ¹/2 cup brown sugar
and vanilla and mix well. Add the eggs 1 at a time,
mixing well after each addition. Stir in the Kahlúa.
Add ¹/2 cup flour and salt, stirring until smooth.
Fold in ¹/2 cup pecans. Pour into the prepared
pan. Bake at 350 degrees for 25 minutes; do not
overbake. Cool in the pan.

Frost the cooled brownies with Kahlúa Butter
Cream Frosting. Chill for 1 hour. Cut into squares.

Yield: 3 dozen.

Kahlúa Butter Cream Frosting

2 tablespoons butter, softened
2 cups sifted confectioners' sugar
1 tablespoons Kahlúa
¹/4 cup cream

⚷ Combine the butter, confectioners'
sugar, Kahlúa and cream in a bowl and mix until
smooth and creamy.

*Bake guilt-free brownies by replacing the
¹/2 cup oil and 2 eggs called for in the brownie
mix with ¹/2 cup each nonfat yogurt and
unsweetened applesauce.*

Triple Chocolate Mousse Bars

1/2 cup (1 stick) butter
3/4 cup confectioners' sugar
1 egg yolk
1/2 teaspoon vanilla extract
1/2 cup baking cocoa
1 cup flour
2 cups semisweet chocolate chips
1 1/2 cups heavy cream
2/3 cup sugar
2 teaspoons vanilla extract
4 eggs
8 ounces white chocolate
2 tablespoons shortening

Line a 9x13-inch baking pan with foil and coat with nonstick cooking spray. Beat the butter, confectioners' sugar, egg yolk and 1/2 teaspoon vanilla in a mixer bowl until light and fluffy. Beat in the baking cocoa and flour until crumbly. Press over the bottom of the prepared pan. Bake at 350 degrees for 12 minutes.

Place the chocolate chips in a bowl. Bring the cream to a simmer in a heavy saucepan. Pour over the chips, stirring until the chips are melted. Whisk in the sugar, 2 teaspoons vanilla and eggs. Pour over the prepared crust. Bake for 32 minutes.

Heat the white chocolate and shortening in a saucepan until melted, stirring frequently. Spread evenly over the baked layers. Chill for 2 hours or longer. Dust lightly with additional baking cocoa. Cut into triangles.

Yield: 2 1/2 dozen.

How To Melt Chocolate

Melting chocolate to use as a baking ingredient, for candy work, or decoration requires gentle heat. Chocolate that is overheated may scorch, lose flavor, and turn coarse and grainy. Stir melting chocolate after it has begun to liquefy. Because of the sensitivity of milk solids to heat, milk and white chocolates should be stirred almost constantly while dark chocolate need only be stirred frequently during melting.

Here are two good methods for melting chocolate so that it is smooth and glossy:

· In a microwave oven–place coarsely chopped chocolate in a microwave-safe container and microwave on Medium (50 percent power) for 1 1/2 to 4 minutes, until the chocolate turns shiny. Remove container from the microwave and stir the chocolate until completely melted. Stir milk and white chocolates after about 1 1/2 minutes. Because of their milk proteins, they need to be stirred sooner than dark chocolate. (If overheated, these chocolates may become grainy.)

· In a double boiler–place coarsely chopped chocolate in the top of a double boiler over hot, not simmering, water. Melt the chocolate, stirring until smooth. Remove the top part of the double boiler from the bottom.

Pecan Chewy Squares

2/3 cup confectioners' sugar
2 cups unbleached flour
1 cup (2 sticks) butter
2/3 cup butter, melted
1/2 cup honey
3 tablespoons heavy cream
1/2 cup packed brown sugar
3 1/2 cups pecan halves, coarsely chopped

Sift the confectioners' sugar and flour into a bowl. Cut in 1 cup butter until crumbly. Press over the bottom of a greased 9x12-inch baking pan. Bake at 350 degrees for 20 minutes.

Combine the melted butter, honey, cream and brown sugar in a bowl and mix well. Add the pecans, stirring until coated. Spread evenly over the crust. Bake for 25 minutes. Let stand until completely cooled. Cut into squares.

Yield: 3 dozen.

Pralines

1 1/2 cups sugar
3/4 cup packed brown sugar
6 tablespoons butter
1/2 cup milk
1 1/2 cups chopped pecans
1 teaspoon vanilla extract

Combine the sugar, brown sugar, butter, milk and pecans in a heavy 3-quart saucepan. Bring to a boil over medium heat, stirring constantly. Boil for 1 1/2 to 2 minutes or until mixture reaches 220 degrees on a candy thermometer, stirring constantly. Remove from heat. Stir in the vanilla immediately and beat with a wooden spoon for 4 to 6 minutes or until mixture begins to thicken. Drop by teaspoonfuls onto waxed paper. Let stand until firm.

Variation: For Chocolate Pralines, add 2 ounces unsweetened chocolate before boiling.

Yield: 2 1/2 dozen.

Measurement Equivalents

Liquid Measures

1 gallon	=	4 quarts	=	8 pints	=	16 cups	=	128 fluid ounces
$1/2$ gallon	=	2 quarts	=	4 pints	=	8 cups	=	64 fluid ounces
$1/4$ gallon	=	1 quart	=	2 pints	=	4 cups	=	32 fluid ounces
		$1/2$ quart	=	1 pint	=	2 cups	=	16 fluid ounces
		$1/4$ quart	=	$1/2$ pint	=	1 cup	=	8 fluid ounces

Dry Measures

1 cup	=	8 fluid ounces	=	16 tablespoons	=	48 teaspoons
$3/4$ cup	=	6 fluid ounces	=	12 tablespoons	=	36 teaspoons
$2/3$ cup	=	$5 1/3$ fluid ounces	=	$10 2/3$ tablespoons	=	32 teaspoons
$1/2$ cup	=	4 fluid ounces	=	8 tablespoons	=	24 teaspoons
$1/3$ cup	=	$2 2/3$ fluid ounces	=	$5 1/3$ tablespoons	=	16 teaspoons
$1/4$ cup	=	2 fluid ounces	=	4 tablespoons	=	12 teaspoons
1 cup	=	1 fluid ounce	=	2 tablespoons	=	6 teaspoons
				1 tablespoon	=	3 teaspoons

Ingredient Equivalents

One (1) pound of		is equivalent to	One (1) pound of		is equivalent to
Butter	=	2 cups	Potatoes	=	2 cups diced or 2 large whole
Cheese	=	4 cups grated			
Cornmeal	=	3 cups	Raisins	=	3 cups
Flour, all-purpose, sifted	=	4 cups	Rice	=	2 cups
Flour, all-purpose, unsifted	=	$3 1/2$ cups	Sugar, brown, packed	=	$2 1/4$ cups
Macaroni	=	4 cups	Sugar, confectioners'	=	4 cups
Meat	=	2 cups chopped	Sugar, granulated	=	2 cups

Substitutions

If the recipe calls for	You can substitute
1 cup buttermilk	1 cup whole milk plus 1 tablespoon vinegar
1 cup half-and-half	1 tablespoon melted butter plus enough whole milk to equal 1 cup
1 cup sour cream	1 cup plain yogurt
1 cup whole milk	$\frac{1}{2}$ cup evaporated milk plus $\frac{1}{2}$ cup water, or $\frac{1}{4}$ cup powdered milk plus 1 cup water
1 cup light corn syrup	1 cup sugar plus $\frac{1}{2}$ cup liquid
1 cup honey	$1\frac{1}{4}$ cups sugar plus $\frac{1}{4}$ cup liquid
1 cup molasses	1 cup honey
1 cup sugar	1 cup packed brown sugar, or 2 cups sifted confectioners' sugar
1 teaspoon lemon juice	$\frac{1}{4}$ teaspoon cider vinegar
1 teaspoon lemon peel	$\frac{1}{2}$ teaspoon lemon extract
1 cup tomato juice	$\frac{1}{2}$ cup tomato sauce plus $\frac{1}{2}$ cup water
2 cups tomato sauce	$\frac{3}{4}$ cup tomato paste plus 1 cup water
1 teaspoon baking powder	$\frac{1}{4}$ teaspoon baking soda plus $\frac{1}{2}$ teaspoon cream of tartar
1 tablespoon cornstarch	2 tablespoons flour (for thickening purposes)
1 ounce semisweet chocolate	3 tablespoons semisweet chocolate chips, or 1 ounce unsweetened chocolate plus 1 tablespoon sugar
1 ounce unsweetened chocolate	3 tablespoons cocoa plus 1 tablespoon shortening or vegetable oil
1 garlic clove	$\frac{1}{8}$ teaspoon garlic powder
1 tablespoon prepared mustard	$\frac{1}{2}$ teaspoon onion powder, or 1 tablespoon dried minced onion
$\frac{1}{4}$ cup finely minced onion	1 tablespoon dehydrated minced onion
2 tablespoons minced parsley	2 tablespoons dehydrated parsley flakes

Quantities to Serve 100

Baked beans .... 5 gallons
Beef .... 40 pounds
Beets .... 30 pounds
Bread .... 10 loaves
Butter .... 3 pounds
Cabbage for slaw .... 20 pounds
Cakes .... 8 cakes
Carrots .... 33 pounds
Cauliflower .... 18 pounds
Cheese .... 18 pounds
Chicken for chicken pie .... 40 pounds
Coffee .... 3 pounds
Cream .... 3 quarts
Fruit cocktail .... 1 gallon
Fruit juice .... 4 (No. 10) cans
Fruit salad .... 20 quarts
Ground beef .... 30 to 36 pounds
Ham .... 40 pounds
Ice cream .... 4 gallons
Lettuce .... 20 heads
Meat loaf .... 24 pounds
Milk .... 6 gallons
Nuts .... 3 pounds
Olives .... 1³/4 pounds
Oysters .... 18 quarts
Pickles .... 2 quarts
Pies .... 17 pies
Potatoes .... 35 pounds
Roast pork .... 40 pounds
Rolls .... 200 rolls
Salad dressing .... 3 quarts
Scalloped potatoes .... 5 gallons
Soup .... 5 gallons
Sugar cubes .... 3 pounds
Tomato juice .... 4 (No. 10) cans
Vegetables .... 4 (No. 20) cans
Vegetable salad .... 20 quarts
Whipping cream .... 4 pints
Wieners .... 25 pounds

Garnishes

Bell Pepper Garnishes . . . . Accent rice dishes with sautéed julienned red, yellow, and green bell peppers.

Butter Curls . . . . Dip the blade of a vegetable peeler into hot water and pull firmly over a slightly softened stick of butter. Chill the curls in ice water.

Carrot Curls . . . . Scrape raw carrots to remove the tough outer peel. Use a potato peeler to make thin strips down the length of the carrot. Roll up the strips, secure with wooden picks, and place in ice water until crisp and curled.

Celery Curls . . . . Cut celery stalks into short pieces. Slice the ends lengthwise; both ends may be cut if desired. Chill the cut celery in ice water and let stand until the cut ends curl.

Chocolate Curls . . . . Pour melted chocolate onto a baking sheet lined with waxed paper. Spread the chocolate into a 2- to 3-inch strip. Let stand until the chocolate is cooled and slightly sticky but not firm. Pull a vegetable peeler slowly across the chocolate until a curl forms, allowing the chocolate to curl on top of the peeler. Use a wooden pick to transfer the curl to a plate. Chill until needed.

Cooked Vegetable Garnishes . . . . Decorate large platters with bundles of julienned carrots and celery tied with chives, slices of baked sweet potato, or thin wedges of baked acorn squash.

Cookie Trimmers . . . . Coat rolls of chilled cookie dough with minced candied fruit, chopped nuts, or candy sprinkles before slicing and baking.

Fluted Fruit Wheels . . . . Cut thin strips of peel evenly from the stem ends to blossom ends of lemons, oranges, and limes. Cut the fruit into slices of the desired thickness. To make twists, cut from one side to the center and twist. For fans, cut fruit into slices, cutting to but not through the bottom side; fan out the slices.

Fluted Mushroom . . . . Select firm, round white mushrooms. Rub gently with lemon juice to prevent discoloration. Press the flat tip of a knife into the center of the mushroom cap in a star design. Continue making indentations in rows around the mushroom cap.

Garnishes

Frosted Fruit	Rinse and dry grapes, cranberries, or cherries. Dip in egg whites beaten until frothy, then in granulated sugar; shake off excess sugar and let dry.
Grape Ice Cubes	Make ice cubes for party beverages using white grape juice and freezing a green grape in each.
Green Onion Frills	Cut off the root end and most of the stem portion of green onions. Make narrow lengthwise cuts at both ends with a sharp knife to produce a fringe. Chill in ice water until the ends curl.
Herb Bundles	Decorate meat platters with bundles of herbs used in preparing the dish, such as watercress, parsley, thyme, rosemary, or sage.
Kumquat Flower	Cut a canned kumquat into six wedges to but not through the bottom to make petals.
Radish Accordion	Select long, narrow radishes. Cut a thin slice from each end. Cut crosswise into slices, leaving the bottom intact. Chill in iced water until the slices open.
Radish Mum	Select round radishes. Trim off the root ends. Make several thin crosswise cuts almost to the bottom of the radish. Make additional cuts perpendicular to the first cuts. Chill in ice water until the radish opens.
Radish Rose	Select round radishes. Cut a thin slice from each end. Cut 4 or 5 thin petal-shaped slices around the outer edge from top to bottom, leaving the bottom intact. Chill in ice water until the petals open.
Strawberry Fans	Select large firm strawberries with caps. Cut several parallel slices from the tip of each berry to just below the cap with a sharp knife. Spread the slices gently to form a fan.
Tomato Rose	Cut the peel gently from a firm tomato in a continuous 14-inch strip with a sharp knife. Shape the peel into a rose, starting at the base end and placing the skin side out. Add fresh herb leaves such as basil to resemble rose leaves.

Food and Wine Pairings

The pairing of good food with fine wine is one of the great pleasures of life. The rule that you drink white wine only with fish and fowl and red wine with meat no longer applies—just let your own taste and personal preference be the guide. Remember to serve light wines with lighter foods and full-bodied wines with rich foods so the food and wine will complement rather than overpower each other.

The best wine with which to cook is the one you will be serving at the table. The real secret is to cook with a good wine, as the alcohol evaporates during the cooking process, leaving only the actual flavor of the wine. A fine wine with rich body and aroma will insure a distinct and delicate flavor. When used in cooking, the wine should accent and enhance the natural flavor of the food while adding its own inviting fragrance and flavor.

Semidry White Wines

These wines have a fresh fruity taste and are best served young.
Serve with dove, quail, or shellfish in cream sauce; roast turkey, duck, or goose; seafood, pasta, or salad; fish in an herbed butter sauce.

- Johannisberg Riesling – *(Yo-hann-is-burg Rees-ling)* • Frascati – *(Fras-kah-tee)*
- Gewürztraminer – *(Guh-vurts-trah-mee-ner)* • Bernkasteler – *(Barn-kahst-ler)*
- Sylvaner Riesling – *(Sihl-van-uhr Rees-ling)* • Fendant – *(Fahn-dawn)*
- Dienheimer – *(Deen-heim-er)* • Kreuznach – *(Kroytz-nock)*

Dry White Wines

These wines have a crisp, refreshing taste and are best served young.
Serve with chicken, turkey, and cold meat; roast young gamebirds and waterfowl; shellfish; fried or grilled fish; ham and veal.

- Vouvray – *(Voo-vray)* • Chablis – *(Sha-blee)* • Chardonnay – *(Shar-doh-nay)*
- Pinot Blanc – *(Pee-noh Blahn)* • Chenin Blanc – *(Shen-ihn Blahn)*
- Pouilly-Fuissé – *(Poo-yee Fwee-say)* • Orvieto Secco – *(Ohr-vyay-toh Say-koh)*
- Piesporter Trocken – *(Peez-porter Trawk-uhn)* • Meursault – *(Mehr-soh)*
- Hermitage Blanc – *(Ehr-mee-tahzh Blahn)* • Pinot Grigio – *(Pee-noh Gree-jo)*
- Verdicchio – *(Vehr-deek-kyoh)* • Sancerre – *(Sahn-sehr)*
- Sauvignon Blanc – *(Soh-vihn-yohn Blahn)* • Soave – *(So-ah-veh)*

Food and Wine Pairings

Light Red Wines

*These wines have a light taste and are best served young.
Serve with grilled chicken; fowl with highly seasoned stuffings; soups
and stews; Creole foods; veal or lamb.*

- Beaujolais – *(Boh-zhuh-lay)* • Bardolino – *(Bar-doh-lee-noh)*
- Valpolicella – *(Vahl-paw-lee-chehl-lah)*
- Moulin-à-Vent Beaujolais – *(Moo-lan-nah-vahn Boh-zhuh-lay)*
- Barbera – *(Bar-beh-rah)* • Lambrusco – *(Lam-broos-koh)*
- Lirac – *(Lee-rak)*
- Nuits-Saint-Georges "Villages" – *(Nwee San Zhawrzh)*
- Gamay Beaujolais – *(Ga-may Boh-zhuh-lay)*
- Santa Maddalena – *(Sahn-tah Mahd-dah-leh-nah)*
- Merlot del Ticino – *(Mehr-loh dehl Tee-chee-noh)*

Hearty Red Wines

*These wines have a heavier taste, improve with age, and are best
opened thirty minutes before serving. Serve with game including duck, goose,
venison, and hare; pot roast; red meats including beef, lamb, and veal;
hearty foods; cheese and egg dishes, pastas, and highly seasoned foods.*

- Barbaresco – *(Bar-bah-ress-koh)* • Barolo – *(Bah-roh-loh)*
- Burgundy – *(Ber-gun-dee)* • Zinfandel – *(Zihn-fuhn-dehl)*
- Chianti Riserva – *(Kee-ahn-tee Ree-zehr-vah)* • Bordeaux – *(Bohr-doh)*
- Côte-Rotie – *(Koht Roh-tee)* • Hermitage – *(Ehr-mee-tahzh)*
- Taurasi – *(Tow-rah-zee)* • Merlot – *(Mehr-loh)*
- Syrah – *(See-rah)* • Châteauneuf-du-Pape – *(Shah-toh-nuhf-doo-Pahp)*
- Petite Sirah – *(Peh-teet Sih-rah)* • Côte de Beaune – *(Koht duh Bohn)*
- Cabernet Sauvignon – *(Ka-behr-nay Soh-vihn-yohn)*

Herbs and Spices

Allspice . . . . Pungent aromatic spice, whole or in powdered form. It is excellent in marinades, particularly in game marinade, or in curries.

Basil . . . . Can be chopped and added to cold poultry salads. If the recipe calls for tomatoes or tomato sauce, add a touch of basil to bring out a rich flavor.

Bay leaf . . . . The basis of many French seasonings. It is added to soups, stews, marinades, and stuffings.

Bouquet garni . . . . A must in many Creole cuisine recipes. It is a bundle of herbs, spices, and bay leaf tied together and added to soups, stews, or sauces.

Celery seeds . . . . From wild celery rather than domestic celery. They add pleasant flavor to bouillon or a stock base.

Chervil . . . . One of the traditional fines herbes used in French-derived cooking. (The others are tarragon, parsley, and chives.) It is good in omelets or soups.

Chives . . . . Available fresh, dried, or frozen, chives can be substituted for fresh onion or shallot in any poultry recipe.

Cinnamon . . . . Ground from the bark of the cinnamon tree, it is important in desserts as well as in savory dishes.

Coriander . . . . Adds an unusual flavor to soups, stews, chili dishes, curries, and some desserts.

Cumin . . . . A staple spice in Mexican cooking. To use, rub seeds together and let them fall into the dish just before serving. Cumin also comes in powdered form.

Garlic . . . . One of the oldest herbs in the world, it must be carefully handled. For best results, press or crush garlic clove.

Marjoram . . . . An aromatic herb of the mint family, it is good in soups, sauces, stuffings, and stews.

Mustard (dry) . . . . Brings a sharp bite to sauces. Sprinkle just a touch over roast chicken for a delightful flavor treat.

Oregano . . . . A staple herb in Italian, Spanish, and Mexican cuisines. It is very good in dishes with a tomato foundation; it adds an excellent savory taste.

Paprika . . . . A mild pepper that adds color to many dishes. The very best paprika is imported from Hungary.

196

Herbs and Spices

Rosemary ....A tasty herb important in seasoning stuffing for duck, partridge, capon, and other poultry.

Sage ....A perennial favorite with all kinds of poultry and stuffings. It is particularly good with goose.

Tarragon ....One of the fines herbes. Goes well with all poultry dishes whether hot or cold.

Thyme ....Usually used in combination with bay leaf in soups, stews, and sauces.

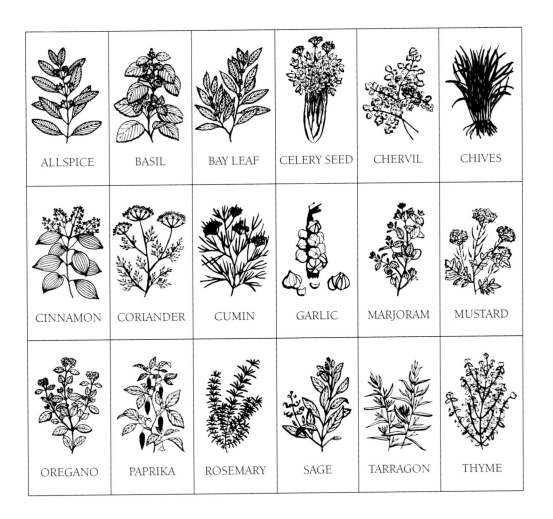

ALLSPICE	BASIL	BAY LEAF	CELERY SEED	CHERVIL	CHIVES
CINNAMON	CORIANDER	CUMIN	GARLIC	MARJORAM	MUSTARD
OREGANO	PAPRIKA	ROSEMARY	SAGE	TARRAGON	THYME

Cooking Meat and Poultry

Roasting . . . . Use tender cuts of beef, veal, pork or lamb, and young birds.

Place meat fat side up, or poultry breast side up, on rack in foil-lined shallow roasting pan. Do not add water; do not cover.

Insert meat thermometer in center of thickest part of meat, being careful that end does not touch bone, fat, or gristle.

Roast at 300 to 350 degrees until done to taste, or for pork and poultry until cooked through.

Broiling . . . . Use tender beef steaks, lamb chops, sliced ham, ground meats, and poultry quarters or halves. Fresh pork should be broiled slowly to insure complete cooking in center. Steaks and chops should be at least 1/2 inch thick.

Preheat oven to "Broil." Place meat on rack in foil-lined broiler pan.

Place pan on oven rack 2 to 5 inches from the heat source, with thicker meat placed the greater distance. Brush poultry with butter.

Broil until top side is browned; season with salt and pepper.

Turn; brown second side. Season and serve at once.

Pan Broiling . . . . Use the same meat and poultry cuts suitable for broiling.

Place skillet or griddle over medium-high heat. Preheat until a drop of water dances on the surface.

Place meat in skillet; reduce heat to medium. Do not add water or cover. The cold meat will stick at first, but as it browns it will loosen. If juices start to cook out of the meat, increase heat slightly.

When meat is brown on one side, turn and brown second side.

Pan Frying . . . . Use comparatively thin pieces of meat, meat that has been tenderized by pounding or scoring, meat that is breaded, and poultry parts.

Place skillet over medium-high heat. Add a small amount of shortening— 2 tablespoons will usually be sufficient.

Add meat or poultry when shortening is hot. Cook as in pan broiling.

Braising . . . . Use for less tender cuts of meat or older birds. You can also braise pork chops, steaks, and cutlets; veal chops, steaks, and cutlets; and poultry legs and thighs.

Brown meat on all sides as in pan frying. Season with salt and pepper.

Add a small amount of water—or none if sufficient juices have already cooked out of the meat. Cover tightly.

Reduce heat to low. Cook until tender, turning occasionally. Meats will cook in their own juices.

Cooking in Liquid . . . . . . Use less tender cuts of meat and stewing chickens. Browning of large cuts or whole birds is optional, but it does develop flavor and improve the color.

Add water or stock to cover meat. Simmer, covered, until tender.

Add vegetables to allow time to cook without becoming mushy.

Acknowledgements

The Junior League of Alexandria, Inc.
Presidents during the production of *Secret Ingredients*

1997–98	1998–99	1999–2000	2000–01
Ginger W. Brown	Kristina L. McBride	Nancy C. Stich	Tracy O. Cicardo

Cookbook Executive Committee

Chairman:
Carman Luneau

Distribution:
Sissy Jones, Tammi Salazar

Chairman Elect:
Merrilyn Norem

Treasurer:
Sandy Patton

Development:
Denise Wood, Chrys Thompson

Sustaining Advisors:
Ginger Brown, Kristina McBride

Cookbook Committee Chairmen

Design:
Merrilyn Norem, Catherine Pears

In-League Fundraising:
Lee Ann Leckie, Christy Mayo, Traci Raiff

Collection:
Deborah Mason, Brenda White

Marketing:
Carman Luneau, Camille Robison

Testing:
Brenda White, Suzie Wagner

Public Relations:
Patti Jo Pearson, Denise Wood

Corporate Underwriting:
Tammi Salazar, Pat Texada, Patricia Upton

Media: Lelia Roy
Events: Sissy Jones

Cookbook Committee Members

Melissa Augustine
Lynn Barrett
Fran Bates
Jan Bordelon
Ann Brewer
Wendy Castille
Patti Colwell
Nan Cowan
Martha Elliott

Linda Ellis
Rhonda Fontenot
Kim Gist
Susan Goodwin
Carolyn Guidry
Evelyn Jones
Lou Ann Jordan
Rachal Karam
Cathi Kirk

Stacey Leglue
Krista Lombardo
Frances Ann McMullen
Jennifer Munsterman
Joni Oates
Nancy Owens
Diana Hobbs Richard
Angie Roberts
Cindy Sadler

Vickie Smith
Angelle Stringer
Debbie Triche
Janis Villard
Ashley Vincent
Cathy Wilder
Christina Wilkins
Kay Wood

Acknowledgements

Special Thanks

The Alexandria Zoo
Jean Blake
Bird Deville's Garden
Tracy Cicardo
Mary Duncan Crockett
Nancy and Bubba Flournoy
Rosemary Gist
Hill-Harris Gifts — Sandra Kearny
Joy Hodges
Inglewood Plantation
Sissy and Bart Jones
Lucy Karam
Krewe of 12th Night
Margie McBride
Pat Moore
Kathleen Nolen
The Odyssey Shop — Colin Riggs
Stems Floral Shop — Bob Luna
Nancy Stich
Mr. and Mrs. Michael Traylor

To the active and sustaining membership of the Junior League of Alexandria,
the Cookbook Committee would like to extend a special thanks
for all of the recipes submitted and tested, stories and ideas shared
and your endless patience with this special project.

Acknowledgements

Cookbook Contributors

Lou Aertker
Margaret Allen
Jennifer Badeaux
Fran Bates
Lorraine Bath
Annie Bejach
Jean and Henry Blake
Mary Ann Brame
Kathryn Brocato
Lynelle Brocato
Ada Bryant
Marjorie Bucklew
Debbie Burns
June Chandler
Mildred Chandler
Reneé Chappell
Mamie Jo Cheneval
Patti Colwell
Annette Curley
Billie Dawson
Ruby Leigh Edgerton
Debbie Erwin
Angie Farrar
Kasey Fiscus
Michele Fontenot
Eloise Gardner
Karen Garner
Susan Goodwin
Nella Guilbeau
Adair Gwinn
Lynne Hyde
Betty Ingrish

Shirley Joffrion
Zelda Kaplan
Lucy Karam
Sandra Kearney
JoAnn Kellogg
Ann Kingrey
Carol Kirkikis
Missy Laborde
Lee Ann Leckie
Krista Lombardo
Merriam Lowther
Carman Luneau
Karen McBride
Kristina McBride
Kenda McGilvray
Frances Ann McMullen
Mary Jo Mansour
Deborah Mason
Eloise Meginley
Melinda Mikell-Wilder
Anagene Mobley
Doris Moriarity
Rebecca Morris
Kathleen Nolen
Merrilyn Norem
Joni Oates
Lee O'Dell
Linda Ortego
Nancy Owens
Susan Owens

Charlotte Parrott
Sandy Patton
Patti Jo Pearson
Grace Ponthie
Ruth Prince
Barbara Provosty
Diane Hobbs Richard
Elizabeth Riley
Cathy Robinson
Camille Robison
Pam Rubin
Jane Shank
Kendall Smith
Lisa Smith
Annelie Smolenski
Nancy Stich
Angelle Stringer
Suzie Talley
Chrys Thompson
Deborah Tillman
Patricia Upton
Esther Vanderlick
Kathryn Van Hoof
Ashley Vincent
Lynn Wheelis
Brenda White
Frieda White
Sarah Willis
Peggy Wilson
Denise Wood
Nona Yeager
Winona Yeager

Index

Index

Index

Index

Index

Index

Secret Ingredients

The Junior League of Alexandria, Inc.
P.O. Box 13086 • Alexandria, Louisiana 71315-3086
318-443-6975 / 888-830-6975
via fax: 318-443-6927
via Internet: www.jlalex.com

Name _____

Street Address _____

City _____ State _____ Zip _____

Telephone _____

Your Order	Quantity	Total
Secret Ingredients $24.95 per book		
Shipping & Handling $3.50 per book; $1.50 each additional book		
Sales Tax $2.00 per book		
Total		

[   ] Check enclosed payable to The Junior League of Alexandria, Inc.
[   ] Charge to: [   ] VISA   [   ] MasterCard

Account Number _____ Expiration Date _____

Cardholder Name _____

Signature _____

Photocopies accepted.

Order Form Key Sponsor